THE FINAL CH

EDITED BY DONALD KENRICK

The Final Chapter

EDITED BY

DONALD KENRICK

UNIVERSITY OF HERTFORDSHIRE PRESS

The Gypsies during the Second World War
Volume 3

First published in Great Britain in 2006 by
University of Hertfordshire Press
Learning and Information Services
University of Hertfordshire
College Lane
Hatfield
Hertfordshire AL10 9AB

British Library Cataloguing in Publication Data
A catalogue record for this book is available from the British Library

ISBN 1-902806-49-2 paperback

Design by Geoff Green Book Design, CB4 5RA
Cover design by John Robertshaw, AL5 2JB
Printed in Great Britain by Antony Rowe Ltd, SN14 6LH

Contents

Contributors

TED HANISCH has been engaged as a social worker with Roma and indigenous Travellers in Norway. His article is part of a longer treatment of their relationship with the State.

MILENA HÜBSCHMANNOVÁ taught Romani at the University of Prague. Her contribution is based on original interviews with survivors from Slovakia. Sadly, Dr Hübschmannová was killed in a car accident in 2005 shortly after completing her chapter.

VALDEMAR KALININ is a writer and educational consultant. His published works include (in Russian) *The Mystery of the Baltic Roma*.

KATALIN KATZ is at the Paul Baerwald School of Social Work of the Hebrew University of Jerusalem. Her article is based on original interviews with survivors in Hungary.

DONALD KENRICK published (with Grattan Puxon) the first book in English on the Gypsies in the Nazi period in 1972: *Destiny of Europe's Gypsies*.

HEIKE KROKOWSKI is a historian from Hanover. Her doctorate was on *Die Last der Erinnerung* (The Burden of Memory).

REGULA LUDI is a historian with a doctorate from the University of Bern. She has written widely on contemporary political issues.

DENNIS REINHARTZ is at the Department of History in the University of Texas. His publications include *Milovan Djilas: A Revolutionary as a Writer*.

PETER SANDNER works at the Central Archives for the State of Hessen in Wiesbaden. His publications include local studies of the National Socialist period.

SUSAN TEBBUTT is a Head of German Studies at Mary Immaculate College in Limerick. Her publications include *Sinti and Roma. Gypsies in German-speaking Society and Literature*.

SUSAN TEGEL is a historian and at one time was Head of History at the University of Hertfordshire. She has published widely on the historical aspects of film in the Third Reich.

WOLFGANG WIPPERMANN lives and teaches in Berlin. His writings include *Das Leben in Frankfurt zur NS-Zeit*.

MICHAEL ZIMMERMANN is on the academic staff at Bochum University. His book *Rassenutopie und Genozid* is the standard work on Gypsies in the Nazi period.

Illustrations

Glossary

Gadjo (pl. Gadje): The word for non-Gypsy in the Romani language

German: In the Second World War the German people as a whole were identified with the Nazis by the victims. Generally, survivors' accounts use the term 'German' rather than 'Nazi'

Gypsy: The term is used when discussing policies and translating documents (e.g. *Zigeuner*)

Rom (pl. Roma) and Romani (pl. Romanies): These words are used as synonyms throughout the text

Sinto (pl. Sinti): A clan of Romanies living mainly in Western Europe

Preface

This is the final volume of what was planned as a four-part series. Parts 3 and 4 are bound together.

I remind readers of the words of Henriette Asséo in the Introduction to the first volume of the series, that it has not been the intention of this series to give an exhaustive region-by-region table of the extermination of the Gypsies. The aim is to present a global vision of our knowledge of the genocide acquired thanks to the contributors of authors from many European countries.

Part 1 continues from volume II and deals with the period leading up to and during the Second World War. It includes previously unpublished material about the situation in Slovakia and Hungary. In particular, the picture of events in Hungary – based on interviews with survivors – is very different from that which appeared in Hungarian publications.

Part 2 – The Aftermath – looks at how Germans and others have come to terms with and remember the Romani Holocaust.

Donald Kenrick

Introduction

When the Nazi party came to power in 1933, it inherited laws against
nomadism that were already in operation. From the beginning, the
National Socialists considered the Romanies and Sinti – whether nomads
or sedentary – as non-Aryans. Together with the Jews, they were classed
as alien and considered a danger to the German race. Already by 1935
they had been deprived of citizenship and given the second-class status of
'nationals'. In the same year, the Law for the Protection of German Blood
made marriages between Gypsies and Germans illegal. There was no
place in the image of Germany under the New Order for a group of
people who travelled around the country freely, worked as craftsmen and
sold their wares from door to door. A quasi-scientific research
programme was set up in Berlin, under the leadership of Robert Ritter.
Later this programme was carried out at the Race Hygiene and Population
Biology Research Centre. The researchers had to accept the historical and
linguistic fact that the Romani and Sinti peoples came originally from
India and, therefore, should count as Aryan. However, they claimed that
on the route to Europe they had intermarried with other races and as a
mixed race had no place in Nazi Germany. Allegations were made against
them in pamphlets and articles.

Internment camps were set up on the outskirts of towns in Germany,
and both caravan- and house-dwelling Gypsies were sent there.
Discipline was strict and the internees were only allowed out to work. In
1938 several hundred Gypsy men were deported to Buchenwald and
Sachsenhausen concentration camps as "people who have shown that
they do not wish to fit into society" under the Decree against Crime of the
previous year. Volume I of this series deals with this period.

Heinrich Himmler, who became police chief in 1936, was particularly interested in the Gypsies and led the campaign against them. In 1938, he signed the Decree for Fighting the Gypsy Menace under which Ritter's Research Centre was linked with an established Gypsy Police Office and the new combined institution was put under the direct control of police headquarters in Berlin. The first task of this institution was to classify all nomads by their ethnic origin. To be classed as a Gypsy of mixed race it was sufficient to have two great-grandparents who were considered to have been Gypsies, which meant that part-Gypsies were considered a greater danger than part-Jews. In general, a person with one Jewish grandparent was not affected in the Nazi anti-Jewish legislation whereas one-eighth Gypsy blood was considered strong enough to outweigh seven-eighths of German blood – so dangerous were the Gypsies considered.

Alongside the programme of registration and classification, new laws were imposed on the Roma and Sinti. Any children who were foreign nationals were excluded from school; the German Gypsies could be excluded if they represented a moral danger to their classmates. The race scientists discussed what should happen next. Eva Justin proposed sterilisation, except for those with pure Gypsy blood, while Ritter himself wanted to put an end to the whole race by sterilisation of those who were at least one-eighth. In fact, a law of 1933 had already been used to carry out this operation on individuals.

In the end, the Nazi leaders decided in 1940 that deportation was the means to clear Germany of Gypsies. Adolf Eichmann was responsible for the transporting of Gypsies alongside the Jews. In the first operation, 2,800 were sent to Poland and housed in Jewish ghettoes or hutted camps.

In 1941, however, the Nazi leaders had carried out an experiment at Auschwitz with Zyklon B gas, where they had murdered 250 sick prisoners and 600 Soviet POW's in underground cells. The discovery of this cheap and rapid method of mass murder led to a change in the treatment of the Jews. Deportation was replaced by death, and in 1942, Himmler decided that the same 'final solution' should be applied to the Gypsies.

On 16 December 1942, he signed an order condemning all the German and Austrian Gypsies to imprisonment in Auschwitz, and in February of the following year the police began rounding up the Roma and Sinti. Within the first few months, 10,000 persons had been transported to the camp. Children were taken out of orphanages and

Germans were asked to inform the police of any Gypsies living in houses that might have been missed. We may never be in a position to say how many remained outside the camps in Germany. They can be numbered in the hundreds and lived under strict police control.

When Austria was annexed in 1938 it was announced that the Gypsies there would be treated as those in Germany. Two years later in Lackenbach a camp was opened for the Austrian Roma and Sinti. The western part of Czechoslovakia was also annexed, but many Romanies succeeded in escaping across the border to the puppet state of Slovakia. Two internment camps were opened in 1942 in the German-controlled provinces of Bohemia and Moravia. The majority of the nomads were immediately locked up in the new camps. Later, when they were closed, several hundred of them were sent to Auschwitz together with the sedentary Gypsies who were rounded up. Only a handful of the Czech Gypsies survived the occupation. Articles in Volume II describe these camps and much of the following.

The comparatively small numbers of Belgian and Dutch Romanies were also arrested and sent to Auschwitz, where the majority died.[1] In France and Italy, Romanies and other nomads were interned in camps with poor conditions, where many died, but there were no deliberate murders. In France, no attempt was made to seek out the small number of Roma living in houses. It is well known that Bulgaria resisted attempts by Germany to deport its own Jews to the camps and the Gypsies, too, survived. This can be contrasted with the actions of the Romanian fascist government, which sent Gypsies east to their death. Yugoslavia was divided up by the Axis nations and an article in this volume describes what happened in that country.

The Romani population in Eastern Europe was mainly sedentary and integrated into the life of town and village. Many had been to school and had regular work. They had cultural and sports clubs and had begun to develop Romani as a literary language. Nevertheless, the German troops carried out the same policies of murder against these populations as against the nomads. The Romanies who lived in Poland were crammed into the Jewish quarters of towns and villages. The Germans forced the Jews to give up their houses and move in with other families, and then the Romanies were allocated the empty houses. Many Gypsies, however, were murdered on the outskirts of the villages where they lived. The Auschwitz Museum is preparing a volume on the fate of the Gypsies in Poland and we do not attempt to cover that country in this series.[2]

The task of murdering the Romanies in the occupied areas of the Soviet Union was allocated to the so-called Task Forces (Einsatzgruppen) who were given their orders soon after the invasion. Their orders were to eliminate 'racially undesirable elements' and most reports of the Forces mention the killing of Gypsies. In all, they murdered over 30,000 Romanies.

In most of the countries that came under German rule the alternative was often between death on the spot and a journey without food or water to a concentration camp. Nearly all the larger camps had their section for Romanies: Bergen-Belsen, Buchenwald, Mauthausen, Natzweiler, Neuengamme, Ravensbrück, Sachsenhausen, Theresienstadt and others. From 1943 on the camps were merely waiting rooms for the journey to death by gas or shooting. Chelmno, Sobibor and Treblinka were extermination camps, which meant immediate death on arrival. From all the camps where Romanies and Sinti were held, the best records available are for Auschwitz, where Jewish prisoners kept secret notes.

It is also known that Romanies and Sinti were used in the camps for experiments with typhus, salt water and smallpox. Perhaps the most horrifying experiments were the attempts to find new quick methods of sterilisation. These were to be used on all the races considered inferior so that they could be used as a workforce while preventing the birth of a new generation.

As Soviet and Allied troops advanced in 1944, the last tragic phase began in the life of the concentration camps. The remaining prisoners were evacuated on foot in the direction of Austria and Germany. Anyone who could not keep up during these marches was shot.

During the Hitler period, the Romanies and Sinti of Europe suffered a terrible blow from which they have not yet fully recovered. Some estimates of deaths are as high as 500,000. It should not be forgotten that even this figure does not give the whole extent of the persecution of the many thousands who suffered internment or other repressive measures.

PART 1

The Killing Fields

CHAPTER ONE

Roma in the so-called Slovak State (1939–45)

Milena Hübschmannová
Translated by Valerie Levy

Introduction

The following paper is based partly on literature dealing with the history of the years 1939–45. Among the basic works concerning the fate of the Roma in this period are numerous publications by Ctibor Nečas.[1]

The main source is, however, an analysis of the accounts of Romani men and women who lived through the war in the so-called Slovak State. Between 1970, when I began recording accounts, and the present time, we have compiled more than 500 testimonies. In the early years, my Romani Studies colleagues conducted some of these interviews about the war. From 1992 students of Romani Studies[2] also joined in. With a few exceptions, we recorded these dialogues in Romani.[3]

Accounts of Romani survivors are mostly consistent with the facts described in the literature on this subject. They also contribute important information not mentioned in the literature, e.g. testimonies about Roma recruited into Slovak President Tiso's[4] army, that fought side by side with the German army on the Eastern Front and later in Italy; testimonies about Roma who, from Russian prison camps, joined the First Czechoslovak Army, established in Russia by General Ludvík Svoboda; information about Roma in the partisan movement and in the Slovak National Uprising.

Several witnesses tell of local authorities who kept 'their Gypsies' from being deported to forced-labour camps, from being shot or from forced evacuation from their villages. Women in particular describe terrifying days during the last year of the war, spent in the woods where Roma – and Slovaks – hid from the approaching frontline and from German soldiers who were raping women.

Witnesses speak more eloquently and extensively than archive documents about the extensive sufferings of the Roma during the Second World War, and of interpersonal relationships within the Romani community and within the Gadjo villages. If we locate their accounts in a sociological and cultural model, we will understand better why the Roma in Slovakia – despite all kinds of persecution and discrimination – did not become victims of Nazi genocide during the Second World War, as Roma elsewhere did.

In contrast with the Jews, whom the fascist Tiso regime almost completely liquidated, the Roma in Slovakia were not victims of genocide. Of the 80,000 Jewish inhabitants of prewar Slovakia, less than 6,000 people survived to the end of the war. Official statistics and witnesses confirm that, on the other hand, Roma in Slovakia did survive the Second World War not only as individuals but as a group.[5] Of the similar population of 80,000 Roma in pre-war Slovakia about 79,000 were to survive.

Although Roma were not victims of genocide in the Slovak State does not mean that they were spared discrimination and persecution. Immediately after the forced partition of Czechoslovakia, following the declaration of an independent Slovak Republic (14 March 1939), various anti-Gypsy decrees were issued and these gradually multiplied. While in the first relatively peaceful years the decrees often remained on paper, towards the end of the war that was soon to be lost and they were put more drastically and passionately into effect. When the Nazi army invaded Slovakia after the Slovak National Uprising was suppressed (29 August 1944), it seemed that the fascist motto "After the Jews, the Gypsies" would soon take effect. Only the end of the war prevented this.

The place of Roma in prewar village society in Slovakia

The directives and practices directed toward the Roma by the central representatives of political power, as well as local functionaries and the Slovak public, were not uniform. This was the main reason why the Roma were spared complete liquidation in Slovakia. The discriminatory attitude toward Roma was, at least in the early years of the war, significantly moderated by their solid place in the prewar, rural, class-based Slovak society. I believe that the social integration of Roma into the society of that time was more complete and natural than in the totalitarian postwar 'socialist' society that forcibly disintegrated the extended Romani family, deprived them of their traditional trades and, by brutal means, tried to assimilate Roma linguistically and culturally.

The Roma in Slovakia still belong to three main sub-ethnic groups. The so-called Slovak and Hungarian Roma had already begun to settle in the sixteenth century. The third group is composed of Vlahi Roma, who were nomads until 1959 when the Communist government forcibly settled them.

The number of travelling (Vlahi) and settled (Slovak and Hungarian) Roma is indicated in a detailed 1893 census of Gypsies in Hungary. Roma in Slovakia numbered 36,623, of whom 36,231 were settled and only 400 were nomadic.[6] Data taken from the census shows an important phenomenon – the productive professional incorporation of Roma into society. Professions existed that were generally known as Gypsy professions. The main professions were music and the blacksmith trade, each of which fed over 4,000 families. Another important job, which provided for nearly 2,000 families, was the production of adobe bricks (*valka*s). In addition, there was basket weaving, rope making and brush making – trades plied by 1,200 Romani men and women. At the end of the nineteenth century more than 1,100 Roma worked as farm workers or day labourers. Most of the rest worked in other trades and services. Only a negligible number of Roma worked on the edge of society. The census claimed that theft was the source of income for 42 men and 81 women; 2 men and 107 women were fortune-tellers; 2 men and 14 women were fraudulent healers.

Theft – apart from occasional stealing from fields – and palmistry did not appear among the *dharmas*[7] of settled (Slovak and Hungarian) Roma. As part of their livelihood, travelling Roma, who were not permanently linked with a Gadjo (non-Gypsy) neighbourhood, might indulge in petty theft.

The census document shows the social integration of Roma into the feudal-like Slovak agricultural society at the end of the nineteenth century. Although Roma lived in Gypsy settlements outside of villages, segregation expressed by a multitude of horizontal and vertical boundaries was a characteristic of the feudal society and did not apply only to Gypsies.

Therefore, although Gypsies lived in isolated settlements, they associated with Slovak villagers according to precisely delineated rules. The Roma exchanged their products and services for foodstuffs, but also became entitled to paternalistic protection. Most Romani families had their Gadje and most Slovak farmers had their Gypsies. These bonds were often confirmed by having a farmer or his wife as godfather or godmother to the children of their Gypsy families. This paternalistic relationship was, in its way, a European modification of the Indian *jajmani* system in which members of a higher caste have the unwritten obligation of taking complete care of the members of those *jatis* (castes) who provide their patrons with the caste's services. The exchange of services for payment need not be immediate but depends on the needs of one party or the other at the time.

Therefore, the term 'begging' did not have the same social implications in India and in Gypsy/Gadjo relationships in Slovakia, as did the begging of anonymous beggars in a European town. Our Slovak witness from Lutila, Mrs Mikušová reports:

> When a Gypsy woman came asking (pytat) we always gave her something because she would come later and sweep the farmyard, split wood or do whatever we needed. Our Gypsies weren't Gypsies, they were Jožko or Janči or Ondrej.

The position of Roma remained the same, even up until the first third of the twentieth century. Nevertheless, political and socio-cultural changes in society as a whole gradually began to influence Romani society. Technical development reduced the need for Gypsy blacksmiths: some blacksmiths tried to take up the music profession, which was always in demand, as well as being prestigious and relatively profitable. We hear from many survivors the same sentence describing their father's or grandfather's way of earning a living: *During the week he hammered iron and on Saturday and Sunday he went to work playing music.* In some localities Gypsy blacksmiths set up as specialists in wrought iron, particularly in the area around Bratislava.[8]

After the establishment of the Czechoslovak Republic in 1918, a new specifically 'Gypsy' profession arose: the pig trade. A few communities of traditionally settled "Slovak" Roma in the area of Prešov made their living selling pigs. Traders bought swine from Slovak farmers, took them to Prešov and, from there, representatives of various firms took them to Bohemia. The pig traders soon became very rich and their material status often surpassed that of their Slovak neighbours. They owned, for example, automobiles and trucks – which were very rarely seen in Slovak villages in the thirties. On the other hand, the growth of a multitude of so-called 'hungry settlements' *(bokhale vatri)* made it impossible for the inhabitants to find work. Urban quarters arose in Bardějov, Humenné, Michalovce, and elsewhere, inhabited by Roma who could not find a demand for their traditional products or services and who tried to find some job in the city – as porters at train stations carrying goods from wholesale stores to retail stores and similar work. The increased number of beggars in localities with too many 'foreign' Gypsies annoyed the Gadje.

On the other hand, unemployed Gypsies functioned as a reserve pool of labour in case of need. These Roma performed communally necessary unclean work: they cleaned out cesspools and dug wells, crushed stones for road building or took jobs as seasonal agricultural workers. The depression in the Czechoslovak Republic, deepening from the mid-twenties, hit the Roma twice as hard. Many survivors begin their accounts of old times with this typical sentence: *Te o gadžo mardo, o Rom mardo duvar* (If a Gadjo is beaten, a Rom is beaten twice). *There was no work; there was nothing to eat; I went bare-foot and naked.*

Settled Roma, like nomads, took any work that was offered to them, even for ridiculously low pay, and the quality of the work they performed often made them more successful than non-Roma. Hunger often forced them to steal and do some minor swindling.[9] Those who did not wish to steal tried to earn a living by peddling. Even earlier, this profession had been the main or supplementary means of earning a living for a few Romani families. There were professional organizations of Gadjo door-to-door salesmen and small businessmen who repeatedly asked the authorities to prevent Gypsies from doing business and travelling. The term 'travelling' generally covered not only the mobile way of life (in caravans) characteristic of Vlahi Roma, but also the temporary movement of settled Roma who could not find work near their homes.

One result of the reaction of the majority to the depression was that Roma were again targeted. In 1927, a law was passed "concerning travelling Gypsies". The law limited their right of movement. It required 'travelling' Gypsies to submit to police inspections. It forbade Gypsies from entering some Czech and Slovak towns, although many of those towns in Slovakia were the permanent homes of their own Gypsies. Often those Gypsies themselves wanted to prevent a flood of 'foreign' Gypsies, who could worsen relations with their Gadjo customers. In 1928, a survey was taken throughout the whole Czechoslovak Republic of travelling Gypsies, and Gypsy identity cards were issued based on that survey. A total of 36,969 people received them, among who were a number of "vagabonds living the Gypsy lifestyle". There were 7,000 Gypsy travel permits issued. Most of the travel permits were given to Roma in

Bohemia and Moravia (so-called Czech Roma and Sinti), of whom only a small number (mainly in Moravia) had permanent housing.

In various regions of Slovakia, discrimination against Roma communities was dependent upon the local conditions. In western and parts of central Slovakia, where industry and education were better developed, the proportion of integrated Romani communities was greater than in very poor, non-industrial eastern Slovakia, where the greatest concentration of Roma lived. As late as 1970 a census showed that 45 per cent of the entire Romani population of the Czechoslovak Republic still lived in eastern Slovakia.

When comparing existing data on this subject, we are surprised at the high number of Roma who, according to the testimonies of our informants, had already completed eight years of elementary school or even attended secondary school during the so-called First Republic (1918–38). The educational level of western Slovak Roma was, on average, higher than that of Roma in eastern Slovakia. This was true not only of Roma but also of 'whites', that is, non-Roma.[10] For example, in the western Slovak district of Šariška župa – one of six districts in Slovakia – at the end of the 1920s, 68 per cent of the Slovak population was illiterate.[11]

Two factors determined the differing approaches toward Roma in the Slovak Republic during the Second World War. First, differences between professionally qualified and unqualified Roma, the rich and the poor, and the level of integration. Secondly, whether the areas were full of problems of general poverty and backwardness or were relatively prosperous.

Before we look at the Gypsy policies, however, I wish to spend a few lines on one question: Why did the Slovak State deport and liquidate its Jews, who were also fully integrated into Slovak society, while Gypsies were spared the worst?

We suppose that two factors were important: continuous pressure from Nazi Germany for the liquidation of the Jews and the different nature of Jewish integration into Slovak society. The historian Ivan Kamenec states that the independent Slovak State which, with the support of Nazi Germany, arose with the fall of the Czechoslovak Republic, was forced to sign the so-called Protection Pact (*Schutzvertrag*) of 18 March 1939. This bound Germany to assume the "protection of the political independence of the Slovak State and the integrity of its territory" on the condition that Slovakia fulfill Germany's demands.[12] Formally independent Slovakia agreed to obey mainly out of fear of the incessant territorial demands of Horthy's Hungary. Germany and Italy, on the basis of arbitration in Vienna (2 November 1938), permitted Hungary to occupy 10,400 km^2 of Slovak territory and, in March 1939, Germany did not contest Hungary's invasion of an area containing a further 1,600 km^2 of Slovakia. Kamenec describes the role of Nazi Germany in relation to the rivalry between the two satellites Slovakia and Hungary thus:

> Territorial disputes between Hungary and Slovakia led to competition between both lands to win the favour of Germany. Sending military contingents to the Eastern Front and persecuting Jewish citizens were considered to be points in their favour. Pressure from Nazi Germany to carry out anti-Semitic policies was non-stop. In the first wave from September to October 1942, 57,628 of the 80,000 Slovak Jews were deported to Nazi concentration camps and a further 13,500 people were deported after the German occupation of Slovakia between September 1944 and March 1945.

Although the main ideologists and implementers of the anti-Jewish policies were right-wing Slovak politicians – the Minister of External Affairs and Prime Minister, Vojtech Tuka, and the Minister of the Interior and Commander of the main fascist organization Hlinka Guard, Alexandr Mach – the spokesman for the more moderate wing, President Josef Tiso, a Catholic priest, did not prevent deportation. In several public speeches he, in fact, justified it. Some Romani survivors mention that they personally heard Tiso speak about the Gypsy question when, in the first half of 1943, he visited the forced-labour camp in Hanušovce nad Topl'ou.

Josef Horváth said:

> *He stood like this next to me, the way you're sitting now. On his thick neck he had a big cross and said, 'I've given up Jews, I won't give up you Gypsies because you are Christians. A hundred percent of you have to work. Otherwise ninety percent of you will be beaten. You are branches and we Slovaks are the fruit of the nation.*

Anti-Semitic politics not only had a political function. In addition, the confiscation of Jewish property, 'aryanization', was intended to strengthen the economic independence of the Slovak State. The Jews in Slovakia were bankers, industrialists, owners of agricultural land. In the villages, the shops and taverns were Jewish property. The percentage of Jews who were doctors and lawyers was not negligible.

The potential liquidation of the Roma would decidedly not have brought any material or social advantages to the Slovak Nation collectively or individually. Which Slovaks would have been able to provide the music in the villages or in the town taverns? Who wanted to or could replace the work of Romani blacksmiths? Who would have wished to crush stones on the roads or empty septic tanks instead of the Gypsies?

The same conclusion to ours was also formulated by Kamenec:

> In the so-called solution of the Jewish question by means of aryanization, there was planned confiscation of personal property and immovable assets (enterprises, artisan and businesslike services, houses, land, cash, securities, jewellery and objects for daily use)... This gain did not exist among the Romani population and, therefore, the issue of the Gypsy question had a much slower tempo.[13]

"Roma-Gypsies" and "Roma-Slovaks"

The constitutional law of 25 September 1939 concerning citizenship in the state divided the population of the Slovak Republic into two groups: citizens and 'foreign elements'. Only citizens were entitled to civil rights; the others were deprived of them. While the Jews were all classified as foreign elements, the approach toward Gypsies varied.

> If it is ascertained that [Gypsies] live an orderly civil life, if they have decent dwellings and employment in a fixed locality and if their behaviour and morals, political reliability and public activity have reached the level of an ordinary citizen, they may be included in the community of the Slovak nation. If not, i.e. if they work sporadically, if they communicate among themselves in the Gypsy language, if their morals and political reliability are doubtful, it is impossible to consider them as members of the Slovak nation.[14]

According to a law issued on 29 February 1940, by the Ministry of National Defence, Jews and Gypsies were excluded from military units and drafted into separate labour detachments. From the colours of the facings on their uniforms, the Jewish regiments were labelled 'the blue army' (belavo armada and the Romani regiments were called 'coffee' (kavejovo), 'cocoa' (kakaovo) or 'chocolate' (šokoladovo). While all Jews were excluded from military service, shorthand reports from the January congressional meeting of the Slovak Republic testify to how the Roma were viewed.

> It is known that one part of this (Gypsy) race has become so acclimatized that they think of themselves as Slovak men and women and they don't see the Gypsy in them in the true sense of the word. The Defence Commission … decided to ask the honourable administration to characterize the term Gypsy.[15]

The term Gypsy was then determined by a special decree of the Ministry of the Interior on 18 June 1940: A Gypsy is defined, according to §9 with the power of Law number 130/1940 S.l only as a member of the Gypsy race whose two parents are of that race and who leads a travelling lifestyle or a settled lifestyle and dodges work.[16] The decree's approach toward Roma backed by the highest authorities enabled all sorts of local authorities – mayors, notaries, local police, military draft boards and school directors – to decide which Gypsy deserved to be "raised to the position of Slovaks" and who should be treated as a 'Gypsy'.

And so it happened that in some communities all Roma were spared deportation to forced-labour camps because their Gadje, the mayors where they lived insisted that "Gypsies are decent citizens and work well", while elsewhere – for example, in the Prešov region – the authorities sent all men from the ages of sixteen to seventy to labour camps without making any exceptions. While some Romani recruits were chosen for army military units, the committee sent others to perform hard labour in the 'Chocolate' Army, "perhaps only because their dark skin betrayed their Gypsiness". According to the testimonies of many survivors, it seems that 'black skin' itself decided how they would be dealt with, more than whether a Rom was 'acclimatized' (the terminology of the time) or 'asocial'. For decision-making, a range of social and political factors determined who was a Gypsy and who a Slovak, but perhaps even more decisive factors were purely subjective: fear, revenge, personal dislike, personal acquaintanceship, and so on. As the general situation in Slovakia worsened during the course of the war and general poverty, uncertainty and fear for one's life increased, an ever growing number of Roma were classed as and treated like 'Gypsies'.

Roma in the army

According to the Protection Pact with Germany, Slovakia was required to "carry out its foreign policy in close agreement with the German administration and organize its military strength in close cooperation with German military power."[17] Immediately after the German invasion of the

Soviet Union in June 1941, Tiso supplied a combat division and a rear division, in all 60,000 men. Even Roma were recruited into the army. As previously mentioned, draft boards allegedly based their decisions on statements of notaries and other authorities from the communities where the Roma in question came from – whether the Gypsy recruit qualified for military units or for Gypsy labour regiments. According to the accounts of survivors, anyone who was chosen for the regular army was identified as a Slovak in his papers whereas Roma sent to the 'Chocolate' or 'Coffee' Army were labelled as members of the Gypsy race.

According to Vojtech Bendik, Roma were recruited into the Coffee Army based in Čemerné (district of Vranov nad Topl'ou) in 1942. In that town there were about 800 Roma. In Čemerné there was also a Jewish military work camp. Mr Bendik, as well as Jewish survivors,[18] refers to it. The camps were strictly separated. Bendik says that new recruits spent approximately a month in Čemerné. During that time they learned to practice using shovels and pick-axes as weapons. Jewish survivors describe this absurd exercise in detail.[19] Then the Roma were separated and sent away to various labour sites. Bendik and sixty other Roma worked in the Borkutos forest near Prešov. They built bunkers.

At Christmas time 1943, in contrast to the Slovak soldiers who had served out their two years in the army, the Gypsies learned that they would not be released, but would remain in the military labour detachment one more year. They did not even receive Christmas leave. A few Roma organized a strike and the whole unit refused to go to work. According to Bendik, eight of the strike organizers were led away to Poprad in chains and there they were sentenced to death by a military court. Bendik did not know what happened to them. According to Ilona Lacková[20] the organizers of the rebellion were granted mercy by Tiso. Among the insurgents originally sentenced to death and later granted mercy were her cousin and another Rom, J. Kaleja, from Velký Šariš, Lacková's hometown.

When the Slovak National Uprising later broke out, many Roma from the 'Cocoa' Army participated. Along with many other Roma, Bendik reached Liptovský Hrádok. *Somewhere they got hold of machine guns, I don't know where*. They joined the uprising and repelled German attacks twice.

The men who guarded the Roma in labour detachments were Slovaks. *Some were decent; some harassed us as much as they could*. Bendik mainly complained about one terrible little Hlinka Guardist who chased

Roma out into the night, sometimes in rain, and forced them to exercise barefoot and naked.

> *Once they gave me such a thin little piece of bread for three days. I went to complain to the lousy Guardist and he beat me till I bled. There was a sergeant major from Sabinov there and he saw what happened. He went to the commander – and he was from Velký Šariš, too. A first lieutenant. And he had that killer transferred to the Russian front. Because of me.*

According to Mr Bendik, there was a Romani guard "with a rifle" in his work battalion. That would have corresponded to the testimony of Kolomán Pompa-Emelik, who was originally inducted into the 'Coffee' Army, but, because he found one of his former Slovak neighbours there, he got into the normal army, where he was assigned to supervise Romani work troops. Then he was transferred to the Italian Front, which will be discussed later on.

This account of a Jewish survivor[21] is interesting:

> *I joined up in Sabinov. Then I was transferred to the headquarters division in Prešov and there they found out I was a teacher. There was one Gypsy company of a work battalion, all illiterate. So the work load I got was to teach the Gypsies to read and write for three hours every morning.*

In Bendik's company, no literacy courses took place. Bendik himself had completed the fifth grade of elementary school "in Masaryk's time" – i.e. during the First Czechoslovak Republic. In school, the Czech teacher[22] wanted Bendik to continue his education. *Then they expelled all the Czechs and we got a teacher who was a hlinkovec[23] and he kicked me out of school because I was a Gypsy.*

Bendik is one of those who personally experienced a visit from Tiso to the Cocoa Army:

> *So Tiso was the Slovak President, and he said: 'You are Slovaks – There are no Gypsies'. As if we were just Slovaks of Gypsy origin.*
> We asked: Did Tiso come to your work battalion?
> *Yes, he was there, he was. He saved us... Next to us were Jews, about four hundred Jews. And one day they weren't there any more. They had already taken them away somewhere. And we were afraid they would take us away, too. Only Tiso said we were Slovaks.*

Although – as we have already said – undoubtedly the greatest percentage of Roma were sent to Gypsy labour detachments, we were surprised to meet a great number of Roma who were sent to fight in Russia or, later, in Italy, or who served in Slovakia. Among them were Otto Baláž and many others. Ernest Daško, Kolomán Pompa and Vojtěch Fabián (who was transferred from Russia) served on the Italian Front.

The testimonies of former Romani armed soldiers are so fascinating and informative that they could fill this entire paper. Therefore, we will limit ourselves to the most basic information

Otto Baláš says:

> At that time, few Gypsies were in fighting units. They put Gypsies into labour detachments. But they took me into a fighting unit. Of us they also took my cousin Pal'o. He didn't look like a Gypsy – he was white, and also Mikulaš and Jan from Herlice. They took us four from our neighbourhood.

Dark skin – that is, a racial characteristic — undoubtedly played a role in the draft. Apart from very dark Ladislav Tancoš and Tibor Gombár, the rest of our witnesses who were called to arms are light-skinned. Vojtěch Fabián had told a recruiting doctor that he was a Gypsy. *But please, just never say you're a Gypsy. You don't look like one. They would send you to a camp and it would be bad for you.* So, Fabián was recruited and travelled with the Slovak army to Russia and then, later, to Italy.

Tibor Gombár was sent to Russia with a military unit: as a so-called 'farm boy'. Gombár came from a family with many children. His father had been disabled since the First World War. His parents gave their seven-year-old son to a farmer as a labourer. He remained there until he was drafted into the army. Instead of the son of the family where he worked, he was enrolled into a twenty-one member Gypsy company of 'farm boys' – that is, Romani labourers who were sent to the Russian Front instead of young Slovaks.

Ladislav Tancoš was a trained metalworker at the time of induction. They took him as a Slovak – although he was markedly dark-skinned – and put him into a Gypsy anti-aircraft company in Žilina. In Žilina, Mr Tancoš was active at the beginning of the uprising: Partisans invaded the barracks and captured them without a fight; the warehouse keeper gave over the keys; a fascist major, Čilek, was shot, and Laci Tancoš, along with the others, marched toward Banská Bystrica where the uprising began.

Josef Pešta was inducted into the army from the Petič work camp where they sent Roma from the Prešov region without distinguishing between 'asocial' and 'assimilated'. Pešta had married into a Romani family of pig traders in Kapučany. He worked as a truck driver and transported pigs. His hobby was motorcycling. In 1938, he became a motorized messenger in the Czechoslovak army. Although he had had a decent job, professional qualifications and a permanent home, he was sent to Petič during the mass recruitment of Gypsies. A month later, military headquarters in Prešov transferred him from there.

An officer came with a driver and immediately picked me out. They put a uniform on me and in three days I was at the front. We arrived at Malinovka-Kalinovka in Russia and, there, First Lieutenant Karpov captured us. They took us to Rostov, from Rostov to Buzuluk, and, in March 1943, we had already joined Svoboda.

In Buzuluk, Czech Lieutenant-Colonel (later General) Ludvík Svoboda formed a Czechoslovak unit that, towards the end of the war, grew into the First Czechoslovak Army and distinguished itself in Sokolov, Žačkov, Dukla and elsewhere. Josef Pešta served as one of the motorized messengers with Svoboda himself.

Apart from Vojtěch Fabián, all of the witnesses we interviewed either deserted (like Otto Baláž) or they were captured. Many allowed themselves to be captured (like Štefan Kočko) and later reached the Svoboda army. Svoboda recruited his army in prison camps, among other places. The story of Josef Diro is interesting. He was drafted as a Slovak:

I tell the doctors that I'm from a poor family and have to support my sick father, that I'm a Gypsy and I myself am not well. The doctor kicked me in the rear end: Healthy, capable, perfect, that's all! And so they sent me to non-commissioned-officers' school in Prešov, six months later to the Dolný Kubín training camp before going to the front. So we went though Ukraine and Belarus to Rostov. We had good officers, Slovaks. The Germans went ahead and we were in the middle or the back. And when we kept low and some German raised his head, bang, and a Slovak shot him – instead of the Russian shooting. Well, then they didn't trust us and made us dig trenches. We got as far as Rostov and there we were captured, the whole battalion. [Then Svoboda's men came to the camp]. They wrote down our names, how many Czechoslovaks there were and who wanted to go with him, with Svoboda. We all wanted to. At night we shaved, bathed, got ready and, in the morning, when Svoboda's men were to come for us, the Russians took us somewhere else. And they did that to us three times. We were already in Romania, in Bucharest. There Svoboda's officers also came to us; they brought us money, razor blades, soap and cookies so we could be prepared. And, early in the morning, the Russians took us over to New America –Nový Donbas. That's some place! Nothing but mineshafts, and we had to work in the pits and that's all. I didn't get home until 1946.

From Jozef Diro we have a unique account of the conditions in a Soviet prison camp: Little food, worms swimming in the soup, inadequate hygiene. Diro saw a guard beat a prisoner to death because that prisoner had caused the guard to be punished by a superior officer. Diro was one of the few who survived a gas explosion in a shaft.

The German military leadership stopped trusting the Slovaks because many individuals and whole groups deserted. Captain Nálepka brought his whole unit over to the Russians. In autumn 1943 two thousand soldiers of the Slovak army crossed over to the Russians in Melitopol. So, at the end of 1943, both Slovak divisions were pulled out of the Russian Front. The combat division was transferred to Transylvania and the rear division to Italy.

In Italy

In Italy the fighting intensified; the number of allied air-raids increased; the Italian army was decimated; anti-Nazi revolts occurred, and finally, on 13 October 1943, Italy declared war on Germany. The Slovak division that had been pulled out of the Eastern Front was, of course, no longer provided with weapons, but was assigned to clear away unexploded bombs and dig ditches.

While Vojtěch Fabián reached Italy from Russia, Ernest Daško and Kolomán Pompa-Emelik were sent there directly from Slovakia as Slovak soldiers. Mr Pompa remembers:

> We came with guns, but a couple of days after that we had to put our rifles 'in a pyramid' and, instead of rifles, they gave us shovels and we had to clear away unexploded bombs. The Germans gave Slovak soldiers the most dangerous work of all.

Vojtěch Fabián's account of Roma in Italy is extremely interesting:

> We were in Rocca Gorga, seventy kilometres from Rome. And, at night, the Americans bombarded us, right at Easter. They destroyed everything, everything; about ten of us survived, me too. I tell you, girl, I have always been lucky. We went to another regiment; we got there at three in the morning. We got up early, I wash, comb my hair, look around at the terrain. And, girl, what do I see? Only Roma! I had no idea there were so many Roma among the Slovak soldiers! And those Guardists who were among the Slovaks, I beat them to a pulp. One sergeant, Baláš was his name, from Michalovce says: 'Gypsy, c'mere. Why didn't you go to peel potatoes?' That Rom was from Trnava, from Bučany. I go to that sergeant – I was a

*staff sergeant – and I say: 'Sergeant, come here! Why did you beat that
Gypsy kid like that?' And he said: 'What's with this Gypsy! He doesn't
want to peel potatoes. Everybody has to.' And I ask, 'Are you allowed to
slap people here?' 'Well, he's only a Gypsy!' And I gave that sergeant such
a whack that he staggered. He never knew that I was a Gypsy, too. Not
even my commander knew it. Then I went to the commander. His name
was N'an'ák and I tell him, "Captain, yesterday we were bombarded. We
came to you and I see how you treat Gypsies. I would be glad to watch
over these Gypsies. And N'an'ák says, 'I'd be delighted, I'd be delighted.'"*

From that time on Vojtěch Fabián was in charge of a Gypsy company –
thirty men. They continued doing the hardest work – as did the ordinary
Slovaks as well – but Fabián intervened in order to ensure better
treatment of the company by their superiors.

Ernest Daško and Kolomán Pompa-Emelik colourfully describe their
fate on the Italian Front. At the end of the war, when the army was
already demoralized, Daško managed, with help from his Italian
girlfriend, to join the Italian partisans. Pompa-Emelik's recalls that the
famous Romani musician, Rinaldo, was on the Italian Front. He was
released from his work duties – unofficially, of course – and Slovak
officers took him on their staff to play for them during their drinking
bouts. Daško tells of seeing a black American for the first time in his life
during an encounter with the American army. He spoke Romani to him
and was surprised that the man was so black and still did not understand
him.

We have talked a great deal about Roma in the army because, so far,
we have not come across any literature on this theme and we feel it
necessary to publicize how, for example, in the liberation of
Czechoslovakia, a significant number of Roma served beside the soldiers
of Svoboda's First Czechoslovak Army. Ilona Lacková, Bartoloměj
Daniel and the survivors we interviewed refer to Roma who fell on the
Eastern Front. Of our witnesses, several were commended for their
courage: Kočko, Gombár, Pešta, and especially Otto Baláž who, in 1996,
received a commendation of gratitude to the "Slovak co-fighters" directly
from the then USSR President Boris Yeltsin.

Roma in forced-labour camps

Ctibor Nečas writes in detail about forced-labour camps based on a range
of archive material. The following section draws on his writing.[24]

According to a February 1941 notification by the Ministry of the Interior of the government to the Prime Minister of the Slovak Republic, there were to be "labour detachments in concentration camps with required residence and compulsory labour." Their role was "to quarantine and punish people for political, racial and moral reasons".[25]

From 1941 until December 1944, eleven forced-labour camps were gradually established. Most Romani men who were sent to labour camps went through those that operated in eastern Slovakia from 1942 until December 1943. None of the forced-labour camps were exclusively Gypsy but, in them, Romani detainees dominated by far. For purposes of orientation, we will present some of the figures that historian Nečas found in the archives: During the first recruitment campaign in July 1942, 750 people, 95 per cent of whom were Gypsies, were added to the labour detachment in Hanušovce nad Topl'ou (in Petil').[26]

From other tables of Nečas concerning labour detachments in Bystré nad Topl'ou, we have selected some data:

1 April 1943: 83 non-Gypsies/218 Gypsies (= 301)
15 April 1943: 168 non-Gypsies/341 Gypsies (= 509)
1 May 1943: 192 non-Gypsies/314 Gypsies (= 506)
1 July 1943: 10 non-Gypsies/34 Gypsies (= 44).

In Dubnica nad Váhom in December 1943, out of 331 detainees, there were 156 non-Gypsies and 175 Gypsies.[27]

The labour detachments in eastern Slovakia mainly built railroad tracks that were important for links to the east, where further military transports were destined to go. When work in a certain location was finished, the regiment was transferred to a further section. According to survivors, large numbers of them were transferred from Hanušovce nad Topl'ou to Bystré nad Topl'ou and to Nižný Hrabovec, for example.

The camps were supposed to be materially equipped and provided for by the construction firms. A subsidiary police office was responsible for the operation of the camp and the work of the prisoners. Mayors and notaries were supposed to choose people "fit for re-education work". The votes of members of the Hlinka Guard, and, occasionally, the votes of local police played a significant role. According to testimonies of our interviewees, a Gadjo mayor, in some cases, entrusted the job to a Gypsy leader (*vajda*) – in order to transfer that unpleasant responsibility to someone else. Of course, the *vajda* of a Gypsy settlement was thus placed in a very stressful situation. According to the testimony of Vasil Demeter, his own uncle took advantage of a long-time family feud with his brother-in-law, Vasil's father (a professional feud between two music groups fighting over the same jobs in one region). He, being a Gypsy *vajda*, had Vasil, the strongest and most feared adversary of the enemy relatives' branch, arrested as a communist and sent to Legan'a, the hardest labour camp within the borders of Hanušovce nad Topl'ou.

According to the account of Tibor Cica of Pavlovce nad Uhom – site of one of the largest Romani settlements – a Romani *vajda* also chose to send to the camp *anyone he wanted; anyone he didn't want to he didn't send.* Cica's family was protected because the *vajda* was his grandfather's brother. *Of course, those families where he chose someone for camp, they were mad at us. But what choice did uncle have? But he couldn't send his own blood to camp.* The regime caused a conflict between the traditional Romani imperative of kinship solidarity and the need to obey Gadjo orders.

On the other hand, according to the testimonies of Jolanka and Aladár Kurej of Podskalka u Humenného, a Gypsy *vajda* was brutally beaten by a local policeman because he refused to send any Roma to a labour camp. *He was just, but he also was afraid that, if he took away the boys of those families, they would get their revenge.*

Accounts of interviewees show the varying approaches of authorities towards Gypsies in individual communities and, more particularly, in individual regions of Slovakia. While, in many localities in eastern Slovakia, people were taken away in great numbers, in central and western Slovakia, many mayors or notaries "didn't give up their Gypsies". František Kotliar of Richnava, district of Spišká Nová Ves, for example, states that their engineer stood by the Roma saying: *I need the Gypsies for reclamation of the stream and, because they are hardworking, I won't send them to the camp.*

The Romani historian Dr Bartoloměj Daniel says that not one inhabitant of his hometown, Šaštín, was sent to a camp. Nor were any from some other nearby Romani communities because Roma made their living as musicians, blacksmiths and field workers. In Šaštín, they worked on lands belonging to the Order of St Francis. Their village mayors protected them "as honest citizens".

Jozef Horváth of Železník, tells how their mayor also stood by his Roma. Apparently, no one from Železník was in any work camp. Horváth, though, was unfortunate that his legal domicile was in Kapušany where he had been married, and from there almost all Roma between 16 and 60 years old were sent to a camp.

Songs of the camps

Conditions in the work camps were terrible. In one of the camps a song was composed. Based on a traditional song Čhajori roman'i, it became the hymn for Roma all over the former Czechoslovakia. After 1990, Romani political meetings, conferences and congresses in Slovakia began or ended with this song and they still do today.

Čhajori roman'i	Romani girl
ker mange jagori	Make me a bonfire
na cikn'i na bari	Not large not small
Čarav tro vod'ori[28]	Urgently I beg you
Andr'oda taboris	In that camp
phares but'i keren	people work hard
mek mariben chuden	and still here people are beaten.
a bokhate meren	And they die of hunger
Ma maren ma maren	Don't beat me don't beat me
Bo man murdarena	You are killing me
Hin man khere čhave	I have children at home
Ko len l'ikerela	Who will support them?

A less known song that we recorded by Ján Horváth of Mirol'a and by Marynda Kešelova of Litomn'ice goes:

Devla mro gulo Del	God my sweet God
som adaj korkoro	I am here alone
e lopata mri phen'ori	The shovel is my sister
krompačis phraloro	The pick-axe my brother

Labour camps were not extermination camps but many died there. According to Nečas, "fourteen men met their death in the eastern Slovak labour detachments."[29] These official figures, which Nečas had confirmed by a regimental doctor, are very much an underestimate. Nečas himself accepts this. According to the accounts of our witnesses, many more Roma died: of hunger, as a result of beatings; from illnesses and exhaustion; of fatal injuries. For example, while building a tunnel in Hanušovce, a Romani worker was buried alive (related by Vasil Demeter and Nečas). Demeter speaks of a case in which prisoners smothered a fellow-prisoner who was an informer. *Nobody was punished because who would work for the fascists?*

More than one prisoner died soon after returning home, his health destroyed by the conditions in the labour camps. Roma – and Gadje – deliberately maimed themselves to avoid being sent to a camp. According to Vojtěch Grundza, Roma exchanged disabling techniques with each other and with Slovak villagers, who occasionally felt threatened and with whom the Roma felt a sense of solidarity. One commonly used technique, for example, was putting drops of chewing tobacco into the eyes, which then became infected and swollen. Grundza did this and, as long as he lived, his eye never healed.

According to all of the survivors, the worst suffering in the camp was from chronic hunger. On the way to or from work, the starving prisoners, when unobserved, picked turnip leaves, sorrel, and any kind of edible greens. If a guard saw them, they were beaten.

Relatives of 'detainees of the first category' (those who worked properly, did not rebel, and did not try to escape) were allowed to take food to the camp for them. Usually these would be mothers, sisters or wives. The mother and the young wife of Vasil Demeter would walk to Hanušovce from Ladomirová, which was eighty kilometres away; they slept in the woods overnight. The problem was that families that had lost their breadwinner also suffered from hunger and it was extremely difficult to obtain food for their imprisoned relatives. Nobody could take food to prisoners from distant areas of Slovakia. Sometimes, more fortunate prisoners shared their food with them.

The *dereš* – the punishment bench where four local policemen beat them brutally until they were unconscious – was the most common punishment for any kind of transgression.

A further source of suffering was the inadequate clothing. The prisoners worked in their own clothes, the clothing they had been wearing when they came from home. They also slept in these clothes. Mr Synáč and Mr Kešel told of how cement sacks tied at the waist served as their only clothing; underneath they were entirely naked. A number of Roma had no shoes or had shabby shoes that tore after a few days of work. They worked barefoot. The testimonies of survivors are even confirmed by police reports: "The Gypsies are insufficiently clothed... therefore it would be better to obtain some clothes, at least for the winter months."[30]

Overfull barracks – where the prisoners slept on straw mattresses and sometimes only on scattered straw – swarmed with insects: bedbugs, fleas, lice. *When I got home, my mother scraped off the lice with a piece of wood,* said Vojtěch Grundza.

The conditions in the camps were so terrible that, in a letter sent to the Ministry of the Interior on 11 April 1943, a member of the Slovak parliament, M. Hun'ka, wrote: "The camps were established to re-educate asocial elements and not for people to be tortured and to be reduced to even worse moral decay"[31]

Escapes

A number of prisoners attempted to escape from camp. Escape was clearly not easy, but, unlike from concentration camps, it was possible. If the escape succeeded, the local policeman came to search for the escapee and very often found him. Punishment for escape, or for attempting to escape, was a drastic beating on the *dereš*. The first time Grundza ran away, he hid in a cemetery between the tomb of his grandfather and that of his aunt. His mother took food to him at night. One day he could not bear the hunger, cold and fear and went home to eat. The policeman on guard descended upon him. He was taken away to the camp and beaten so badly that for two days he was unable to move. When he fell unconscious, the guards poured water on him and beat him further. Despite this, Grundza tried to run away again. This time he was not caught. He hid in a brick-lined well and leaned on protruding stones with his hands and feet. He could hear the local police walking around the well and looking for him.

Anna Cinová related the escapes of her son Jan Lacko in detail. Like Grundza, Jan, who was hiding in the forest with his cousin Štefan, once came home to eat.

> *The moment he started eating halušky, bang, a policeman was at the door. We jumped, but the policeman was startled, too. 'Lacko, you're not watching out. Now I have to take you away!' I started to beg him: 'What would your mother have done if they had taken you away to the camp?' 'I understand you, mother,' the policeman says, 'but if I don't take him, they'll punish me. The people saw your Janek creep through the window. Try to go to the notary and pray for him. But I have to take him with me.' 'At least promise me that they won't beat him.' 'I can only promise that I'll*

say that he gave himself up to me and then maybe they won't beat him so much.'

During one of Jan Lacko's escapes, both he and his cousin Štefan, who regularly ran away with him, were caught. Their hands and feet were bound and they were driven back to the camp in the rear of an open truck. At a sharp curve, the helpless Štefan rolled out of the truck, hit his head on a stone and was killed. His name is not mentioned in any lists of victims.

The conditions in the camps harmed the prisoners physically, mentally and morally. One of the demoralizing methods was the use of informers. The local police received direct instructions on that subject from the Ministry of the Interior: "...it is necessary to have a well-organized news service. It is necessary to win over informers from among the detainees."[32] As mentioned earlier, one night one of the informers in the Hanušovce camp was smothered with a blanket by other prisoners. A further demoralizing method was to force prisoners, instead of policemen, to beat their fellow prisoner. Vasil Demeter says:

Many people ran away. They couldn't stand it there. There were these kinds of wooden barracks, I can't even talk about it (cries)... Lice, fleas, bedbugs. And if a man didn't do what he was supposed to, a policeman took a shovel or a pick-axe, whatever fell into his hand, and he whacked him. I was the foreman of a gang of workers. I behaved myself. I didn't try to run away. And there were Roma from Mirošová, and they tried to escape. And they were caught. Well, they ordered me to beat them. Only how could I beat them? I didn't have the heart to whack them. So I pretended to punch them twice and a Guardist said, 'Can't you do better than that?' I say, 'I don't have the strength!' 'I'll show you how it's done!' I got mad at those Roma from Mirošová that I was beaten because of them, but then I felt sorry for them. They tied them to a rack and whacked them. One vomited on a policeman's boot – and they made him eat it.

Forced-labour camps contributed to the decimation and pauperization of many Romani families. The detainees received negligible pay. None of our interviewees received any. Meanwhile, prisoners from the camp in Hanušovce nad Topľou who built the Prešov-Strážké section of train lines earned 2,767,235.80 crowns for the construction company.[33]

Pauperization understandably led to 'criminality'. Romani families, especially those with many children, deprived of their most capable worker, had to look for a livelihood wherever they could, which often meant theft. Letters from local and regional authorities calling for the improvement of the situation reached the Central Labour Office of the Ministry of the Interior: The district head of Humenné wrote that sorting out the question of detainees' income was necessary in the interest of peace and for limiting theft of food from fields by the children and families of the deported men.[34] The petty criminality into which Roma were impelled, through discriminatory measures, then justified more and harsher discriminatory measures: a vicious circle of cause and effect.

Regulation and Ghettoization

On 20 April 1941, the Ministry of the Interior issued a decree to regulate the lifestyle of Gypsies. In the first place, the decree definitively invalidated travel permits and ordered their owners to return to the town where they were born or to the town where they had lived for the longest period of time. There they were placed under police supervision and could only leave their homes with permission from the local police commander.[35]

The decree affected not only travelling Roma. According to Ilona Lacková, Františka Zimová and other interviewees, not even settled Roma were permitted to leave their hometown without permission. In her autobiographical account, Ilona Lacková describes how she slipped out in the night with her six-month old son in her arms and walked twenty-eight kilometres through a forest from Kapušany, where she lived after her marriage, to her mother in Velký Šariš. Once she was stopped in her native village. As she had lost her residency permit, the local police – because they did not want to beat a breast-feeding mother – beat Ilona's husband instead.

Františka Zimová reports that, in Kopčany, the local police beat up a Rom who had got married there, without changing his official residency. As a result of the harsh beating, the Rom died a few days later.

From the literature on this subject, we learn that various regional and communal bureaux issued their own directives limiting the movement of Gypsies, prohibitions against entry into a town, and permission to enter a district only during limited hours of the day, generally from noon to 2pm.

Vladimír Gecelovský quotes a decree from the Chief Administrator of the district of Dobšiná from 19 May 1944, in which he states: "In a decree by this office of 15 June 1943, I forbade Gypsies to linger in the streets of the town of Dobšiná. As my prohibition has not been followed and town police have not done their duty in this matter, with my notice of

4 February 1944 (number D-5928/1 – 1943) I have again pointed out that this prohibition is valid. And it is to be consistently obeyed. Therefore I point out that the streets of the town of Dobšiná... are swarming with Gypsies without the town police noticing them or doing the right thing. If it comes to my attention once more that the police are not doing their duty, there will be consequences."[36]

The question arises whether the police did not follow their orders to arrest Gypsies in the town out of laziness or whether the local police depended on neighbourly relations in the town and ignored at least some Roma.

The worst were those outside police and Hlinka Guardists, said Štefan Gašpar. *Ours didn't even hurt us that much. But those police higher up saw it and so they began to change them around. They got someone from Zvolen to do bad things to us and they sent ours to do harm somewhere else.*

This actually happened when, after the occupation, the position of the fascist wing was strengthened with German soldiers, policemen and special anti-partisan units.

The prohibition against entering a town was enforced most in eastern Slovakia, mainly in Prešov. Ilona Lacková describes the situation in detail. The police drove around town in a car called Eržička, named after a famous prostitute. In this car they took away the Roma who had disregarded the prohibition and come to town to go shopping or to sell at the flea market, which was an important supplementary source of income. At the police post, they punished them by shaving a cross on the heads of the men and cutting off half the hair of the women. Beatings during interrogations were usual. If a man was caught several times, they sent him to a labour camp.

Long after the war, Slovak Roma were still singing a stanza they added to the popular czardas song *"Duj duj duj duj deš-u-duj."* In it they made fun of their bitter fate.

> Two two two two twenty-two
> I won't go I won't go to town
> In town they would nab me
> Cut off my lovely hair
> All the whores in Prešov would cry.

The previously mentioned decree of the Ministry of the Interior of

April 1941 contained an order that, if Gypsies lived along a public road, they must remove their home and rebuild it far from the rest of the inhabitants in a remote area.[37]

The fact that the decree was reissued on 21 July 1943 in itself indicates that it had not been obeyed. We encountered only one case of Roma expelled from their town after the issue of the original decree of 1941. This does not necessarily mean that there were no more such cases. Romani artist Jaroslav Cicko, a native of Bodorov, who was two years old at the time, remembers "as in a dream" how his whole family dragged themselves a long way to the fields, and there they slept in the open air until they built a temporary hut. Apparently the whole village was moved because it lay on the route from Bratislava to Žilina, and Minister of the Interior Mach, "who didn't want to look at Gypsies", travelled along that road.

Mass expulsion of Gypsy settlements out of towns began in autumn 1943 and continued until the Slovak National Uprising in August 1944. The drastic forced resettlement of more than six hundred Roma from the town of Velký Šariš to a distant slope, on a hill called Korpáš, is described by Ilona Lacková.[38] The frightening experience became the theme of her first play *The Burning Gypsy Camp*.[39]

Nowhere in the literature is there mention of the number of Romani communities forced out of a town or those who then suffered hardships in much worse residential and economic conditions. Lacková, Verona Gin'ová and her son, the writer Andrej Gin'a (from Šariské Dravce, district of Prešov), told us about the displacement of settlements in detail. František Klempár and others also mentioned this. On the other hand, we recorded many other survivors who were not given up to the camps by their mayors. Anna Mižkarová of Hromoš could not praise her Gadjo mayor enough because he looked after her and her brother when their father died and their mother became very ill.

None of the villages near the south Moravian border relocated their Gypsy citizens, according to the testimonies of both Dr Bartoloměj Daniel and Františka Zímová. Various reasons were given for relocating settlements or not relocating them. Some of these reasons are mentioned in archive material. Vladimír Gecelovský in his monograph on the situation in Gemer quotes, for example, the July 1944 report from the police station in the town of Betliar in the district of Dobšiná:

> Those same Gypsies from the town of Vel'ká Poloma were to have been relocated to the Slaná stream... but they were not transferred to that place

because many of them work in a paper factory in Slavošovice and come to Vel'ká Poloma only once a month... Gypsies from the town of Betliar like those from Vel'ká Poloma cannot be considered as travelling because they are all employed either by the Rimomuránská Company in Nižná Slaná or by the paper factory in Slavošovice.[40]

Of eleven communities in the described region, only three settlements were relocated; the others, according to the police station's records, remained in their original place. Of course, there were not only neighbourly, humanitarian or pragmatic economic reasons for some villages not relocating their Gypsies. They may have lacked suitable land or had a slow moving bureaucratic administration.

Although the majority of settled Slovak and Hungarian Roma in Slovakia lived in Gypsy settlements before the War, these were not ghettos in the true sense of the word, but could perhaps be compared to *basti* quarters in India.[41] Generally, Roma could leave their settlements freely and were not limited in their movement.

Moving around on the land was tremendously important, economically, as well as socially and culturally. Music bands played not only in their own villages but also throughout the region. It would have been difficult to make a living in one town alone. Of course, they played in villages that didn't have their own Gypsies. Wives of blacksmiths sold the metal products made by their husbands *pal o gava* (from village to village). *Te phirel pal o gava* (to walk from village to village) is an expression with a deeper social significance than the combination of words indicates. The expression implies to go farther for food, because one village alone could not support several Romani professionals. Large groups of men and women went to work in the distant villages on landowners' properties during harvest or to do other work the landlord ordered.

Several times a year they walked to fairs, sometimes even 80 kilometres away. At the fairs, they made important social, business and cultural contacts. For example, they looked for suitable brides from groups that were socially close although not related by blood.

In my opinion, we can label not only resettlement but also the widespread limitation of movement as ghettoization. This limitation was made legal after the birth of the Slovak Republic, but mostly put into practice at the end of 1943.

Conditions in the settlements

Living and hygienic conditions worsened with the forced displacement of settlements. The standard of living of individual families varied in the original settlements. For example, Verona Gin'ová, the wife of the Romani mayor of Šariské Sokolovce, had a wooden floor – which not even the houses of poor Slovaks had. She had a brick house – a sign of high status compared to the hovels made of adobe bricks. Even a few eastern Slovak towns were built with adobe bricks. When she told about her expulsion from villages, she cried again and again because she had to leave a new house with a wooden floor. Like everyone, she lived in a ramshackle hut in a forest outside of the village. Ghettoization made earning a legal, honest living impossible. It led to further pauperization and, with it, forced criminality.

In Eastern Slovakia, authorities solved the problem of hygiene – in displaced settlements as well as in those that were not displaced – by mass haircuts for men and women: on the head, under the arms, on their private parts. Haircutting interfered profoundly with traditional culture; it was an unimaginable shame (*ladž*). In a traditional Romani community, a woman's hair was cut as punishment for adultery, and unfaithfulness was one of the worst crimes a woman could commit.

Typhus broke out in a number of settlements. The Romani author Margita Reiznerová, who sent us a recording about the war period dictated to her by her mother, writes that seven members of her family died of typhus.

Displacement of Romani settlements from the village to a forest also had its advantages. Lacková writes about a sympathetic doctor who had had signs "Watch out: Typhus" pasted on Gypsy homes, and after that neither police nor Germans bothered the Gypsies – and this lasted until after the occupation by the German army.

After the Slovak National Uprising was crushed, many of the fighters who had not been killed or imprisoned by German units withdrew to the forests and fought further as partisans. The Germans did not know the terrain and more than a few Romani survivors agree that the Germans were afraid of the woods. Mr Ridaj of Rimavská Pila says:

> The Germans didn't move around through the woods. They would rather have burned down a whole town, than chased after partisans in the woods; they didn't much feel like doing that. Our village threw us out into the

woods to live, and we actually had an advantage there because the Germans were afraid and they left us alone.

In many places, the ghettoization of Roma broke the previously good and mutually advantageous relationships between Slovak farmers and their Gypsies. Elsewhere these relationships were strengthened by a common resistance to fascism and Nazism. This will be discussed later.

Ghettoization activated fear, which, in the historic unconscious of Roma, codified the experience of persecution over many centuries. Etela Kompušová of Medzev says: *Fear, constant fear was the worst suffering.*

I surmise that this fear contributed to the emigration to Bohemia and Moravia after the end of the war, and was reinforced with economic and political inducements. The musician Luboš Horváth of Krásna Lúka says:

For two or three years people still didn't believe that the war had really ended. They were afraid; everyone was afraid; they wanted out of the place where they had experienced so much suffering. When the first recruiter came from Bohemia and said we could move to the homes left by the Germans who were chased out, we went.

It is tragic that the displacement of Gypsy settlements and ghettoization in some places in Slovakia did not end even after the war. In Richnava (region of Spišká Nová Ves) Roma lived right in the village. The Nazi army burned down the whole village in punishment for partisan activity. After the war, the Slovaks did not allow Roma to move back and today the gigantic Gypsy settlement nearly three kilometres from the town spreads along two steep slopes.

In the village of Sása-Lomné (Zvolen region), according to Mara Hakelová, a German garrison that went to Roma for entertainment saved them from being displaced. Their colonel was the lover of the then sixteen-year-old Mara. It was only after the war that Roma were displaced to unapproachable hilltops "where the Lord God himself gets lost" in the words of a Slovak who showed us the way there.

Exclusion from education

The exclusion of Romani children from schools was perhaps based on a central decree – we do not know. We have not found this information in the literature on this subject. Until 1939, many Czech and Jewish teachers were teaching in Slovak schools. Romani survivors have praised both groups. After the fall of Czechoslovakia and the creation of the independent Slovak State, the Czechs (numbering some 12,000) were expelled from Slovakia. Czech teachers, policemen and other functionaries were replaced by Slovaks, who often, either out of conviction or fear, sympathized with the fascist regime. We heard first-hand testimony about Gypsy children being excluded from school from Luboš Horváth and Maria Danielová of Podunajské Biskupice. We have three detailed recordings about courageous teachers who risked their jobs and continued teaching Gypsy pupils privately. One teacher was Mr Markuš of Krásna Lúka who taught Luboš Horváth in the evening in his own flat after receiving the order to send the Gypsies home from school. *He was my second father. Even today I telephone him at Christmas and we both cry,* said Luboš.

The Gypsy community in Krásná Lúka was saved from being evicted in a peculiar way. The local Catholic parish priest was secretly seeing Markuš's sister. Because the fascist Slovak State was a clerical state (the head of it was a priest, President Tiso), Catholic priests had an important say. The parish priest continued his secret romance and thus showed readiness, in consultation with the teacher, Mr Markuš, to announce that the local Gypsies were good Catholics who went to church and, through his intervention, the Roma continued living in the town.

Thanks to the brave director of the high school in Rimavská Sobota, Ján Cibula was accepted into secondary school despite the prohibition against teaching Gypsy children. After the war, he graduated, and studied medicine.

The historian Dr Bartoloměj Daniel finished secondary school during the war. His teacher joined the Hlinka Guard – apparently out of fear of losing his job – but he did not expel the Gypsy Daniel. These cases, of course, were exceptions rather than the rule.

The Partisan movement and the Slovak National Uprising

The literature is full of material about the partisan movement and the Slovak National Uprising. However, only a few isolated passages mention the participation of the Roma in the resistance.

The partisan movement as a whole arose in mid-1944. Soviet partisans, who were dropped down into Slovakia as paratroopers, took part in instructing the rebels. Roma were among the paratroopers. We recorded first-hand testimony of Štefan Kočka about this. Ladislav Goral told us about his father, who was a paratrooper.

Groups of partisans destroyed important communications, blew up bridges, liquidated individual fascists, and mobilized a wide section of the population to resist. On 29 August 1944, the Slovak National Uprising was proclaimed in the central Slovak city of Banská Bystrica. The preceding day, before the uprising was proclaimed, President Tiso and the Slovak Republic agreed that German army units would come to Slovakia "to give aid against the partisans". In the SS training schools in Brno and Olomouc (in what was then the Protectorate of Bohemia and Moravia) anti-partisan commandos were quickly set up – death squads such as the SS Edelweiss and the Horst Wessel Commandos.

In October 1944, the Slovak National Uprising was suppressed. A study by Zita Janotková mentions the participation of Romani partisans in the uprising. It is limited to the situation in the Banská Bystrica region. "Citizens of Gypsy origin bravely joined in the fight against fascism. Two of them died in battles at Martin-Priekopa. These partisans were Gustáv and Štefan Bučko."[42] Names of Roma also appear on a few monuments (Bystrany, Žehra), but without ethnic identification.

We recorded detailed first-hand testimony of a few Romani partisans and many testimonies in which witnesses mention their partisan activities or talk about other partisans who had been executed, tortured or decorated later with medals, or who, at the time of our conversation, were no longer alive. As an example, we offer an excerpt from the account of František Klempár:

In 1943 I was recruited. In October they took me into the army, but to the Coffee Army, to a labour detachment. Military clothing, but without arms. Three months later, an officer came and picked boys out. He said to me and my cousin – he's already dead, a man my age – 'You should have been on the front long ago.' And so I was drafted and in January 1944 we went to Italy. Before Christmas they gave us something like passports. They didn't take anyone who had "Slovak nationality – race Gypsy." And those who didn't have 'Gypsy' written down, even if he was one, he went to fight in Italy. I had 'Gypsy' so they returned me; my cousin Mirga didn't have it in his papers – "aryan" – and so he went to Italy.

I got sick, bad rheumatism, I couldn't move, two months I lay in the hospital in Ružomberok. They should already have let me out of the army but then the uprising of 29 August broke out and partisans, ours and Russian, came for us; at the porter's office they detached the telephones and then the Tiso leader had to give up.

Then the partisans said to us soldiers: 'Which of you will join us?' And right away all of us Roma because we all have a few brains, we went with them. They took us with them to the forest near Ružomberok, Bielý Potok it's called. And then the Germans came; they advanced from Poland and directly to us. The whole German army descended on us. They drove us back to Banská Bystrica and from there to Prašivá. There we didn't have anywhere to go. The uprising was crushed and so the Russian commander Jegorov – but we also had our Slovak commander, Josef Podhora was his name – so Jegorov and Podhora talk it over so we can escape and go home.

There were plenty of Roma in our group, but only three of us ran in the same direction: me from Stará Lesná, then one from Spišky Čtvrtok, Kroščen, and one from Poprad. He died in '48 because he was wounded in the leg, he limped, it dried up and then he died. As old as me. Born in '25.

When Klempár returned home having survived a period of wandering, hiding and getting lost, he learned that his settlement had moved from the village to the edge of the woods. They had let only one family stay: his rich father-in-law, who had a large house and was one of the few Romani landowners. *When I came home and saw that we lived in the woods, I burst out crying and said: 'So this is what we fought for?'*

We have another account from Ján Tumi-Koro (the Blind one). I recorded Tumi's testimony in 1995. By that time he was blind and hard of hearing.

Mrs Tumiová helped us during the interview; she knew her husband's story by heart and reminded him of events he had forgotten. Tumi volunteered as a partisan in the town of Valaská (region of Brezno), where they had a base. Mr Tumi's story, due to his state of health, was fragmentary.

Tumi: *The Germans had heavy weapons and our heaviest was a machine gun. A light machine gun.*

(Were there many Roma among the partisans? We asked.)

Tumi: *There weren't many in our group. We were four from around here: one from Mišana, Andro Boldi, and the second – God, where was he from, I'm old and sick, I'm already forgetting a lot. I volunteered in Valaská. There was an agricultural school there, and there a Russian general, Tchernov, took us.*

(Did you get some kind of compensation for fighting as a partisan?)

Tumi: *Nothing. And meanwhile I fought in my own clothing.*

(What did you eat?)

Tumi: *Good heavens! Every two or three days, maybe also nothing. And we drank water from puddles.*

Mrs Tumiová: *And they slept in the woods.*

Tumi: *Out in the open.*

Mrs Tumiová: *But there wasn't snow yet. Only autumn.*

Tumi: *But the rain, the rain! It poured.*

(How long did you stay in those woods? When did you return home?)

Tumi: *In May, not until May. But we weren't fighting any more…*

Mrs Tumiová: *They were blowing up bridges.*

Tumi: *We blew up bridges. And roads. And you know how the Germans got us? We were in a village, Močjari near Zvolen. And our parish priest betrayed us. A Catholic priest.*

Mrs Tumiová: *A Catholic priest betrayed them.*

Tumi: *They got us there, shot at us. But some were able to escape. I could also escape.*

(You were lucky.)

Mrs Tumiová: *Do you hear that you were lucky? We were lucky; we have nine children. All are alive. They live fine. They have their own houses. We built ourselves a house; he (my husband) built it himself. During the day he worked in a quarry; at night he built. He wore his skin off. He later went blind. But, God be praised, we're alive.*

One of the most prominent anti-fascist fighters was Anton Facuna. Although we were in frequent contact with him while doing political work in the Union of Gypsies and Roma, the problems of the time engulfed us so much that we left talking of the war for a later time. Alas, the interview did not take place because Mr Facuna became seriously ill and died in 1980.

We recorded accounts of his activity in the resistance from his sister, Anna Virágová, in 1998 in Martin. Anton Facuna, known under his pseudonym 'Novák', was mentioned with respect and admiration by many other Roma, in detail by Mr and Mrs Abraham of Budča. In May 2001, we visited the Museum of the Slovak National Uprising in Banská Bystrica in order to find out if Anton Facuna was mentioned in archive material. We found his photograph and other material confirming that he was a prominent anti-fascist fighter who used the name Novák and that there was a reward of 100,000 Slovak crowns on his head. Museum workers were amazed when we told them that Facuna was a Rom. They did not have any idea of that. No records had been kept about Romani partisans and participants in the uprising. We could not even find information about the independent Romani Ján Oračko partisan group from Chmel'ov (Poprad district). Both Ilona Lacková and Helena Gašparová of Chmel'ov told us about that six-member Romani partisan group which was part of the Čapajev partisan unit.

Our interviewee, Laco Petík, also took part in the uprising. The interview with him concentrated on his stay in the Sachenhausen concentration camp, where he was taken after he was captured. Those participants in the uprising who were not killed either fled and tried to go home or stayed longer in the woods as partisans. Those who were captured were transported to German concentration camps. Mr Petik relates:

> *I was an active soldier in Trnava and, when the Slovak National Uprising broke out, we joined the partisans. We got to Banská Bystrica, from there to Staré Hory and then to D'umbier and Prašivá. And then there was no longer anywhere to go. There was nothing to eat. We shot horses and we ate horses. We drank water from puddles. We were quite a few Roma. If any of us was caught, straight to Germany. Ravensbrück, Sachsenhausen ... In the concentration camp with us were many Roma from Slovakia, captured partisans. In the cell with me was one of our old men with two sons. They shot all three of them because they tried to escape. We spoke Romani with each other only secretly because we were afraid that they would shoot us. When the Russians conquered Berlin, the Germans evacuated us to the west. They sent us on marches and the Russians kept following us by plane. At night, we broke green brushwood and slept on it; it was cold. The Germans were so cold, one who was guarding us gave us matches so we could warm up by a fire... We were able to escape from the convoy. We were four: one old Gadjo from Čirče, one Rom from Hanušovce, me and one Romani musician – what was his name again? I don't remember any more.*

Emil Šarközi of Svätý Križ (today Žiar nad Hronom), as a prisoner of the uprising, was taken to Berlin, where apparently a concentration camp had been built in a hurry. When he returned home, he found SS units had burned down his settlement and his Romani neighbours had been murdered. His closest family survived because, at the time of this mass murder, his father and another brother were in the Gypsy internment camp in Dubnica nad Váhom, and his mother and his youngest brothers and sisters and another few Roma were hiding in the woods.

Apart from active participation in the anti-fascist resistance, a number of Roma provided partisans with lodgings and shared their meagre food with them. Elsewhere, on the other hand, well-supplied groups of partisans shared their food with Roma. Roma shared their news of the situation in the town with the partisans and oriented them to the terrain. This coexistence, which carried enormous risks of brutal reprisal, took place mainly in those settlements that had been thrown out of villages to the edge of the woods.

For cooperation with the partisans or only on Nazi suspicion that the "Gypsies are partisans", a number of Romani communities were murdered; their settlements were burned; captured individual Romani partisans were brutally tortured to death similarly to partisans of other nationalities.

Reprisals after the German occupation

The occupation of Slovakia by German troops and the suppression of the Uprising led to brutal reprisals. Official propaganda against "domestic traitors, Czechoslovaks, Czechs, Jews, Jewish Bolsheviks, and thieving bands", as the insurgent fighters were termed, literally had the characteristics of a pogrom and in some way explained and justified the cruel repression by the occupying and Guardist units. They left behind them mass graves of nearly 4,000 victims; they arranged for transports to concentration and prison camps where a further thousand people died; they filled the prisons and internment camps in Slovakia.[43]

During that era, the greatest number of Roma died. Individuals who were caught as partisans – or only on suspicion that they were partisans – were murdered; whole Romani communities were burned and shot.

Nečas, in his chapter 'Murdered Gypsy populations in the years 1944–1945',[44] names Romani communities that were slaughtered almost in their entirety. We recorded a few first-hand testimonies of Roma who, for some reason, were not at the place of the murder at the time or survived the massacre. We obtained other indirect accounts from Slovak neighbours or Roma from nearby towns.

Roma in Tisovec (Rimavská Sobota) were almost all murdered. According to concurring accounts of Mrs Hudecová, a former school inspector who had begun to work during the war as a young teacher, and Mr Ridaj (a Rom), of the nearby town of Rimavká Píl'a, a German informer Antek came to the Roma dressed as a partisan and asked a group of Tisovec Roma if they would go with the partisans and blow up a bridge. All the men agreed and waited until they could join the sortie. Instead of partisans, an SS commando invaded the community. Fourteen men were shot; ten women and twenty children were executed the next day in Nemecká nad Hronom. In Tisovec there is a memorial at the edge of the town with 44 Romani names. The ethnicity of the victims is not mentioned.

During the raid in Tisovec, one single fourteen-year-old girl, the future Mrs Mušuková, saved herself. She hid in a pile of potatoes under her bed. She died two years before we came to Tisovec (1994) to collect testimonies about the events.

We heard about Tisovec through the narration of Koloman Sendrej. Mr Sendrej was in a unit of the Slovak army – again one of those Roma who were not classified to be enrolled in the Gypsy labour detachments – and, after the Slovak National Uprising erupted, the Germans arrested their whole battalion that was based in the town of Palota near the Polish border. Everyone was deported to a temporary concentration camp near the French border. Mr Sendrej told us:

> *A Rom from Tisovec was with us, Dono was his name. And that Dono, when they stuffed us in trains in Michalovce, he said he was going to escape. He and I were travelling in the same wagon. When they slammed the door from the outside and the train started, he pulled up a floorboard and let himself down. Nothing happened to him because the train was high. When he got back home in Tisovec, the settlement had been burned down and his whole family had been murdered. When I returned from Germany, the first thing I did was find out if Dono was alive. He was. But how did he live? When he got home he didn't find anything or anybody.*

None of the some 45 Roma survived in the town of Lutila. On 2 November they were murdered for collaboration with the partisans.[45] Mrs Mikušova, whose father was the mayor of the town at the time of the pogrom, recounted:

> *Those Gypsies weren't bad. They went around playing music; two of them worked as blacksmiths. When they didn't have anything to eat, they came and asked us and we gave them. They didn't steal, they were not used to stealing. And when that had to happen, when they were taking them away, my father had to be there and they fell to their knees and begged: 'Mr Mayor, save us, Mr Mayor, save us.' But he said: 'What can I do? I am powerless in this! I can't do anything about it.'*

Could? Could not? Who can judge? The truth is that many mayors, police, employers, even members of the German Army did save Roma from being massacred.

In the town of Ilija (Banská Štiavnica), out of a 111-member Romani settlement, one woman and her child were saved. The Roma were murdered here on 22 November 1944, along with Slovak anti-fascist fighters. The names of all the victims are carved onto a monument, above which rises one of the oldest churches in Slovakia, a monument under UNESCO preservation.

According to Janotková, "on 14 November sixty citizens of Gypsy origin were murdered in Čierny Balog. Women and children were burned alive in wooden hovels, men shot in the valley of Vydrovo. On that very day [SS units] burned down the Gypsy settlement of Pusto."[46]

In Polomka (Brezno region) the Romani settlement was burned, but, according to the account of our witness, 98-year-old Mrs Helena Grl'áková, "good Germans" let Roma escape through windows and, in the hovels, set fire only to the corpse of a man who had been shot and one infirm person. There were numerous other pogroms – for example, of the Romani men in Kremenička.

We will end with the story of the burnt-down settlement in Svätý Kríž. We recorded an interview with Koloman Šarközi in 1994. We present a slightly shortened version of the interview:

I was thirteen years old. The time came when we had to evacuate to Bystrica. A drummer drummed out that anyone who wanted to leave for Bystrica should and anyone who didn't could stay. My family went. All of us Roma went except those who lived here and were musicians, well-known musicians who played in hotels and cafés. Well, they went only to Svätý Ján with us, and from there they returned home. And there were partisans with them. And the mayor said that this treason had been committed by Gypsies!

(What kind of treason?)

The partisans attacked a German at the gate-house in town. The Roma hadn't done anything; they were completely innocent. Roma were musicians, excellent musicians, and musicians are fine people. Only the village committed that 'treason'. And the Germans didn't ask who really did it. No investigation. They came to the settlement and burned and burned. If we had returned with them, they would have burned us, too.

(How many days before that did you leave?)

About three days. We went to Svätý Ján, to Dúbrava, Budča, Zvolen, Bystrica. On foot. Gadje and Roma. And that trupák, that German plane from above, it shot at Roma like at dogs. Then we escaped into the forest and then they couldn't get us any more. We came to Bystrica, from Bystrica to Kremnica and then the Germans caught us. They took us away to Štubn'a and there they beat us. From Štubn'a to Martin and there they kept my father and my older brother. They took them to Dubnica to a camp. They let us go home. But there the tunnel was blown up, so we went home on foot. And a German took us with a rifle in our backs. But my grandmother knew German. That German – he was a Slovak German, Krekáč, who was going to shoot us in the woods. But a German from Germany came along. He saw we had dismissal papers from Martin and he pushed that Krekáč away. He asks Krekáč what he wants to do with us ? he says 'shoot' – but that German from Germany told him not to shoot us and to let us go. We came home, houses burnt down, Roma murdered. Everybody, everybody, everybody we had left. We made ourselves some sort of huts, hovels, as best we could and we survived in them until the end of the war.

(How many members of your family were killed?)

From my father's family there were four: his sister, her husband and their children. The Germans burned them. From his family nobody was left alive. We were lucky that our mother evacuated with us little ones. My father and one brother survived in Dubnica nad Váhom. They beat them with handles of tools – but they stayed alive. And my brother Emil, they captured him in the uprising, delivered him over to the Germans, but he survived, too... Here they burned seven families to death. Over there in the corner, a mother sat with her child. All that was left there were her bones...

(What happened, after the war, to that mayor who let Roma be killed?)

Nothing. He went on living. When the Russians came, there was a communist here, Morat, and he said what the mayor had done. Only what good was it? A member of the committee said we couldn't throw all the Guardists into one sack, that there were some who fought on the side of the partisans. And the one who had us burned went on living. Then he became a notary. We have not been lucky.

There were many other Romani families who lost several members who were murdered. No-one has counted them. In their memory, we present an excerpt from the account of Ladislav Goral of Ihráč:

My father, the father of my mother, their brothers – my uncles lived in Ihráč. Six little Romani houses. Before the war, we had a good life. My father was a blacksmith; he made chains, tracing wheels, horseshoes. He shod horses for the farmers and they gave us food and money for it. We children helped him from the time we were small; we operated his bellows.

Other Roma earned their living by gathering wood and selling it to the farmers. My grandmother, my father's mother, was a rich lady. She had a cow and a field. And that in itself meant something. My mother's father was an outstanding musician of the Senáš clan. My father and my uncles could read and write. My grandmother had given them a proper education.

During the war they drafted my father into Tiso's army. They sent him to Russia, but Dad deserted and got into Svoboda's parachute unit. When the uprising began, they threw him out of a plane somewhere near Banská Bystrica. He wanted to see his family and at night he somehow got home. But someone saw him and went and reported that a partisan was with the Gypsies. And so they came to shoot him, only Dad managed to escape through a window and disappear into the woods. When they didn't find him, they took four of our men instead of him. Grandpa, my dad's father, dad's brother, a cousin and mum's brother. They asked where my dad was. The Roma wouldn't tell, so they shot them before our eyes.

In the spring of '45, they took my mum, my grandma and my oldest sister – she was seventeen. We had a little boy at home; he wasn't a year old yet. Grandma says to mum: 'Take him with you. Maybe they'll let you go when they see you have a little baby.' And so mum took my little brother with her. Five of us stayed home: my sixteen-year-old brother, then two sisters, I and our three-year-old sister. We didn't go to school; we were afraid and anyway, they didn't take Romani children. I began to go to school when I was ten – and I graduated from an industrial school.

When they took my mum and grandma, our other grandmother took care of us. The war ended and mum didn't return. Dad came back from Russia two months after the war. He had been wounded; he had bullets through his arm and leg. He returned and the first thing he did was go look for mum. Then our whole family got ready to go to Horní Štubn'a, where there was a mass grave of murder victims. The Germans threw everyone they shot into it. There might have been some six hundred people there. After the war German prisoners had to dig out the grave, and the Gadje and Roma looked for their relatives there. We looked, but we didn't find mum. Later we went to Vrútky; there was also such a common grave there. Dad searched for three days; he finally found mum. He recognized her from her scarf. And grandpa recognized grandma from her shoes.

From our settlement, in our family two men were in the resistance, my dad and my uncle. Eight of my closest relatives were murdered.

We recorded a number of cases where a Romani community was saved from murder at the last minute by one of the influential Slovaks, and even by Germans. From them we have chosen the testimony of Mrs Anna Čonková:

One evening, three partisans came to our settlement, Roma. My brother-in-law – my sister's husband – the son of my cousin from Ostrofa, and one more boy from Lomnice, called Bombarda. And one such evil-doer, a Gypsy, may the devil scatter his flesh all over the world, went to the Germans to inform them that my brother was drinking with the partisans. And so the Germans came at night and captured those partisans. They lit a fire, tied them to branches and turned them over that fire. They burned them alive. To this day I still tremble.

Then the Germans came to us: 'Who has a gun?' We didn't have any guns. They grabbed my dad – he had just had surgery – stuck a rifle into him. Dad's wound opened. I ran to him – I might have been twelve years old – but they hit me with the rifle and I fell down.

Then they chased us all out of our huts, lined us up, the old people on one side and the young ones on the other, us children to the side. The parish priest came. Everyone had to confess like in church. Three times they played a funeral song to us.

At Šarpanec near Rakúsy there was a German commander. They telephoned there and asked what they were supposed to do with us. But a farmer, a Guardist, was with the German, and he rescued us. My brother worked with him; he was very satisfied with my brother. He ran to the place where they were planning to shoot us. 'Nicht schießen! Nicht schießen!' Because we worked for the farmers and, if there weren't any Gypsies, who would work on the fields and throw dung and stuff? He says we aren't partisans. They had thrown the children onto a pile and so we all had to pick up our children – infants were there, too. And they told us to go home. But they stood in front of us and made a speech, that if partisans happened to come to our homes – whether they're our own father or son or brother – then we have to inform the mayor immediately. And if we don't do that, then they'll shoot us.

The partisans came that very night. They were starving. And we had bread at home. Dad was a blacksmith. He worked for farmers. For his work they gave us food – such tiny loaves of bread, ones that had cracked crusts or were burned. So what about the partisans? Quick, quick, we gave them two balls of tobacco, three boxes of matches, half a bag of those little cracked loaves and quick, run away and don't let anyone see you.

In my family, they only shot my brother. He was with the partisans. They found him in the woods. Anyone who lives through such fear, the way the Roma did during the war, he can never get rid of it. It's like a bedbug: During the day, when it's light, it crawls away, but, as soon as it's dark, it crawls back and bites and bites.

Mr Cicko of Kl'ačno (Western Slovakia) describes a similar situation:

> *I remember when I was a child, I could have been seven years old. The Gadje hired us to build roads somewhere near Pezinok. Farmers didn't do that work; they worked in the vineyards. A number of us Roma went. We crushed stones for the roads. The Germans thought we were partisans. One night, they surrounded us, loaded us on a car – men, women, children, old people, young people, all of us who were there. They took us to Pravno. We had to march through the town 'til we got to the police station. Something like a camp was there. They kept us hungry, the children naked. It was cold; we were already expecting snow to fall. Then came an order: 'Dig a pit.' And the Germans: 'Anyone who wants to can bind his eyes.' The crying! The sobbing! Well, but then another order came: 'Don't shoot! Those are our workers. They're building us a road!' I still remember that soldier, the one who was supposed to shoot, then he shot the whole load from his machine gun into the rock because he was so angry. He was angry because he couldn't shoot Gypsies.*

In Medzev (Košice), a settlement of ethnic Germans, an official of the fascist Deutsche Partei (German Party) saved the Roma from being murdered: "They work for farmers and they don't do anything wrong." Etela Kompušová presented testimony to this.

According to Helena Dunková of Badín, a German soldier came to the Roma one night – *but not with that death-head; they were the worst!* – and warned them never to say that partisans went to them for entertainment or they would be shot.

The Roma of the settlement in Sása-Lomné (Zvolen) was rescued by Mara Hakelová who was 'friendly with' the commander of a German garrison. The Roma do not condemn her for it. According to Mrs Kompušová of Medzev, apparently the Romani community chose two young girls and asked them to go and prostitute themselves with the German soldiers in order to save the Roma. Margita Reiznerová's mother told her daughter about a similar case.

In the testimonies of Romani interviewees about the Germans, tremendous fear of the gruesome brutality predominates, mainly of those *with the death-head* (the SS). On the other hand, the witnesses repeated more than once: "The ordinary soldiers didn't do anything to us. They came to us for a good time. We had to play for them. They brought the children chocolate." According to Verona Fečová, who was from a clan of rich pig traders, a high German officer was billeted in her home.

> *He helped me drive the pigs back when they escaped; he liked my children. He said, 'I also have children at home, so I know what that means.'*

Internment camp for Gypsies in Dubnica nad Váhom

Six months before the end of the war, under the influence of Nazi soldiers, the slogan "After the Jews, the Gypsies!" began to take hold. A step towards its realisation was the establishment of the internment camp for Gypsies in the western Slovak town of Dubnica nad Váhom. This was initiated by the German military and security section in the region.[47]

One of the forced-labour camps was originally in Dubnica. In it were Gypsies as well as 'Aryan asocials' who performed hard labour.

An order for the transformation of the forced-labour camp into an internment camp was given on 2 November 1944. The camp was supposed to hold "detained Gypsy people without regard to sex or age". From 2 November 'Aryan' detainees began to be released; on 15 November only Roma remained. The status of the camp was changed. By 23 December, 729 Romani prisoners were squeezed into this camp. Among them were approximately 250 children.[48]

We recorded one short and two extremely extensive accounts of the conditions in the camp. Here we will quote only the brief one. We recorded it in 1980 with the couple, Ján and Mária Telvák, both of whom experienced the camp:

In our village, Dlhé nad Cirochou, there was a Gypsy settlement, Romani homes, and that's where we lived. In '44, it was already cold and some German came in the night on a horse and said he had to take us away. Early in the morning, the Germans came, all of them on horseback. They surrounded the whole settlement. Then they took us, all of those who were there, one after the other. They came with cars, loaded us in and took us to Humenné. Then from Humenné we continued in trains that were like cattle trucks.

So we got to Dubnica. People were there from various parts of the country, a lot of people. At first, Gadje were there but, afterward, they let them go so only Roma were left. They herded us behind a kind of wire – men, women, and children – the men here, the women there, and the children there.

We had to work, but what hard work that was. In the winter we worked in an excavator to excavate sand and stones from water. And we were barefoot in the water. What can you get on a shovel in water? Nothing. Water splashes it away.

They beat us on our backs and across our faces with clubs, and we worked from early morning till night and had only an hour for lunch. And, besides, we had to sing. Even the children worked – for a while they had to work or exercise. They were dying of hunger and they didn't even care if they died or not. One woman gave birth to a little boy there and he died because she didn't have any milk.

There was no food, terrible hunger. We ate everything we found, whatever they threw on to the dung heap, garbage, rotten potatoes, calfskin. And we were terrified that they would see us because then they would beat us. It was a horrible life!

They cut off our hair, under our arms, between our legs, everywhere. Then they took a kind of brush and spread an anti-scabies ointment on us because some of the children there got scabies. After that, there was typhus. They took the sick away, as if to a hospital. Only they shot them. We learned that from Gadje when we escaped later. The Gadje told us how the Germans threw our people into carts like timber, and, in addition, threw in machine guns, shovels, and pick-axes, and drove them to the woods. There they had to dig themselves a pit. I've heard that they grabbed each other by the arm, brother with brother, father with daughter and begged each other's forgiveness for the bad things they had done. They forgave each other and cried. The Germans shot them. They fell into those pits, some still alive, and there they hit their heads with pick-axes and threw earth on them.

We learn, from Nečas's publications, that 27 Romani victims were massacred, and this was on 23 February 1945. The camp was dissolved on 8 April 1945, the day before the liberation of Dubnica nad Váhom.[49]

Mrs Alžbéta Demeterová, fourteen years old at that time, walked with her extended family for six whole weeks to the same town in eastern Slovakia, Dlhé nad Cirochou, from where the Telváks, too, had come. Three members of her family lost their lives on the way. Although the Red Army had reached eastern Slovakia, Germans were hiding everywhere in the woods, and, during a chance encounter with the lost Roma, they shot the uncle of Mrs Demeterová and his little daughter, who tried to protect her father. Mrs Demeterová's cousin died of exhaustion on the way.

Mr Ladislav Dudi-Kot'o, also of Dlhé nad Cirochou, tells about the end of the painful journey from the camp in Dubnica nad Váhom thus:

When we finally reached home, we found our little house in ruins. And yet my father fell to the ground and kissed it and thanked God that we had survived. We also cried because our boy, my older brother wasn't with us – they had killed him in the camp – but otherwise God kept us alive. If the war hadn't ended, the same thing would have happened to the Roma in Slovakia as in Bohemia and Moravia. May God not allow any more wars.

Postscript

In 2001 – 55 years after the end of the war – the Fund for Czech-German Understanding paid reparations to Romani victims of Nazism. Nearly two thousand Roma living in the Czech Republic received financial compensation for the suffering they experienced.

In Slovakia, no financial restitution has been announced for the Romani survivors.

Conclusion

Roma in Slovakia, for the most part, survived the war, but the majority of them were affected economically, socially, psychologically and morally. Traditional bonds with the Slovak villages were broken. On the other hand, new bonds arose based on the common resistance of Slovak and Romani partisans or soldiers. However, the prewar process of integration of the Roma into the whole of society was interrupted and their further incorporation into postwar society was extremely difficult.

Thus the fate of Roma in Slovakia during the Second World War, more enviable than those of Roma from states that sent Gypsies to their death, contributed to the realisation of the old saying: *Rom Romeha – gadžo gadžeha* (Rom with Roma – Gadje with Gadje).

The coffins. In memory of the Lety internment camp (see Volume 2) (etching by Barbara Scotch, Montpelier, USA)

The Roma of Hungary in the Second World War

Katalin Katz[1]

Introduction

Hungary was an ally of Nazi Germany both through its taking part in the Second World War and through the racist ideology that decided its internal politics. Collective persecution of the Romanies began long before the War. During the War, it was carried out more strongly up to the point of trying to destroy them entirely. The critical year in which the Hungarian Roma were persecuted to the point of annihilation was from March 1944 to April 1945.

Although the heightened persecution lasted only for one year, by this time the Nazi extermination machine had already been constructed and tried out. The Hungarian Roma suffered all forms of the horror of persecution, internment and registration, the enlistment of the men for compulsory labour, death marches and massacres on the spot, as well as being deported to concentration and extermination camps in all parts of the Third Reich. Within Hungary, there was a castle in the town of Komárom (see below) that served for the internment and selection of Roma from all of Hungary. After the end of the War, the suffering of the Roma was not recognised and they received no compensation. Not until the 1980s were they given the right to hold open memorial meetings.

The following chapter is based on personal interviews with some sixty Roma from different parts of Hungary.[2] I also refer to interviews that have been published in the press and specialist literature, as well as archives and other material. Relevant documents from contemporary sources are largely lacking. Most of the events happened, as already noted, towards the end of the War as the Soviet Army rapidly approached and even crossed the borders of Hungary. There were times when many deeds went unreported. For that reason interviews with the people affected – the victims – are particularly important to bring the events to light.

Hungary – Germany: Alliance and occupation

The links between Hungary and Nazi Germany had a great influence on the events of the Holocaust. As an ally of Germany, from 1941 Hungary took an active role in the war. Hungarians (in the so-called Horthy Regiment) fought on the front with their fellow German soldiers. The civilian population suffered under the wartime conditions but they did not initially undergo occupation by Germany, as was the case for the majority of the countries of Europe. In spring 1944, a change began in the politics of the Final Solution in Hungary. After October 1944, when Szálasi, the leader of the Arrow Cross fascist organisation, took power by force, with the aid of the German Army, this was to lead to a strong local racist terror campaign.

Nazi racist ideology was strong in Hungary, even before the entry of the German Army in March 1944. The Gypsy question was thoroughly discussed in medical and scientific circles. In this connection, they took as a model the theories of German racial science and the possibilities of putting them into practice following Germany's example. Dr Orsös, who was a member of the Upper Chamber in Parliament, delivered a scientific lecture in 1941. Referring to German colleagues, he sought to win the support of the members for a Race Law for the Gypsies – alongside the Law that applied to Jews. "One can learn much from German Gypsy research (he said)... mixing with the Gypsy race destroys the [Aryan] race." The Germans forbade marriage to Gypsies just as to Jews.[3]

With this background, one could have foreseen the escalation from general regulations, arrests by the police and harassment of the Romany population to registration, mass arrest and detention in transit camps, expulsion and murder. The local police, together with the national police and army, generally carried out the checks, arrests and internment. We see an example of this in a circular from the district authorities in Somogy-megye:

> In accordance with the Interior Minister's Circular no. 267.000/1928 concerning nomadic Gypsies, they are to be tracked down and their details recorded ... they should be taken before the court and treated in accordance with the Circular ... to ensure success and cooperation I am informing the general headquarters of the local police and district

headquarters in Kaposvár and Pécs as well as the local offices of the national police.[4]

In the Komárom camp, where during autumn and winter 1944 up to ten thousand Roma were interned and held until April 1945, the guards consisted of Hungarian and German soldiers. That is what Mr Horváth said about Komárom:

The whole place was surrounded with barbed wire. That was our fate at the time and who knew, perhaps we were to suffer more under the Germans... Amongst the guards there were also Hungarians... they were worse than the Germans.

This collaboration led to high efficiency in the machinery of annihilation at the very time when the break up of the German Empire and its ideology was imminent. Hungary was near to the frontline and Soviet forces were advancing rapidly. Looking back one might have thought that such a place and time might have led to a lessening of the collaboration and to a rethink that would bring about the end of the persecution. In fact, such a development did become apparent towards the end of the period when Horthy was Prime Minister [and tried to negotiate peace with the USSR]. As a result, he was replaced by Szálasi in October 1944. With this change the fanaticism increased and with it the determination to complete the destruction of the 'less worthy races'.

The attitude and policies towards the Gypsies before and during the Second World War

In 1907 there had been a wave of hatred and a stirring up of public opinion against Gypsies. They were collectively considered guilty and held responsible in the so-called Danos case, a robbery case, which was never solved. In the same year came the demand from Pörzölt Kálmán:[5] "Wipe them out! That is the only way."

The journalist Lucidus argued in a similar way:[6]

Wipe them out! That's the only possibility. For what is the aim of civilisation? In essence it must mean the destruction of those races which civilisation does not suit and therefore are not suited for civilisation. The cultured nations outside Europe, everywhere, in America in Asia, in Africa as well as in Australia, eliminate races which have no civilisation and are not capable of developing a culture. And in the middle of Europe can we not destroy a race, the wandering Gypsies who rob and kill us. That is Hungary's shame.

Between the two world wars various proposals were made to deal with the Gypsy Question. Among them was the proposal of Vassanyi in 1936, a judge who wanted to have a separate discriminatory legal code. In his view, all Gypsies should be compelled to settle down. To make this easier, he proposed confiscating their wagons and horses, cancelling all permits for horse dealing, trading and handicraft. Instead, they should only be given physical work for wages that would only just give them the bare minimum to live on. All of this should take place under the watchful eye of the police. He recommended corporal punishment as the effective means of bringing law and order to the Gypsies. The best, he thought, would be beatings for the men and for the women, humiliation such as cutting their hair, solitary confinement and withholding food.[7] Imre Almasi in 1937 wrote: "It would be desirable to sterilise the Gypsies here, too, as is common in other countries."[8]

Racist, quasi-scientific arguments were advanced with the demand to free Hungarian society from the Gypsies. The 'experts' in this matter were doctors and from the 1940s medical journals were full of articles which analysed the Gypsy question. These articles were later quoted in the popular press. In 1942 Dr Jozsef Szekely wrote an article, the conclusion of which recommended introducing the prohibition of mixed marriages between Gypsies and Hungarians and a law for the compulsory sterilisation of all Gypsies. He wrote: "I do not believe anyone is against sterilisation... only by this means can we save society from the burden and curse of useless descendants?"

In 1941, the result of a medical experiment was published.[9] The reaction of several persons to varying doses of arsenobenzole was tested and it described how the chemical was injected into 124, then 48 and finally 36 Gypsies, including children. The results were described including jaundice, skin eruptions and damage to the nervous system.

The same doctor who carried out these experiments also wrote an article on the Gypsy Question. Several versions of this article appeared, and it was spread in the medical community and other forums at a local and national level. He maintained that "Hungary had to be saved from the scroungers" and "one must strengthen the race that is master in the country and start a preventative attack on the parasites".[10]

As already mentioned, there were also 'experts' in the Parliament, such as Dr Ferenc Orsös. He made a speech in the Upper House and put forward his proposal, with the help of racist theories, that the Law for

Preserving Racial Purity (relating to Jews) should also apply to the Gypsies.[11]

From April 1938 laws concerning Jews had been discussed and passed. At the same time there were voices who demanded that the opportunity should be taken to "solve the Gypsy problem". However, in the case of Gypsies no new laws were needed. There were laws that had already been passed in the 1920s and 1930s but had not been put into practice and they permitted control, mass actions and brutal interference in the life of the Gypsies.

Compulsory military service for Gypsy men

When at the end of June 1941 Hungary entered the Second World War and general mobilisation followed, young Gypsy men were also recruited to regular units and above all served on the Soviet front. The men who remained at home were either below or above the age for military service or were not conscripted for various reasons. Many Hungarian Roma fought as front line soldiers alongside the German army while their relatives were being assembled ready for massacre.

Jakab Orsös said:

> At that time I was a soldier. When in 1944 the Gypsies were being arrested I was fighting 'for the fatherland' and at the same time my parents had packed their things while a fascist Nyilas [a member of the Arrow Cross] stood watch at the door of their hut. With black uniforms the Nyilas were the rubbish of the village, they were ready for anything.[12]

By 1944 there were already many Roma who had completed their military service, or had been released as wounded, and returned home after experiencing fighting. So, for example, Antal Sárközi who survived the massacre in Lengyel: *I was at the front, far away at the front, I had breathing problems [from asthma] and I was sent home. I was twenty when I went away. I served for two years.*

With the increase in persecution came the enrolment of Gypsy men in Forced Labour Brigades within the army, similar to Jewish brigades. The idea was to recruit every Romani man between the age of 16 and 60 in an unarmed unit without any rights. There they were subject to the will of merciless and often sadistic officers and, at the same time, they had no weapons with which to face the Soviet soldiers who saw them as enemy soldiers. Service in these units was called 'Labour Service' and, in practice, the recruits were allocated heavy work and given a minimum amount of food. They carried out these tasks in the hardest conditions, sometimes on the frontline, in bad weather without suitable clothes, without food or weapons with which to defend themselves. Many of them were engaged in the clearly hopeless defence of the Third Reich. They constructed the so-called Lower Danube Line, which stretched from Bratislava to Kőszeg. By March 1945 they had built some 558 kilometres of trenches and some 163 kilometres of defensive bunkers.

Eyewitness Sándor Nagy said:

I was still young during the War when we were taken for work service. I was 17 at the time. I spent a year there. I was arrested in Miklósfa... the family remained behind and were taken to Germany afterwards. After they had taken the Jews they took our parents, they wanted to destroy them...the Germans. Hitler took me. His orders were everywhere. The Jews, the Gypsies, they took them. We were taken to Germany, to Berlin. We went to Berlin through Czechoslovakia. We worked there, we were made to work, they were very bad to us. After two or three weeks we were almost dead.
[and what work did you do?]
We built tank traps. Trenches.
[and did you have weapons?]
No, we did not have any weapons. We had a terrible life. I would never have believed how much men can suffer... standing outside in the cold. Work. Digging ditches.

Soviet forces then captured many of the recruits and their freedom was delayed by further years of suffering.[13] Mrs Gy recalls the people she knew who were called up for the Labour Brigades but never came back:

In November 1944 I was 14 years old and in Újakna when they took my husband for work service. My husband returned after some years but from those who were taken to the Ukraine many disappeared for ever, they died. As far as I can remember from the Gypsy settlement in Újakna and Pécskő there was György Botos and eleven others.[14]

Mrs F. was another who described the recruitment into Labour Brigades:

The fascist guards and the appointed Gypsy representative came to fetch my father. They had to go to the police station and they were told that they would be sent for labour service and then several hundreds of these men were collected in the school... On December 20 a few days before the arrival of the Russians they sent them towards Slovakia. After a short while there they were captured by the Russians and imprisoned... My father was a prisoner of war in Germany and later in Russia. He was also in a camp there and died still a prisoner in 1946.

Erdos[15] quotes a soldier who guarded and led a labour brigade: *There were some who had special privileges and were not sent to Dachau or Auschwitz but to Slovakia.*

The suffering of the recruits and the death rate were generally very high. The various units differed only in the arbitrary attitude of the soldiers to these conscripts. The first brigades of the Jewish Labour Service (which was not part of the regular army) were set up in 1941. The brigades were an integral part of the Final Solution although they were given a military framework. So the Jewish survivors of these brigades were fully recognised as persons who had suffered the Holocaust. Many Gypsies were drawn into the Labour Service in small groups but they were not regular soldiers.

A survivor said:[16] *I was recruited into the Labour Service in 1943. We were taken to the border to build trenches for the Germans. This lasted for about a year.* After this year the witness returned home and a few days later was deported via Komárom to Auschwitz.

On 23 August 1944 a joint decision of the Defence and Interior Ministries decided to set up large scale Labour Brigades for Gypsies. The plan was to set up between 50 and 60 brigades each with between ten and twelve thousand men. The recruitment was ensured by mass arrests of the Gypsies who were still in Heves, Komárom, Pest and other districts.[17] Amongst the interviewees for our study was Mr Horváth from the town of Kapuvár in the district of Győr-Sopron.

> There were about ten or twelve of us from Kapuvár but they had brought Gypsies from the whole area and assembled us in the police station... then further afield... when there were air attacks we had to fill in the holes and we also had to dig the long trenches which the German and Hungarian armies needed... as soon as the Russians came we were taken to the frontier in Szentgotthard... then a German officer came and looked at us. We were at the end of our tether, our clothes too, you understand. And we were full of fleas and everything, and so he looked us over and spoke to the captain who was our leader, the one who gave the orders, and said to him. 'We don't need these people. The Russians are coming and we have no time to burn them and we can't take them with us as they are so weak. Take them into the woods and do what you wish.'

What the guards wished was to save themselves. Therefore, these Gypsies were freed and they survived.

Kálmán Farkas described what happened to him:

*I was a young man when the German army marched into Hungary. We
were living in Csisznyikó Törökszentmiklós in the Gypsy settlement. It
was a terrible autumn, horrible, wet and cold, 1944. The rumour spread
like fire. The settlement was surrounded by SS and police. Lorries stood at
the street corner. That same morning they took all the men from
Csisznyikó, young and old. Armed guards watched us so we could not
escape from the lorries. The police accompanied the train as far as Szajol
on motorbikes. There were several hundred Roma there as well as non-
Gypsies, Jews from Labour Brigades also... we were forced to dig tank
traps. That gave them the hope that the advance of the Russians could be
held up. But the more that time passed and the deeper the trenches were, so
the number of those present decreased.*

Gypsies who were in prison were also conscripted into the Labour
Brigades. As well as those who were sent to the front line, there were also
some special work camps for Gypsies within Hungary – in the towns of
Marcali, Sárvár, Szekszárd, Szentkirályszabadja and Vémend. Those who
fled from the Labour Brigades were treated as deserters and sentenced to
death. Most of those who were recruited into these Brigades, however,
met their death in Germany.[18]

  Mr Krasznai began his labour service in Vémend.

*When they took us in 1944 I was fourteen. We were disinfected and we
were given old uniforms that the soldiers had already thrown away... we
were taken to Mohács, there we met some Jews, later as they were under
pressure [on the eastern front] they brought us to Germany. First to Vienna,
that was Germany at the time, then to Linz... they brought us to Salhausen,
or a name like that, there we were examined by a doctor. I had no idea
whether I was going north, west or south. So I came to Freiburg, I was in
Frankfurt and then in Munich, there were Americans there, they surprised
us, these parachutists, as we were working at the airport. Then we were
taken to Berlin and I saw Russian soldiers. If they had come there a week
later no Gypsy and no Jew would have survived.*

Mr Orsös also felt that they would not have held out, if liberation had
come any later.

*I was in Labour Service, in 1944 after the order came that those between
16 and 60 had to go, but only the men. Sometimes there was food to eat,
sometimes not. We were only Gypsies. And many died. They died from the
conditions. We were brought to Lenti. They threatened us with weapons.
Hands up! Don't move! There was a captain on a horse. He rode around us
and hit us with a stick. It was March 15, the Hungarian national holiday. I
will never forget it. All the men were made to run. There was water there*

and they said we should go into the water. Then we had to lie down in the water. There were two old men, they were well over 70, they too, the poor fellows. Then we were taken inside, there was a kind of army barracks. He hit these two poor old men, there was an officer there, he had a stick and beat them from head to toe. I was 18, I was in Vémend, I was in Szentgotthárd on the [Austrian] border, they brought us to Kondorfa. It was a cold winter there in 1944. We were made to stand outside. Our heads were full of lice. There were peas but in the soup there were more stones than peas... and then the journey to Germany began... if the Russians had come two weeks later – we would have been finished.

Mr Balogh did not wait to be freed by the Allies:

One night there was a sudden knock on the window. Police. They led us through the village as if we were robbers or murderers, a policeman on each side, there were at least three hundred of us, all Gypsies. They gave us old shoes, completely worn out, and they put a red armband on us – with Labour Service on it. What did they do next? The order came to shave us. So there would be no lice. Everyone, wherever there was even one hair, every hair had to go. The Gypsies, these old men, they had such big moustaches. They wept for their moustaches. Three of us had decided to escape at night. It was raining hard, it was night, two o'clock in the morning. We set off, walked and walked, we were already so hungry that we could hardly walk. We supported each other, we threw the armbands away. [Allied] soldiers came, nobody said a word to us... we had survived.

The document containing the order for interning Gypsies and restricting them to their hometown[19] gives the grounds for these security measures. "Amongst the Gypsies who have been recruited for Labour Service... many have deserted and... are an increased danger to general security." The number of Gypsies that were enrolled in the Labour Service has not been completely documented. One reliable document gives information about just four brigades and Gypsy units that were attached to other brigades.[20]

On this subject, narrative accounts are hard to find. In the interviews with surviving Gypsies, I came across some witness statements about Labour Service. These have been partly quoted above, but, on the whole, I came across this information by chance, in interviews with their wives. Because of the military setting the survivors do not always realise they are survivors of the Holocaust. The knowledge that the Jews have spoken about their time in these terrible units has not sunk into the consciousness of the Roma. They do not realise that they too are people who could be recognised as survivors and receive compensation or other help.

Schermann, in her work about breaches of human rights,[21] summarises her conversation with a survivor of the Labour Brigades: Police knocked on the window at night. They took the father and the eighteen-year-old son with them. They brought together a group of some 70 men. In the evening they took them on foot to Szombathely and then, from there, in a goods train to the sugar factory in Sárvár. They were guarded by Hungarian soldiers. The group, now several hundred strong, were taken to the western border and there they were forced to dig trenches. A second eyewitness told Schermann that one of the men was weak and could not work. He was treated as refusing to work and was taken away and tied to a post. This unit, the witness said, was lucky. As the front got nearer the officers in charge took them into the wood and said they should wait there for the Red Army. The officers themselves fled to the west.

The internment of Gypsies inside Hungary

No information has survived concerning any central order for the whole of Hungary for the arrest and internment of Gypsies. However, there are documents that point to regional, district and even local orders. Even these documents do not give the complete picture. On 16 October 1944 on the second day of the takeover of power by the Arrow Cross regime, there was an order from the commander of the southern region saying that "it is forbidden for Gypsies to leave their place of residence... anyone breaking this order will be punished and sent to an internment camp."[22]

We often find that actions took place that suggests there was an order, when the order itself has not been preserved. There are letters from one or another official that describe the carrying out of an instruction to arrest and intern Gypsies in the respective district.

So, for example, there is a letter from the police commander in Kaposvár to his superior officer. He tells of an order as early as 12 October to carry out a raid on the Gypsies in his area. "The raid brought no results as a few weeks earlier on the instructions of the Minister of the Interior we had carried out a raid and moved them to a work camp."[23]

Officials in the Tab district sent a similar message. "The transport of the Gypsies into a work camp has been carried out, so there is no need for any further raids and expulsions."[24] Another example is the announcement and continuing relaying of the central order from the fourth regional command centre in Pecs.[25] "Herewith I am sending you a copy of the list of names of the Gypsies in the village of Lengyel. The Gypsies who are on the list may not leave their place of residence. [If they do] the police will arrest them and despatch them to an internment camp. The Gypsies are to be made aware of this order."

This instruction has special significance in view of the massacre of the Gypsies of Lengyel, which took place some four months after this letter (see below).

The registration of Gypsies and the associated prohibition of leaving their place of residence was also mentioned in our interviews. Some of the witnesses told of sheets of yellow paper that were hung on the doors where Gypsies lived. On the paper, all of the occupants of the house were listed. The authorities as well as the Nyilas came regularly to check the presence of the people living in the house. Mrs Filisi said: *The Nyilas decided to register even us, the musician Gypsies of Baja.*

The Romani poet Károly Bari recounted that the members of his family remained in their houses, behind closed doors on which there was a list of those occupants who were Gypsies. They were not allowed to leave the house and there they awaited their fate.

Everywhere in Hungary there were plans and orders to collect and intern Gypsies. The declared aim was to remove them from the villages of the 'true' Hungarians and make it easier to keep a watch on them. Menyhért Lakatos described what the situation was like at the end of 1944. The life of those Gypsies who had not yet been driven out and who were still in Hungary had little value. Life was full of worry and daily harassment. The Gypsy quarters were surrounded by police armed with bayonets and in some places many became ill from the excessive strength of compulsory injections against typhus.[26]

It seems that the first Gypsy ghetto to be set up was in the eastern town of Nagyszalonta, now in Romania but then part of Hungary. This was set up two years before there was talk of collecting the Jews into ghettos. Later, Gypsies were transported from there to their death.[27] In a report of October 1941 with the title *An Attempt to solve the Gypsy Problem in Nagyszalonta*, the decisions required by the council were detailed paragraph by paragraph. The proposal was to collect the Gypsies in a closed settlement, followed by special laws that would apply only to them. This was accompanied by a so-called scientific discussion of the racial question of the Gypsies and examples from Germany of their treatment. The key decision was to erect a fence around the settlement with only one entrance, which would be closed at night. There would only be one Gypsy named as the responsible person and they would be supplied with a copy of the regulations and would have the key to the ghetto and take over the control. Non-Gypsies would not be allowed to come into the ghetto. The document went into detail about the punishment for anyone breaking the rules. The conclusion of the document said that this was just a temporary treatment and radical measures would be needed to solve the problem.

In an article of 3 December 1941, the newspaper *A mai nap* reported the decision by the local council to lock up the Gypsies in a closed ghetto. The article spoke of the urgent need to remove those Gypsies who were freely moving about the town. It gave details of the plans to set up the "first Gypsy ghetto" and the associated orders that every Gypsy must live in the closed area. If they refuse to move to the closed area, the Mayor would ask for help from the security forces. Elsewhere the place where the Gypsy population was interned was not called a ghetto but a 'Gypsy camp'. Nevertheless, the practice was the same. In the town of Esztergom, in 1942, the order went out to set up a settlement area for all the Gypsies in the town, which they would not be allowed to leave.[28] In spring 1944 all 1,166 Gypsies in the Szigetvár district were put in a camp on the edge of Révfalu village as a first step to their deportation.[29]

In many other places in Hungary, Gypsies were taken out of the districts where they lived and collected in a central spot before they were sent to Komárom or the concentration camps of the Third Reich. Zsigmond Vidak said:

> *In the morning the police who kept a watch on the street where the Gypsies lived in the town of Hatvan woke us. They brought us on to the street, read out our names and then took us to the police station. The commander made a short speech saying that anyone who dared to try to escape would be shot on the spot. Then we were assembled in a factory building.*

Many daily papers reported in September and October 1944 the news that the Gypsies were being collected together in several places in Hungary and sent to labour camps. Most of the reports spoke also of the relieved and happy reactions of the local population.

Some of the transit camps were used for both Jews and Gypsies, often at the same time, as for example the brick factories. Mr Balogh says:

> *As it happens there were no black faces in our family, people of Gypsy appearance. But acquaintances… everyone knew that we were Gypsies and*

we were all affected during the time of the troubles of the Gypsies. What happened to my brothers and sisters and my mother I don't know. They took us to the brick factory in Óbuda and from there to Komárom. We were together, Gypsies and Jews.

From Komárom I was taken a long way out of the country and when I came back in 1945 I found no-one. I was alone in the world.

Mrs Sztojka also began the journey that was to take her to Bergen-Belsen from a brick factory in Óbuda. Nyilas fascists guarded us. Then they took us to the trains, we had nothing to drink, there were crowds of Roma.

There were other transit camps for Gypsies only such as the coffee factory in Nagykanizsa. From there thousands of Roma went on a death march on foot, as Ferenc Nagy related:

We lived upstairs in Szabadság Street. From there we were taken away, the Gypsies, from everywhere, we were crammed into the police stations and stayed there three or four days. Mostly outside. From there one evening we were taken to the coffee factory. By this time there were several thousand of us. We were all together there, we were full of fleas, we were there about one and a half months and then they said they would only take us as far as the Mura river and that nobody would survive as the Fascists planned to eliminate us by the Mura.

From the Celldömölk region, Gypsies were assembled in a camp in Keled. The Gypsies from the district of Zalavár-megye were collected in Csáktornya as well as Kraskovec in neighbouring Croatia. As the front came further west, many of those who had been brought together in camps in the south-west were murdered. Others were assembled in Kőszeg camp and from there they were sent to German concentration camps.[30]

In the district of Heves in the north there was a transit camp operating in Mezőkövesd, as Mr Rácz recounted:

We were brought by train to Mezőkövesd. There we were put in the local school. There were already hundreds of Gypsies who had been brought from different places. There were perhaps around one thousand five hundred of us. We were beaten, they took our clothes and gave us some different ones and it turned out they had belonged to the Jews who had been in the place before us. It was already winter and they took us outside and we began to march towards Germany.[31]

On the western border of Hungary a transit camp at Győr was in operation. Men and women prisoners were held there separately, they were tortured, had to carry out hard labour and some were killed.[32]

Deportation

Many of the Gypsies who were driven out of their houses in Hungary were first deported to Komárom. It was situated on the railway route from Hungary to the concentration camps in Germany. A description of the camp is given later.

Mezey and his colleagues say that two or three transports from Budapest and the surrounding area went direct to Auschwitz. They report also other deportations of some 30,000 Gypsies from the whole of Hungary.[33] In November and December 1944 there were 44 raids to round up Gypsies and deport them.[34] From Komárom most of the prisoners who were Gypsies were sent on to different camps within the Third Reich. They were usually transported by train or – towards the end of the war – with death marches on foot.[35]

Mr Kovács said:

> From Komárom I was taken to Germany, through Austria, to a large pine forest, to Schlossenburg camp. They took our own clothes away. We soon suffered from hunger. We were given a portion of rotten cabbage and a hundred grams of bread and we had to work a whole day on that. Then I worked for three months in a stone quarry in Germany. We all got a number, mine was 35648. We were left to starve here also and were beaten mercilessly. The guards were all criminals, they had been sentenced to ten or twelve years. They were set loose on us. I became very weak here. But worse horrors were to come. I was sent to Auschwitz to the crematorium and worked on the ovens. They burned thousands of people there. It was a terrible sight. A train came, they told the victims they were going to a shower, but they put them in the gas chambers, One day I recognised a woman, Mrs Grün, but I couldn't speak to her. We expected they would kill us too. Every two weeks there was a selection and the weak and sick were sent to the crematorium. We were already so worn out that it did not matter to us whether we lived or died.

Those who were transported in the trains described the long painful journey. In every truck they squashed in as many people as possible. They locked the doors, the people who were inside did not know where they were.[36]

Mrs Sárközi, 21 years old at the time, had been married for a month. She says:

> The last transport of Jews was ready. And they took us with them, the men in a separate truck. Do you know what it was like? The windows in the train were blocked with barbed wire. And the terrible pain, torture, the

dryness and thirst, the small pieces of ice, we sucked on them. I can't speak any more about what they did. They urinated on one another... old women, they were already dead. And then the train stopped and they threw us all out, that's how I got these terrible pains. Then we came to the frontier, you know, we had arrived and they unlocked the truck and my husband shouted 'Goodbye my darling, perhaps we will meet again, perhaps not.' And in fact we never saw each other again.

A survivor recounts:[37]

They took us from the Gypsy camp in Nekeresd by train to Komárom, then onwards in a goods train. We weren't let out till Dachau. A week later we were sent to different workplaces. I was taken to an aeroplane factory in Hamburg. There I was put to work for three months. We had striped clothing and a number on our arms. Even now I can say in German 'achttausenddreihundertzwanzig'. Then we built a railway in Mauthausen, and soon after we found ourselves back in Dachau.

A second eyewitness said:

In Komárom people dropped like flies. We were pushed into goods trains again. We stopped in Dachau in a large holding camp, from there we were transported further like cattle. It was three days before we reached Ravensbrück and could climb out. The number on my arm and on my clothing was 6800. Then they moved us on, we came in a lorry to a small camp, I don't know what it was called. My sister was with me and also my aunt. But my sister was already so weak she couldn't get on the transport again. She stayed there and I don't know what happened to her. Probably she was burnt. The healthy ones, those who could still work were taken back to Ravensbrück. We were hauled out of the train and put in a camp – [possibly] Saasreden. There people ate vegetable skins and weeds, many died of hunger at that time.

Mrs Zsuzsa Holdosi tells of what happened to her after she was transported from Komárom at the age of fourteen:

It was really hell. They did not open the door even once until we arrived at Dachau. We stayed there for two nights. They burnt all the dead there. When we arrived at Ravensbrück there was not even a tent, a hut, there were so many there already. They put us in a sort of cellar where there they had also laid out bodies. They couldn't burn them all at the same time although there were three crematoria. And there were bodies that were just skeletons, just skeletons. I said 'Holy Mary, Jesus, so many dead,' and then to the others, 'come and see how many dead there are here'. They were laid out like firewood. They were all women. The next day we had to take them in a sort of cart with two wheels, we had to take the bodies. They had to be

*brought to the crematorium where they were burnt. Then we began to put
up a marquee. There was room for three thousand, it was so big. They put
some straw down and then we lay down. We got one blanket that was all.
And then buckets at the edge of the tent instead of toilets. It was almost
two months before we were given huts. People came with white aprons,
doctors. They gave us injections. They examined us every day. They hurt,
the examinations, that was terrible. In April 1945 we were brought to
Fuschberg or Wurzberg, or something like that, it was a cloth factory. Some
Jewish friends said to me, 'let's run away', and so we ran away. We were
thirteen girls and one woman. In the evening we reached a very large
forest. We saw lorries, we were in a trap. [We were taken back to the
camp], we cried that we wouldn't run away again. After that it was a
terrible night. They shot Magda in the mouth. Three and a half days later
the Americans liberated us and brought us to Prague.*

Mr Balogh told his story to the poet Karoly Bari:

*In November the Gypsies were collected in the Castle in Komárom. They
assembled us, then separated us from the women and children. From there,
first, to Dachau. There were soldiers and doctors and we were told to
undress. They took our clothes away, they shaved all our hair, then an
important man came, an officer. They made a selection. Those who had to
go to the left were killed. An SS officer said to us, 'you have come this far,
but no-one will ever leave here'. Everything was taken away. They pulled
the gold teeth from the mouths of the Jews. And the Germans, they killed,
as easily as they breathed. As if it was natural. They were so cruel. They
took all our clothes away and they gave us some thin clothing, striped, and
a hat with stripes, like summer clothes although it was already December.
And they brought us into the huts, at least a hundred men. We lay there like
pigs. There was a Gypsy in Dachau called Sanyi from the village of
Nyirbator. He escaped from the camp but he was captured. They crucified
him like Jesus. In the late evening as they tied him on the cross, we were
assembled on the square so we could see him as they crucified him. There
was a cold wind then, as cold as it had been in 1944, it was snowing and
the young Gypsy was freezing on the cross. By the morning he had frozen
to death, he was as blue as a plum. So they killed him. Every week we
were taken naked for medical experiments. They tortured us, they gave us
injections, that Mengele, may the earth spit him out! There was never such
a cruel man as him. In June 1945 I came home. My three uncles had been
deported with me, my mother's brothers – Juzsi, Mati, Peter. But I was the
only one who came back. My mother had also been deported, they killed
her in Poland.*

Mrs Sipos also recalled the medical experiments she had undergone in
the concentration camp:

I was eleven or twelve. My periods had already started. And then they carried out experiments on us. There was a particular room where they carried out these experiments. We were pushed onto a table, next to each other, naked. All we could say was 'Oh, I'm dying. Oh God.' And they were looking at us from all four sides. Many died. Afterwards I was in Czechoslovakia in a hospital. I was taken there because I was very ill. They had to feed me with a spoon, my stomach was damaged and I had to go to the toilet every hour, all the time.

Many Gypsies were deported together with Jews in the same trucks or in special trucks for the Gypsies that were attached to the Jewish trains. Most of the people on these transports ended up in Auschwitz. They were sent directly from the arrival platform to the gas chambers without any registration. But not all.

Kati Sárközi was put into the camp itself:

I married my husband in Püspökerzsébet. A month later I was arrested. They came to our house, there were eight of us. The police came and said we should get ready and bring some clothes and tools as we were being taken to pick carrots, to work. We believed them. I was 21 years old. They took us away with the last transport of Jews, the men in a separate truck. They took us on to Berlin. We were left in the open air, naked for three or four days, the ice froze on our skin. And there was a selection. A doctor came, anyone who was not healthy stayed there. They took hold of us, shaved us all over and then our truck was ready. We were moved on, and came to Hamburg. We were there two to three months. Then came another selection and transport – this time to Auschwitz.

There they began to make us work, but we had to work so much. I couldn't tell you about everything that happened there. They opened the doors, you know, there were cellars full of bodies. Their heads hung lifeless. One day we had tried to take some pieces of turnip. We were taken through the camp, there were so many streets, barracks and then the crematorium. They opened it for us and said if we ever took anything again we would be in the crematorium. You know, we went in the evening to try and find turnip skins. And always after midnight, quick, quick, quick, roll call, so we would go quickly. They cut our hair, we were surrounded, my dear girl, with a high fence and in the barbed wire there was electricity and if anyone touched it or went near, that was that... and then the bins, rubbish bins as you'd find in the street, there were bins like that, black and there were bodies inside and we had to carry the bins. They were dead. On the next day we had to carry them again and throw them on a cart. A cart with four wheels. With a black shelf. And then we were all by the crematorium, but we fainted. You know, the blue flames and the smell. That was something. And I forgot to say, they pulled the gold teeth from

the Jews. I saw that one had his eyes still open and I turned away. I was
frightened and it made me so sad. I had to open their mouths and one of a
'commando' [a working party], a German, came with pliers and took them
out. And there I was hit for the first time with a rubber stick. As soon as I
came back to consciousness I looked for my glass eye that had fallen out
and put it back in its place. There was a large box, full of gold teeth. They
collected them, there were four of them. A German with a big head and
three others, who told us they would hit us if we did not open the mouths
wide enough. I did this for least a week.

Then there were injections in our behinds so we would not have
children, and in the event I didn't have any. Then they took all the Gypsies
away from there. Until the end we were together with the Jewish women.
And no-one from my family came home afterwards. They all died.

Mrs Sárközi's eyewitness report deals with the period of winter 1944–5.
She was deported in a transport of Romani and Jewish women, most of
who were murdered. When they arrived in Auschwitz there was no longer
any trace of the Gypsy Camp that had been liquidated in the beginning of
August 1944. It is clear that, after this, many other Gypsies were brought
to Auschwitz to be killed.

Ms Kolompár tells a similar story:

Then we were in Komárom where there was a selection and we were sent
to Dachau, that was the first camp, Dachau. We were about a month there.
After a month we were taken to Auschwitz. It snowed and rained in the
courtyard for three days and nights, we stood outside for roll call and they
did not bring us into the camp. Then we were taken into the washrooms,
our whole bodies were shaved, they washed us and brought us into the
barracks where we lay four in one bed. They were a kind of three-level bed,
wooden beds. There we all climbed up. There were four of us laying there
and so we got to know each other. The four of us decided that we would
stick together till the end. At three o'clock one night we were driven out for
a roll call. We stood on the square in rows of five. They would not let us
inside for a whole day. We had to stand there. Our feet froze, see how my
legs are swollen, even today I can hardly walk. At eleven o'clock in the
evening they let us back in the barracks. Then they gave us half a litre of
turnip soup, freezing cold turnip soup and a piece of bread. That's all we
had till the next day. We ate the small lump of bread, as for the cold soup,
the turnips, we didn't want to eat it. But the Jewish women who had
already been there a long time said, 'if you're not eating it, give it to me'.
We gave them it. With this bread, maybe 50 grams, we had to last till
eleven the next day, for at eleven we got a piece of bread and again half a
litre of cold turnips, this time we ate the turnips. This went on for three and

a half months. [We were taken to another camp.] Then they brought us back, they brought us back to Auschwitz.

Then they began to take us in transports, all the time we had to move faster. And then they wanted to take us to some town in Germany. And the aeroplanes, there were so many bombers in the sky, perhaps more than there were stars. This was on the way as we were being transported. And these aeroplanes flew so low they bombed the town but the tremors did not reach us where we were. We ran up into the meadows where there was corn growing. As we ran, we picked the corn; the bombs were falling around us and we ate the corn. Then we went back – those of us who had fled from the transport when the bomb attack began, and we were told that the others had been taken out of the town. That was to the place that was also waiting for us, they would have shot us and we would have fallen into the pit. That's what it was like, do you see? If I speak about it I get sick. When I came back I found my mother. My father did not come back, nor my brothers, only me.

Mrs Nemes was another who was told they were going to pick carrots and found herself on the way to a concentration camp:

We were all taken but I was the only one who came back. They did not survive. They took us all, Sinti, Bayash, Lovari, all kinds of Gypsies. And Jews. There were some who gave birth there. They brought us to the transport. They took us to many places. And the Gypsies were always together. In the German camp there were Gypsies who had already been there for some years. Magdi met her cousin. They had taken her there. I was already with the Jewish women. We worked, we pulled carts. We wore clothes with stripes. We also worked underground in a mine. Here is my number, see on my arm. I have been told I should put pickled cabbage on it, it might go away. We suffered a lot. There were also doctors there who examined everybody. And we lay there naked and it was very warm. Then the Russians came, we had no clothes, we lay there with blankets. And our heads were full of scars.

Magdalena (Magdi) Szarka (nee Hódosi) was another eyewitness:

We were twelve brothers and sisters, we lived with our parents. My father was taken a year earlier to serve in the Labour Brigades. On 23 November the police came, they banged on the window. I was sixteen. At ten o'clock in the evening we were brought to the station and they put us in the trucks. The train stopped in Buk. There they opened the doors and brought in more Gypsies. Then they took us in the train to Komárom. Towards the end of November they took the men away and soldiers came to guard us. We were loaded into railway trucks again on the banks of the Danube. We came to [Ravensbrück] camp on 21 December. We were left all day fenced in outside in the open air and it was snowing. I had a cousin who had been arrested in Austria as early as 1939. There was a woman with us who somehow used to slip out in the evening and go over to the Austrian Roma. She told them where she came from and then my cousin asked who else was with her. And when she said my name she knew there was no other Magdi, only me. And then one evening she came to look for me and suddenly I noticed that all the women were shouting, Magdalena Hódosi. That was me so I came there and then I recognised my cousin and she recognised me too. She had already been there six years. It was a camp for women only. And then the experiments began. We were taken here and there. I can't remember exactly what they injected us with but there were large syringes. And then someone died where my cousin was and she got me moved into her place. So I didn't have to go to the experiments again, and so I survived.

Mrs Lakatos can no longer remember the name of the camp where she was deported. But she knows what she underwent there:

I was 15, I had a son and I was also pregnant, and that's how they took me. As we were being put in the train one man tried to bend down to take some snow in his mouth as there was no water and they shot him straightaway, on the spot. And he lay there, no-one bothered about him. And there I gave birth and both children died. And since then I have been ill. Then they took us out of the train and the German guard said, 'alle raus' and then we had to stand in a row like soldiers and they counted us and they put me over where they were burning the people who could no longer walk. I crawled along on my bottom. I couldn't stand up when they found us later and freed us. I couldn't walk. I stayed in the camp and they came to collect us and took us to a hospital and treated us there.

Mr Balogh was sent on after just a few days in Auschwitz-Birkenau:

They took me to Buchenwald and those who could, those who were in a good state, they took them for work. They took me later to a factory, an underground factory. You won't believe it when I tell you, it's unbelievable. Naked, all our body hair was shaved and then we got thin summer clothing like prisoners. And outside in January we stood six hours outside. To do that, a cultured people, the German people. There was a gas chamber there, and they pushed them in and turned on the gas and my brothers were inside. They separated us and there was a doctor there, a Jew, who came from Budapest and he too had been brought there. I asked him, this doctor, 'what about my brothers, what can have happened?' 'It can well be that they are in there, he said, and they will come out through the chimney'.

Mr Kolompár was also in Buchenwald, after he had been taken from one concentration camp to another:

They took all of us from Zalaegerszeg, my father, my mother, us four brothers, they took us all. I was eighteen and a half. They took us to Komárom. We were there two weeks, and from there we were brought to Germany to Dachau. We arrived in Dachau. Any gold that we had, or a watch, they took away. They shaved us bald and gave us clothes with stripes and so into the camp. From there I was taken to Hamburg, a seaport, there I worked in an aeroplane factory. I was also in Mauthausen. There I worked on the railway. We worked as hard as we could. If the work wasn't up to standard, there were SS soldiers standing next to us.

One took a man's hat off, threw it away and said, 'get it'. The poor man went to get it and 'bang', he shot him. And if someone didn't handle the shovel properly there was trouble.

Later I was taken to Buchenwald. There we built barracks, we built them for the other prisoners so they had a place. We were full of lice, you know. There were beds with several levels, four levels, and we lay five or six in one bed. Then by the morning there were several dead. Ten or twelve every day. For everyone it was like this. I am alive now, in ten minutes I might be dead. Either they shot the people, or they beat them. Then we went for a medical examination, perhaps two or three hundred together. The soldiers came into the room and we had to undress. We laid our clothes in a pile. Now, two hundred of us, we waited outside naked until the doctor examined us. It snowed and the wind blew. Completely naked. The examination did not last long. He looked quickly at the person, then said, 'turn round' and he looked again, and then we could go out, so we did not have to wait long but even ten minutes was too long. He just looked to see if we still had some strength in us. He examined us to see who looked weak, and anyone who looked weak could go into the 'shower'. That person went to the crematorium. If he saw that someone still had some strength, he said 'that one can still work'. So, just with one look. He didn't examine us, didn't ask us what medicine we needed. Only to see if we were strong. We went out and perhaps a hundred or a hundred and fifty went to the crematorium. Afterwards I was taken back to Dachau. There the Americans found us on 1 May 1945.

Bözsi Horváth remembered amongst other horrors having to leave her mother and always speaks of the terrible hunger in the concentration camp:

I was sixteen years old and my mother was with me. Before Christmas they took her off somewhere else. I wanted to go with her, we were registered, we were always counted at the roll call, weren't we? And I went behind her and there was a long line of people being transported to another camp. I

went there too but the female officer sent me back of course. And I came
back to the camp at night, and then in the night I was crying. I fell and cut
my knee. I cried the whole way back.

I didn't know where I was. I went into one block and there was a female
officer there. She hit me. My back hurt, she had given me such a blow.

There in the camp we thought all the time about what we could eat.
Would we ever have enough bread, even once. Then we thought about
bread all the time, nothing else only bread. I thought, if only just once they
would give us all the bread we wanted. But they gave us a small thin slice.
Afterwards I said I would agree to be shot in the head. Only bread, bread.
And then we cried. And then we remembered that at home we used to
throw away the potato skins, everything, and water from boiling noodles.
Here even that would be good if there was any. It was always like this, we
never spoke about meat or cake, or anything else.

Mrs Stojka was 17 when she was taken from Csepel to Germany. She
survived Bergen-Belsen camp, was then taken to Munich and was also in
Dachau: *When the Americans came in they brought a lot of food. But I*
was clever, I didn't eat. I just drank a lot of tea. So I didn't die although at
that time I could only crawl around.

Komárom October 1944 –April 1945

Built as mirror images, facing one another across the Danube are the
Hungarian town of Komárom and the Slovak town of Komarno, separated
nowadays only by the frontier. In the second half of the nineteenth
century, fortresses were built in each town to defend against any attacks
on the main highway to Vienna, the imperial capital. Both the Csillag and
the Monostori are on the Hungarian side, and both of them can be seen
from the Slovak side across the river. During the Holocaust these
fortresses were turned into transit camps and prisons for persons that the
authorities wished to dispose of. Csillag börtön functioned as a Ghetto for
Jews and later as an interchange station for the transports to German
concentration camps. Towards the end of 1944 the Csillag was not big
enough and they also used the Monostori-erőd – Fort Sandberg – for the
same purpose.

Alongside Jews, communists and other persecuted groups thousands
of Roma formed the greatest number of arrivals between November 1944
and April 1945.

One eyewitness is Mr Sarkozi:

On 4 November early in the morning our house was surrounded… In Komárom we were held in Csillag. Between eight and ten thousand people were brought there, mostly Roma, from all corners of the country, even from districts in the east of Hungary.

The story of their suffering is not confined to the two castles in Komárom and Csillag and, later, Monostori, where Gypsies were also crammed in. Their deportation from their hometowns to Komárom, and their return home after being freed, will be described later. The imprisonment in Monostori came to light through Mrs Krasznai's detailed evidence in Rom Ofer's film Komárom – March 1999. Her vivid description sheds light on what happened in that fortress on the Danube.

Ferenc Horváth is another eyewitness:

We were nomadic at that time, from one village to the next. I was twelve… the fascist Nyilas came and took us, we were transported in trains. One man hit us from one side and another joined in from the other. They pushed us into the wagons, as many as possible. Then we set off but it took some two weeks before we reached Komárom. I can remember Komárom as if it was yesterday. Anyone who collapsed was immediately thrown into the Danube. They squashed us in. Four or five days later we were selected. Small children were separated, girls, those who were thirteen or fourteen, men, separated, women, old ladies. There were six long underground bunkers. One couldn't see the end of the aisles. Each one was about five hundred metres long. In December when we arrived there was no time to send us further on, as every day there were always more Roma arriving. Every morning when they opened the gates there were two or three railway trucks standing there. Those who couldn't move were put on top of the bodies of those who had died and thrown into the Danube. The castle wall was made of stone, they just dropped them down like sacks into the Danube. There was one Romani woman, she was so beautiful, she had chestnut hair and two pigtails. She was wonderfully beautiful, around nineteen years old, they took her by force. The Germans kept her with them all the time. What they did with her I don't know, who knows. They abused her so much that she could no longer stand. Then they tied a rope between two trees and took a tin of petrol and hanged her by the hair on the rope and put the tin under her. It was petrol or oil, or something. They burnt her alive. She couldn't even scream. Why did they do it? And the Germans laughed themselves sick.

What did we eat? Cabbage. If there had been grass we would have eaten that. We were in our excrement up to our knees, in the dirt. We couldn't sit down. If anyone sat down, it showed. As the clothes were filthy it didn't matter much where we did it… They let the older girls pull out weeds and rake the ground. But there was nothing there, only stones. There was a Hungarian fascist, a Nyilas leader in black uniform. The girls asked him why they had to rake as there was no earth to rake. He said there will soon be beautiful flowers here growing in your ashes. It was a slaughter house, even worse, I can understand it if someone shoots you or kills you with a blow. But letting us have nothing to drink or eat for months, to lie in urine and excrement on concrete! Then the Russians came on the Saturday before Easter. I don't know whether the Russians opened up the gates, or whether the Germans let them in, only that the Russians shouted, 'davai, davai.' It sounded different from the Germans.

According to the eyewitnesses, Roma, together with Jews, were taken to Komárom as early as the summer months of 1944. Assembling them for deportation to the places where they were massacred, however, did not reach its climax until November and December. In those months many thousands of Roma were arrested and taken to Komárom.

A survivor, Mrs Krasznai, reported:

On the night of 3 November, early in the morning, the police came by surprise ... they took us off to Bak like lambs pushed into a courtyard. The police kept watch over us, roll call in the afternoon... in the brick factory in Zalaegerszeg... It was full of lice and fleas...there was a large crowd of us. We were taken to the station, there the frontier police, or whoever it was took over guarding us. We were transported on the railway again... no food, no water. In the train my sister was already in a bad way. I thought she would never get there with us, she would die. We arrived in Komárom. Once again fascist guards took over. They had a long stick of cherry wood in their hands, they hit everyone, whether it was a child, a woman, a man, it was the same... Well, they took us to the bunkers in Komárom. In the evening soldiers came but they were German soldiers. Then they took the men away. Only the children and my mother were left. I was twelve, the youngest was six months old, we were there two weeks. We lay in mud, in the wet, and suffered. One day several aeroplanes came, American or English. God bless them and where they walk. So they flew past and threw out their leaflets. I ran out but my mother said, don't run out, they will kill you, my child. I was outside. I took up a leaflet and went back in. There were some of us who could read. I won't forget, written there were these words. 'Dear brothers, don't be afraid, you won't stay here much longer.' Everyone was very happy. As they took us from Komárom by train, some people escaped while German soldiers were guarding us again.

Mrs Kolompár told her story to Agnes Dároczi:

The police came early in the morning and took us. They said we would never return home again. They took the young men out, all of them. We never saw them again. We didn't see my father again either. I was taken over to the group, my mother saw me from the bunker, made a sign with her eyes, 'run, my little child, come back'. I ran back to her fast. Mother wrapped a scarf round my head and there was a little baby, so she pressed it into my hands, so they didn't take me to Germany... There were so many Roma that they couldn't all fit into the camp. There were so many, like ants. There was a Romani woman, she had a bent stick which she beat us with. She was made a Kapo, and when anyone made a noise or caused problems she would hit us. And she did really hit us. May God punish her. She was bad. The guards were bad but she was worse.

We were in the bunker the whole day, and watched by armed guards. If anyone was caught outside the soldiers beat them, if anyone made a noise, they shot them. We are in dirt all day. Mud. And if anyone went out to the rubbish heap [to look for food] if they were caught they were killed. There was a poor girl who was buried alive in the rubbish. She pulled herself out and ran into the cellar. She smelled, she stank. 'Where were you?' I asked. 'I was buried'. I was sorry for her. She was blond and fat. She ran off all the time. She was captured again and buried in the heap of rubbish. I never saw her again. What happened to her? Dead? I don't know.

Mrs Kovács said:

Many adults died in the camp. The children died like flies. Mother said if we had remained there one more week we would all have died. There was a sort of hut with quicklime where they stored all the dead. Every day they came with a cart... often we lay next to dead bodies.

Nearly a half of the people I questioned in Hungary mentioned Komárom. Some groups of Roma, accompanied by police, seem to have been on their way there on foot, when they were freed by the Red Army. For others, Komárom was just one stop amongst others on a complicated journey. For others it was the main feature in the events from which they could count themselves lucky to survive. From December 1944 mothers with small children were sent home from Komárom. The others, those over fourteen who had not died there, were sent to various concentration camps. From the different interviews in which Komárom was mentioned the following picture emerges.

At the beginning of November 1944, usually early in the morning, police knocked on the doors where Roma lived in the districts that had not yet been freed by the advancing Red Army. At that time most of the men had been called up for Labour Service, others were still living at home. Those who were serving far away escaped from the raids. Those who were at home were arrested. Roma from several places in the district were assembled in one place, usually in a brick factory or a temporary internment camp where Jews had previously been held, or were sometimes still there. From the brick factory the Roma were taken to a nearby station. They were told they were being sent to work on the land, to pick turnips or carrots. Pressed tight and locked in the trucks it could take up to two weeks to reach Komárom. On the way the train stopped at several stations to pick up more trucks. The journey was very hard, there was a lack of water and air, and many collapsed. Arriving in Komárom in extreme cold weather the Roma were pushed into underground bunkers, like cellars, or left in the open air. The guards were armed to the teeth with guns, machine guns and whips. The families were kept together for one or two days. Then they were selected. Men over fourteen, women over fourteen without children, mothers with children under fourteen, then they were taken away from another. They had no idea whether they would meet again.

The guards – mostly Hungarian with some Germans – were cruel. They used their whips indiscriminately. The conditions were terrible. There were no toilets or sanitary facilities. Epidemics broke out, including typhus. They stood, sat and lay in mud, dirt and excrement. Their wet clothes froze to their bodies. Food was just thrown down to them which led to friction and fighting. The main meal was a dry slice of bread with boiled cabbage or carrots.

In these conditions large numbers of Roma died in a short time. Almost all the babies and older people froze to death, or died from illness, hunger or blows. Every day piled up bodies were taken out on carts and wheelbarrows. They were lifted onto the carts with hayforks and thrown into the Danube near Monostori. In Csillag the bodies were buried in a ditch with lime. After several weeks the Roma left this prison. Some were loaded into trains and taken to Auschwitz, Dachau or other extermination camps. Their fate is mostly unknown. Others, women with children who had survived up to then, were taken out of the cellars and courtyard and just sent away. The majority of their relatives who had been sent to other places never came back. All the interviewees who had survived Komárom had lost members of their families in concentration camps outside Hungary.

The raids in the villages, the collection in brick factories, transport in trains, overfull trucks, the journey and the stops in stations, which is a story that is well known to us from the reports of Jewish survivors. I do not know of any particular Jewish reports about Komárom. It seems that Jews were not held there for any length of time but just stopped there in transit. In any case, if there were Jews there, it was not in such a large number as the Roma who were crammed in there between November 1944 and Easter 1945.

A Hungarian woman is quoted by the writer Karsai.[38]

> They even led the poor musicians away, followed by their women and children. It seemed funny to us to see how they took their double basses and clarinets with them... It was as if a crowd was marching to the castle in Komárom with musical accompaniment.

The account of the Roma being held in the bunkers and in the open air, in mud, exposed to rain, snow and winter frost is not in itself unique. Komárom was, however, not an extermination camp, yet so many lost their lives there. It was not a concentration camp with constant roll calls, checking the numbers, registration and allocation to barracks laid out in a pattern and numbered. It was the place where many Roma lived and died under extreme conditions, even in the context of the Holocaust. For others their odyssey continued.

The death marches

Towards the end of the war some stretches of the railway could not be used and trains were one of the targets of allied bombers. The front line in the east was moving further back into Hungary and this also affected the train system. It did not, however, affect the racist enthusiasm of the servants of the regime. Large numbers of Roma had to march to Komárom, to camps in Austria and to unknown destinations. Many did not survive the march and many were killed on the way.

Mr Krasznai was in the Labour Brigade in the Ghetto of Pelportpuszta from which the Jews had recently been taken away: *We were there for a month, five thousand Roma, from there we went to Mohács on foot. We walked for two days. Anyone who could not keep up was shot, like a dog. There was no mercy.*

Other groups of marchers did not reach the destinations the Nazis had planned for them, they were rescued en route by the Red Army. One such group came from Somogy district.

Mrs Orsos said:

I was born in 1927 in Somogyszob: I grew up there and was taken away from there. Everyone who was there, we were surrounded by the Nyilas and taken away. We were mixed, various clans, Sinti, Lovari, Romungro, Beyash, all Roma. They took us to Jánosháza and we stopped in a large forest. There were small children, already starving. We were forced along for three weeks. The little ones, they soon died of hunger. They were thrown away. One of my family, as soon as they sprinkled earth over him, his brain spilled open. The small babies and my aunt's parents died there. I have been ill ever since. And they spoke to the people as if we were dogs. If anyone left the line even a little way they were shot straightaway. So we didn't dare to leave the line, only walk and walk. Many died there. No-one counted how many died, they were just left there; people fell, no-one cared. We marched on. I will never forget as long as I live how we suffered there. We were driven like a herd of cows. If anyone disobeyed, they were immediately hit with a rubber whip. Beaten and beaten until they collapsed. I will never forget the terrible feeling. Setting off from Jánosháza they already knew that the Russians were coming near, we were led quickly to Sárvar. There we were freed by the Russians. The march had lasted three weeks.

Another group was assembled from the surrounding area of Nagykanizsa in the coffee factory and was forced to set off on foot. The brothers Nagy were on this march: Ferenc begins the story:

One night we were taken away together with all the Roma from the area... to the police station in Miklosfa, men, women, children, about eleven hundred in all. From there we were taken to the coffee factory in Nagykanizsa. By this time there were several thousand of us. We were kept there for about a month and a half. One morning they told us we would march to the River Mura, so as evening fell we marched over the main bridge. The long line set off, the local people knew we were being taken away, some kind women came and brought us food but they were pushed away roughly by the guards. By the time we got to the next village the news had spread. People just watched our desperate march from their windows. The guards were Hungarians and Germans, there were thirty or forty of them. They hit us with their rubber whips as hard as they could. Anyone who lagged behind was beaten. I can still feel the blows on my back.

We were taken to Bajcsa, then past Fityeháza and Molnári to the river Mura. A ferry took us over to the other bank. A plane flew in circles over our heads the whole time. One night we came to a building. Bombs fell, I will never forget. I was holding on to my grandmother's dress. Suddenly I saw that she was staring at me. She had been hit by shrapnel and died on the spot. There were pregnant women, I can't describe what happened... a thousand dead, they brought a tractor, God knows! They wouldn't let us look because of the blood. It smelt there for two or three days, then they buried them.

His brother Vilmos continues the story:

After they took us from our homes we were kept in the coffee factory for several weeks, with the family. Sandor was in Germany, Ferenc was with me, so was my sister Ilon, my little sister Mari, my young brother Jozsef and Juli had just been born. 1944 – it was a bad time to be born. The world was bad. They had brought all the Roma from the area. They even hunted them out from under bushes. Then they led us off like cattle. Eight year olds, five year olds, even younger, they had to walk. If anyone slowed down the police kicked them in the buttocks... I was eleven. It was terrible what they did there. Anyone who was smart tried to escape. Useless! They were caught. There was no trial. They were shot on the spot, like a dog and they left their body behind. Then we reached Yugoslavia, through Molnári. We had been taken across a large part of Hungary. There were Germans there. We didn't know whether we would live or die. There were about 150 police as there were so many of us. The police ran up to us, we were surrounded and they marched us for a whole day. [After we had crossed the river], we went on to Kraskovec and were put into a school building. It was late at night. There was a school next to the churchyard. We were all put in the yard or the building itself. A policeman switched the light on. We had heard an aeroplane the whole day and then the bombs fell. Nine came down but only three went off. All those in the courtyard were killed straightaway. A few hundred. And many wounded. One lost his hand, and my dear grandmother died there. I lost my hearing from the bombs. I now have a hearing aid. Then we collected the dead and went into the churchyard and dug a mass grave. They were all buried there.

As early as September 1944 the Eastern Front neared the borders of Hungary. The town of Nagyszalonta, then in Hungary, now in Romania, changed hands several times. The Russians had to retreat twice before at the third attempt they took the town under their control. In the meantime, the local Romani population had been attacked with hand grenades and guns. The survivors were marched to the west by police. The order was to take them, and any Roma picked up on the way, to Doboz or Gyoma. The group, which had numbered seventeen when they left Szalonta, grew to forty at its peak. The rapid march went from Nagyszalonta through Kőtegyán, Sarkad and Sosszik to Doboz. Some of the people were killed on the way, others escaped. They walked from the end of September to 5 October. On the eve of their murder there were still twenty Roma alive.[39]

Roma were also assembled in a camp in Mezőkövesd and tortured. Mr Racz was an eyewitness:

It was winter when they made us set off on foot towards Germany. It was terribly cold, we were hurried along. We hardly got anything to eat and everyone knew that if we didn't manage to escape we would be killed. One day somewhere between Gyöngyös and Hatvan there was a stop. We were put in a school. There were Germans downstairs, we were on the second floor and we managed to escape. One of the guards, a teacher, helped us to flee. May God bless him, he was kind. I won't go into details of how we looked, in rags, full of lice, starving, but we managed to survive because we were young and, to tell the truth, we were used to poverty and hunger.

Finally, those who could not run away, the survivors of this group reached Komárom and Győr, together with some Jews. Those who were weak had been shot en route.

Bársony writes[40] that the order for the mass deportation of the Roma came at the beginning of November 1944 with an agreement with the new Nyilas government to send 50,000 workers to build a line of defences on the road to Vienna. For this purpose on 2 November thousands of Jewish men and women were taken from Budapest, together with the Labour Brigades. On this 180 kilometre long march from Budapest to the German border were many Roma, hungry and with no hope.

The final moments: the massacres

As the front came further west, we find similar actions taking place, probably with some overall organisation. In many places one or two days before the arrival of the Red Army a party of policemen would take the Roma from the town to a grave, often dug by the Roma themselves, and shot them. In other places the Roma were killed in their houses or nearby. The first massacres took place in Nagyszalonta in Bekes district, which was in the most eastern part of Hungary, where the first ghetto for Roma had been built.

There are no figures for these murders. Those who managed to escape from the shells and bullets in Nagyszalonta were caught and taken on foot to Doboz, as described above. On 6 October 1944 twenty Roma and two Hungarian communists were killed in the churchyard in Doboz. The invading Soviet soldiers, who had arrived that same morning, shot two of the police who had carried out the killing and were trying to escape.

There is a mass grave but the names of the victims are not written on the headstone.

On the edge of the town of Baja a large number of nomadic Roma were killed. Mrs Pilisi said:

> *I had never seen so many Roma in my life: It was a caravan, a line without end. Perhaps from Transylvania, perhaps from Yugoslavia, perhaps they had been living there in the woods and we didn't know. With such wagons. Many of them were walking alongside the wagons, only the children were riding, and the old people. The rest ran alongside barefoot. They ran through the fields like madmen. They were running away from the Germans and the Nyilas, so they wouldn't be caught. The fascists had already begun to register us, the Roma of Baja itself. But we hadn't been taken away, thank God. Bella and I saw how the fascists followed them and tried to arrest them. Bella saw a heavily pregnant woman in the gutter at the side of the street. She had begun to give birth. The poor woman had laid down so as not to be seen. As we came up to her the head was already out. Bella helped her give birth, and knew how to cut the umbilical cord. Although she was a girl, she had never seen anyone give birth. She took her white blouse off, tore off a sleeve and washed the baby with rainwater from a puddle. Then she wrapped it in the blouse. The woman sat in the gutter then suddenly she jumped up, thanked us tearfully, murmuring in Romanes and ran off with the baby in her arms to join the caravan. We also ran but towards the town. Luckily we knew the hidden paths of the area and weren't caught. It was autumn. A few days later we heard that the Germans had shot the whole caravan near Baja with machine guns.*

The poet Bari writes about this massacre based on the same eyewitness.[41]

> *Roma were also killed in the village of Nyergesujfalu.[42] In the villages of Váralja and Lengyel (in Tolna district) the local Roma were murdered in November 1944. To make sure they were all present, they had been forbidden to leave the neighbourhood. The murder was ordered by the police and they carried it out. We do not know how many were killed in Váralja. In Lengyel, 14 were murdered.[43] Their names and ages are inscribed on a memorial tablet in the village church. In the records of the Catholic Church in Lengyel, the following entry is found in 1944. Cause of death: Shot by the police.*

I interviewed three of the survivors, members of the extended Sárközi family.

> Antal: *The police came on horseback. They rode into the neighbourhood and said that every family should stand in front of their house. We thought they would announce something.*

Julia: *They said 'Out, everyone straightaway in front of the house!'*
Antal: *They shot them all at once, everyone. Those who could ran away,*
the rest were shot.

In the panic those who didn't know where to flee, they ran into the
houses and the police threw grenades in through the windows and killed
everyone in the house. We ran to the woods and they couldn't find us there.
Mihály: *And then they shot the pigs, ducks, horses; they were also killed.*
And the hens, they killed everything they found.

In the town of Győr there were people on their way in a transport to
Germany. The train was bombed and those who managed to get out were
massacred. Mr Balogh said:

> *They took us to Győr. There were lots of us in the truck... In Győr there*
> *was an attack from the air, they bombed the train... The trucks with the*
> *women and children came to a stop and the people ran out. But as they ran*
> *they were shot. They shot at everyone they could. All the fields around*
> *were black with bodies of the dead... there were few survivors.*

The murder of all the Romani inhabitants of the village of Lajoskomárom
remained a secret known only in the village until it came to light through
a documentary film by the director Jancsó Miklós. The film begins with
the facts, presented by the TV and radio journalist Agnes Dároczi:

> Between December 1944 and March 1945 the village of Lajoskomárom
> was on the front line for most of the time. It changed hands between
> Germans and Russians several times. In the third week of January 1945 the
> police massacred all the Romani inhabitants. Their bones have lain until
> today at the edge of the churchyard and the edge of the village with no
> outward sign.

There were no survivors. The man, who drove the victims and the killers
to the ditch where the murder took place, gives the following account in
the film:

> *I didn't see anything as I was ordered not to look. Otherwise I would also*
> *end in the ditch. But when someone unloads people on the edge of a ditch,*
> *what does he think? They were made to face the ditch, then prrrrr, the guns*
> *loaded and shot. A pregnant woman, she struggled for a long time, they*
> *fired five times before she was dead.*

The daughter of one victim family was married and was in another
village at the time. Mrs Peller says:

> *I was in the market when an acquaintance came and said my parents had*
> *been murdered. I wouldn't believe it, I cried and was worried. Where were*

my parents? Much later I went to look for them. I returned home to Lajoskomárom to look for the graves of my parents, brothers and sisters. I found nothing. Then the farmers came, each one with a hayfork, a spade or a sickle, whatever they had and shouted: Get away, dirty Gypsy, nothing happened here, there is no room here for anyone else. They all gave the same answer. Get out, dirty filthy Gypsy.

This visit by Mrs Peller to the village to look for the graves of her relatives took place after the war was over. The documentary film lists the names and ages of those who were murdered in the village.

At the end of January 1945 a party of soldiers murdered the members of one extended Romani family, some thirty persons, in the village of Szolgaegyház in the Fejer district. In the same month, a similar killing took place in Lenti in Zala district.

The largest single mass murder took place near the area of Szekesfehervár in the districts of Fejer and Veszprém in February-March 1945 and lasted for many long days. Hundreds of Roma were killed, group after group, family after family. The killings were carried out by members of the local police, the army, local officials and the Gestapo.[44] Mr Jonas from the village of Szabadbattyan did not want his interview recorded, but he showed the writer the nearby wood where towards the end of winter in 1945 his relatives were murdered.

Several dozen Roma were murdered near the small town of Várpalota by the Mátyás vár castle. But, more ended up in a ditch, now part of a man-made lake, Lake Grabler. The police stood about 150 Roma in front of a ditch that had just been dug for this purpose and shot them. Two women survived and we have their account.[45] Mrs Lakatos said:

We were taken to Várpalota. There were many of us, they imprisoned us in a pen. It had snowed, the children were shouting, there was no bread. We cried too, what would they do to us? They had taken the men away in the morning to dig a ditch. When we came there all the men were already dead. They shot at us, the women and children. I was pregnant at the time, I was due to give birth in June. I was hit by eight bullets, on my arm, legs and side. In eight places and yet I lived and had the child. When it was quiet they checked us with a torch. I lay there in the ditch and did not move, and when they had left and it was still again I tried everyone around me to see who was still alive. My hand touched a girl she gripped my hand,' Who are you', I said, 'whose child are you?' 'I am Falat,' she said. 'Listen, I said. Pull me out, I can't stand up'.

Mrs Raffael (Falat), who was twelve at the time, said: *As they began to shoot I was so frightened and jumped straight into the ditch. So none of the bullets hit me, only one that had already gone through the person next to me.* After she had got out of the ditch, the two girls walked to the town of Veszprém. Her story continues:

> *My clothes were spattered with blood. As I was walking a woman saw me from a window. She already knew how the fascists had killed many Gypsies. She called me over, took off my clothing and dressed me in some of her clothes. She dressed my wounds, put some ointment on and gave me some money.*

The return home. Home?

At the end of the war the few Roma who had survived the concentration camps set off on the way back home. It was a long and difficult journey, in overfull trains, on foot, or on a lorry when they had the good fortune to get a lift. Sometimes the journey took months. Many Roma came back to Hungary together with Jews who had shared their fate.

A survivor Mrs Szarka said:

> *I came back home 16 August 1946. I was together with Hungarian Jewish women till the end, they said I should come to Palestine with them. I said I wouldn't do that, I was sure that someone from my family was still alive here. There were my parents and many brothers and sisters. Why should I go? And I didn't go. This was Harburg, not far from Hamburg. It was a camp, but we were free, although they kept some control over everybody. We had to wash every day, keep clean and then we got a coupon for dinner. So we got dinner. And there was not much traffic going towards Hungary. Every time there was a transport I missed it and in the end I travelled home alone. I didn't have to pay. I showed them my certificate as a deportee and they gave me food and a ticket for the railway. At home they had already been in mourning for me because the Red Cross had told them that... and my parents were sure I was dead because the Red Cross had sent them a postcard. And I was alive and they didn't know.*

Mrs Kati Sarkozi recounted her journey back from Auschwitz:

> *The Poles freed us, they came in first, and then the Russians, my dear. As we walked home, we slept in tents. We were warm enough with the coats we had, with swastikas, we tore them off. On the Czech frontier we lied that our parents had gone to Germany to work and that we wanted to go back home because of the war. They believed us.* [The women who had been freed in Auschwitz were afraid to identify themselves in Poland. They wanted to get away as fast as possible.] *We went into Czechoslovakia and stayed in Prague fourteen days and the war still hadn't finished. In Brno*

we met Russians. They had clothes like Hungarians and there were bombs, houses were burning and we shouted, 'Are you Hungarians?' and they asked, 'Hungarians?' And we said, Hungarian Gypsies'. Then one said we should tell him his future (she said laughing)... None of my family came back and I was so sad and miserable.

Many attempts to make use of transport, which was organised by Jewish relief organisations for the Jewish survivors, were blocked because of the lack of places. Some were offered help by the victorious allies to emigrate to America, Australia or to other European countries. Those who refused went back to Hungary, back to where they had been living before in the hope of finding their families. The relatively long period of time that elapsed between being freed and arriving home and the trauma of loss were two more elements of the tragic history of the persecuted Roma.

Mr Kolompár said:

I had been brought back to Dachau. There on 1 May 1945 the American soldiers found us. We could hear the shots, then they came in. They had landed by parachute, not in the grounds of the camp but nearby. There were German SS in the watchtowers and the Americans were firing at them. We were afraid when we heard the shots. Then we saw the American soldiers, we shouted, we were very happy, you know... and then we moved ourselves, to where the German SS had been in the barracks, we went there and the soldiers took our places in the huts. We moved ourselves. They gave us chocolate, food, everything. As we went across the courtyard I wanted to run but I couldn't, I was too weak. I weighed perhaps 30 kilograms. No hair on my head. I was there for three to four months more, we waited there, the people from America came, then some other people, then it was arranged and we came home. I found my mother and father, they had been freed from Komárom. They were seventy or eighty years old. Everything we owned had been destroyed while my father was in Komárom. They had stolen everything, I had been away for a whole year.

Mr Balogh told me:

I was not even eighteen when they deported me. When I came back in 1945 I didn't find anyone. My four uncles had been with me, they were killed. They were my mother's brothers, I had nine brothers and I didn't find any of them. When the Americans came they didn't want us to go home, especially the young ones. They wanted me to go to Australia and study there. Not I. I only wanted to go home and to my brothers, father and mother. The American officers said to me: Go, or they might take you to Russia but I had decided. There was a Jewish man there called Wollner and this Jew was with me. I came home with him. And there was another Jewish man from Mármarossziget and one more young Jew, the four of us went home to Hungary. Damn it, why? There's no answer to that question. And when I got back they greeted me and said I was just the man the country needed and they would send me to Moscow to study. He was really a nice man that Wollner, he wanted to take me to Palestine with him, I thought what should I do in Palestine. I'm not a Jew.

There is great similarity between the stories about the homecoming from Komárom and the return from the concentration camps. This similarity makes it clear how much alike their situation was. The relatively short time in Komárom had a strong and bitter effect on the physical, psychological, social, economic and family situation of those Roma, just as if they had spent long months in a concentration camp.

Mrs Krasznai described their return:

When we were freed in Komárom, we set off on the way home... There was a child laying in the gutter, a second and a third. People were so weak that they could hardly walk. I turned to my mother because her sister [was so weak] she couldn't even pull the zip on her clothing, then I said to my mother, 'Mama, if one of us dies or you see that someone can't walk any more then we won't leave them here, even if they are dead we will take them home'. 'My poor mother naturally burst into tears and said. 'No, my girl, don't worry, we won't leave one another, if we have to die we will all die in the same place'. So that was that, and then we came to Ács and the police took charge of us. A military train came and there was an empty coach, so they put us in there. Several children died during the train journey, a one year old, a six-month-old baby, and I am not sure who else. We did the last part of the journey on foot. Imagine, in mud up to our knees, barefoot in December. It was pouring with rain, but when we got home there was nothing there. Not a single bed, no windows, not a teaspoon, nothing at all, only the four walls, even the roof had disappeared. Nothing.

A year later in November my brother came back home. We cried and then my mother asked. 'Well, your father and your brother and the others. Where have they gone?' He didn't know as they had been separated when he was only fourteen, And he came back alone.

Mrs Kovacs said: *On the way home my mother found a couple of biscuits in an abandoned military vehicle. We ate them. We might have died without them. We came home on foot.*

Some of the survivors from Komárom got into trains that were going in the direction of their villages, whilst others went on foot. On the way they had difficult and varied experiences. Hungarians whom they meet on the train or on the road reacted with a mixture of sympathy, loathing, and dislike, fear or hate. Some gave them food to eat. That also brought bad luck. Many after going hungry for a long time died from overeating. Others got problems with their digestion and intestines. Many hid and did not dare go home for fear of persecution.

Mr Horvath continues his story:

> *The Russians shouted 'davei, davei, davei!' It sounded different from the Germans. Then we got out... climbed into the train... they saw where we came from, that was easy to see. We needed no tickets, nothing. There were conductors on the train who had food and they gave it to us. Then we got home and those who had eaten too much died. Who would have thought that one shouldn't eat so much because the stomach was like it was. It was not large enough, we came home with shrunken stomachs.*

As the survivors of Komárom came back to their villages, even those who had only been away a few weeks, they found their houses had been looted. Some of the houses or huts had disappeared completely, others had been robbed of all their contents. Even doors and windows had been stolen. The fortunate ones who found four walls – mothers with small sick children, weak, hungry – had to move back into a house with no doors and no windows, without husbands or older children who could help them. The looters were their neighbours.

The end of the War: The dead and the living

The official date for the freeing of Hungary from the Nazi occupation was 4 April 1945. That was the day when the physical destruction of the Roma ceased. Estimates of the number of Roma killed are not objective. One historian places the number of those who suffered in one way or another as low as 5,000 with 1,000 as the total number of deaths.[46] New information is available today, which was not considered in earlier estimates. We know more about the deportations through Komárom to concentration camps. Csillag Prison could take up to 5,000 prisoners at a time while Monostori Castle again had space for several thousand. Other new information deals with local murders. The belated discovery of the massacre in Lajoskomárom begs the question in how many other places were Gypsies murdered and the facts concealed? The unsolved puzzle of the extent of the destruction of the Hungarian Roma means we have to rely on estimates. The most realistic is the figure of 50,000 suggested by Lakatos.[47]

Remembrance

Until the 1980s the persecution of the Roma in Hungary during the Second World War was completely ignored. Mr Balogh said: *Just to talk about it... for forty years I haven't told anyone I was in Germany. No-one knows about it apart from my wife, I didn't want anyone to know.*
The few early attempts to erect memorials met with resistance. Mr Orsos spoke of the massacre of hundreds of Roma in the vicinity of Szekesfehervar: The Romani organisations wanted a memorial. The local government chiefs said 'no, that won't do, those who were responsible still live here.' So there was no memorial. Nothing came of it.

The first memorial to the Roma victims was erected in 1984 in Ondód (Vas-megye district). The local Romani community has held ceremonies there each year. The day of the liquidation of the Gypsy Camp in Auschwitz, 2 August 1944, has become a general date for remembering the victims of the Romani Holocaust. The first memorial ceremonies in 1995 had a low attendance. Gradually knowledge of the story and the wish to remember has grown. In recent years, there have been ceremonies near the Parliament in Budapest, at the memorial in the town of Nagykanizsa and other places. Every year a bus goes to Auschwitz to lay a wreath in the place that, more than any other, symbolises the persecution.

As long ago as September 1998 the erection of a memorial in Varpolata was planned. There is still no visible indication in the town of what took place there. The site of a mass grave of Roma has been turned into an artificial lake

In the Monostori Castle in Komárom, the authorities have installed a tourist site and a Military Museum that glorifies the military history of Hungary. There is no mention of what Hungarian soldiers did in that castle during the winter of 1944–5.

Katalin Katz and a survivor, Friderika Krasznai, visit Komárom, March 1999 (photograph by Danica Vincze and courtesy of Katalin Katz)

The genocide of the Yugoslav Gypsies

Dennis Reinhartz

From the end of the Ottoman Empire to the end of the Kingdom of Yugoslavia

As through much of Eastern Europe, there has been a continuous Romani presence in the Yugoslav lands since, at least, the Middle Ages. Having perhaps come north from Thrace, the first Gypsies arrived among the South Slavs sometime in the middle of the thirteenth century. Their first documented appearance was probably in Macedonia in 1289. Certainly, after the Turkish conquest of the Balkans in the fourteenth and fifteenth centuries Muslim Roma especially were encouraged to settle in the Yugoslav lands beyond Macedonia, among the Serbs of Kosovo (1348), the *sanjak* (region) of Bosnia and elsewhere. This kind of resettlement was in line with the long-standing Ottoman policies to transplant and thereby mix subjugated peoples to make them easier to control. The Turks were not generally interested in greatly improving their conquered territories, but merely in stabilizing their control over them for the purposes of taxation and conscription.[1]

Many of the Gypsies came to reside in the towns and cities. With gradual elimination of the Ottoman overlordship prior to the First World War, the Roma largely remained and became a part of South Slav life. Gypsies took part in Karadjordje's rising against the Turks in 1803–4, and by 1815 there were about 10,000 of them in the Ottoman *Pašalik* of Belgrade. The majority was still Muslim, but a growing minority of them was Serbian Orthodox. Knižanin's victorious army against the Hungarians in 1848–9 included a legendary squadron of Gypsies.

The sparse and largely anecdotal historical record of the Yugoslav Roma in the nineteenth and early twentieth centuries is marked by periodic discrimination, though, on occasion, favouritism as well. A good number of them were illiterate, and to survive and even prosper, they became very good at not being noticed by officialdom. In the newly expanded Serbia of 1833–4, most towns had flourishing Gypsy quarters where the traditional occupations of blacksmithing, horse-trading, bear-leading, faith-healing, tinkering, cobbling, textile and basket weaving, music, and begging were practiced. Obrenović even had his own Gypsy orchestra.

In the first volume of his memoirs, Montenegrin writer and Yugoslav leader, Milovan Djilas, points out that the employment of Roma in occupations like blacksmithing and even grave-digging was necessary before the First World War. The Gypsies, even Muslims, were therefore generally tolerated. He also reflects that in his town the Gypsy houses were indistinguishable from those of Montenegrin peasants. In Serbia, the Roma were perhaps more tolerated because of Serbian orthodoxy, whereas the Roman Catholicism of the Croats and Slovenes of the Austro-Hungarian Empire to the north may have been conducive to greater discrimination, as it also seems to have been towards the Jews.

The Roma managed much the same under the Kingdom of Serbs, Croats, and Slovenes, proclaimed by the Declaration of Corfu in 1917, and its successor, the Kingdom of Yugoslavia, declared in 1929 under the royal dictatorship of King Alexander. By 1941, there were more than 300,000 Gypsies in Yugoslavia, and most of them, with the exception of those in Montenegro, the *Gurbeti,* were permanently settled, many in ghettoes in the larger cities like Belgrade, Skopje, and Sarajevo. About three-quarters of them were situated in Serbia and Macedonia.

During the first week of April 1941 the recently crowned King Peter II was forced to flee to London. As Yugoslavia fell to the German invasion, with the conquest came the fragmentation of the country and the genocide of the Roma in the Yugoslav lands. Because no real records of the Gypsy killings were kept, this genocide remains for the most part unreported.

Macedonia and Montenegro

Montenegro was divided between Italy and Albania, then an Italian protectorate, and Macedonia was split between Bulgaria and Albania. As in Italy, the Roma in the Italian areas survived comparatively well with little harassment. Their situation, of course, became much more dangerous after the German occupation of Italy in August 1943.

In the Bulgarian-annexed parts of Yugoslavia, the discrimination was greater. For example, as elsewhere in Axis and occupied Eastern Europe, signs appeared in restaurants and other public places, proclaiming "Jews, Gypsies, and Dogs Forbidden!" However, the Bulgarians, Macedonians, and Albanians often protected the Gypsies. They also blended in easily with the local populations. The official attitude of Bulgaria was much like that of Italy. Thus, although Macedonian Jews were turned over to Germany in the spring of 1943, no mass deportations or exterminations of the Roma were forthcoming.[2] Nevertheless, a number of Gypsies from Macedonia and the Bulgarian part of Kosovo joined Josip Broz Tito's Partisans to fight in the anti-fascist resistance.

Serbia

For several days before the actual conquest of 6 April 1941, Belgrade and the large Gypsy quarter located in Zemun, across the Sava River from the old city, were mercilessly bombed by the Germans. Serbia was then divided between Germany, Hungary, Bulgaria, and Albania. However, most of Serbia became a German military occupation zone under the collaborationist regime of the former Yugoslav royalist general and Minister of War, Milan Nedić.

The Nazi racial policies, therefore, were promptly and fully applied to occupied Serbia in May. Similarly to the Jews, Roma were defined as those with at least three Romani grandparents who were married to or lived with a Romani. In early July, the racial classification for Gypsies was changed somewhat, based on social position. Serbian Gypsies who could prove that they came from families that had been sedentary since 1850 and had been integrated into Serbian life were freed of the restrictions imposed in May.

Once identified and registered, Gypsies were required at all times in public to wear yellow armbands with a large "Z" emblazoned on them. What Gypsy professionals and office holders there were, were promptly dismissed from their positions, those between the ages of fourteen and sixty, regardless of gender, were subject to forced labour. They were banned from public places like theatres, baths, restaurants, and markets. Gypsies were restricted by a curfew between 8 pm and 6 am and from leaving their places of residence without official permission.[3]

Their degradation continued with the confiscation of their property by the National Socialist *Volkswohlfahrt* (Office of National Welfare). The

Gypsies were among the first taken and executed as hostages at ratios of
10 and 100:1 for casualties caused by *Četnik*[4] and Partisan[5] attacks on the
German occupation forces. In a memorandum of 26 October 1941 to all
German commanders in Serbia, *Straatstrat* Harald Turner, the chief of the
civil administration and an *SS Gruppenführer* under Böhme wrote:

> The Gypsy cannot, by reason of his inner and outer makeup [Konstruktion],
> be a useful member of international society [Völkergemeinschaft] ... as a
> matter of principle it must be said that the Jews and Gypsies represent an
> element of insecurity and thus a danger to public order and safety ... that is
> why it is a matter of principle in each case to put all Jewish men and all
> male Gypsies at the disposal of troops as hostages.[6]

Many Roma and Sinti were taken as slave labourers to help build the
concentration camps at Semlin-Sajmište (Belgrade fairgrounds), Sabac,
Crveni Krst (near Niš), Jajinici (near Pančevo), and elsewhere in Serbia
and Croatia. The Serbian camps in which many of Gypsies were
eventually interned to be exterminated or deported were manned by
German SS and Croatian Ustaša troops. In Belgrade and some of the
other larger cities, the Roma were often held in neighbourhood collection
centres (mini-camps) for later dispersal to main camps like Semlin and
Banjica, which were already open by July 1941. Very early on, those not
rounded up sometimes bravely protested to the puppet Nedič government
on behalf of their seized brethren. In the camps, in addition to being
executed as hostages, growing numbers of Gypsies also died of starvation
and suicide. Next to Jasenovac in Croatia, Semlin was the most infamous
of these camps. Some reports suggest that up to 20,000 Roma were
slaughtered in Serbia.[7]

Still many did not even make it to the camps to be accounted for and
murdered or deported. Untold numbers of them were disposed of as sub-
human refuse in the process of being rounded up, their bodies often being
left where they fell in unmarked graves.[8] On 29 August 1942, Turner
proudly reported that, "In the interests of pacification, the Gypsy
Question has been fully liquidated. Serbia is the only country in which
the Jewish Question and the Gypsy Question have been solved."[9]

Despite Turner's pronouncements and the horrors in Semlin and the
other camps, the Germans and their allies and collaborators probably
effectively controlled only about one third of Serbia's Roma. According
to their linguistic abilities and physical appearances, some escaped by
posing as other nationalities (e.g. Serbs). Others bribed their way free.
They fled, evaded, hid and were hidden, and/or joined the resistance.

Gypsies were not especially welcome among Serbian royalist Četniks, so many of them like Ibrahim Hasani, Stevan Djorjević Novak (d. 1943), Sotchir Sejdović (d.1941), and Dragiša Stojanović joined Tito's Partisans. Sometimes, especially in the very mountainous regions, the Gypsies formed their own resistance groups apart from the Četniks and Partisans and occasionally fought them as well as the Axis forces.

However, chief among their adversaries were the particularly brutal Yugoslav Prince Eugene, Handschar and Kama, and Skanderbeg SS divisions, formed from Germans living in Yugoslavia, Bosnian Muslims, and Albanians. After the war, however, for the Gypsy contributions to the resistance an autonomous Gypsy region in Macedonia was considered, but never realised. Nevertheless, the Roma were constitutionally recognised in 1953 as a national minority for the first time in Tito's Socialist Federal Republic of Yugoslavia.

Slovenia

Slovenia was split between Germany and Italy. The German part was annexed directly into the Third Reich, and the ethnic Slovenes were declared Aryans. At the outbreak of the war, there were comparatively few Roma in Slovenia, and Germany quickly rounded up most of them and deported them to camps in Croatia or German occupied Serbia.

Others fled into Italian territory. In the Italian zone of Axis Europe, the Gypsies were gathered into refugee camps where they were generally well treated and protected.[10]

Croatia

Croatia lost some Dalmatian coastal territory to Italy. Out of the rest, the *Ustaša* fascist satellite, the Independent State of Croatia, under Pavelić as *Poglavnik* (Leader), was proclaimed by the Axis on 10 April 1941. The Italian Duke of Spoleto, Aimone of Savoy, who would never set foot in Croatia, accepted the medieval Croatian Crown of Zvonimir as King Tomislav II. The new Croatian state also incorporated most of Bosnia-Herzegovina and had a diverse population of 7.5 million Croats, Serbs, Muslims, and others, including 30,000 Roma. A small number of Gypsies were Roman Catholics, while the others were nominally Serbian Orthodox or Muslim. Proportionally, the greatest genocide of the Holocaust was not in Germany, but in its loyal Croatian ally. In 1941–5, over 10 per cent of the population of Croatia – Serbs, Jews, Roma, and others – perished as a result of the Croatian racial policies and programmes.[11] The largest number killed were Serbs, but the genocide of the Croatian Gypsies was almost complete. In Jasenovac alone, up to 30,000 Gypsies from all over Yugoslavia died.[12] By October 1943, only one per cent, 200–300 of the pre-war Roma and Sinti remained.[13]

Croats and Croatia's 750,000 Bosnian Muslims (and the Muslim Roma among them),[14] whose support was needed against Croatia's 2.2 million Serbs, were proclaimed Aryans by the *Ustaša*, but their Nazi masters did not wholly agree. In Berlin, the Croats and their collaborators were pronounced a *Grenzenvolk* (a 'border people'), who because of their long beneficially protective presence against "Orientalism" on a frontier of Europe, were deserving of respect. Croatia's position, therefore, essentially paralleled that of Slovakia in the Nazi "New Order". Croatian Aryanism, which asserted the racial superiority of the Catholic Croats over their fellow (Orthodox) Yugoslavs, Jews, Gypsies, and others, was largely a by-product of nineteenth century extremist fringe Croatian nationalism. It implied kinship with the peoples of Western Europe and is a complex, contradictory, and basically alien phenomenon in modern Balkan history. Yet, it was at the core of the Croatian Holocaust because it was an essential part of the *Ustaša* ideology.

Djilas characterized the *Ustaša* ideology as "an amalgam of primitive Croatian nationalism with modern Fascist totalitarianism … militant separatism to Fascism to total anti-Serbianism."[15] In his observation, he was essentially correct. In the nineteenth century, the militant Croatian separatism of men like Eugene Kvaternik and Ante Starčević was initially in large part a response to Hungarian claims to historical Croatia. Pavelić, the founder of the *Ustaša*, transferred this response to Serbian, Pan-Slav, and/or Yugoslav pretensions in the twentieth century. Starčević has been cited as the "father of racism" in Croatia and as the "ideological father" of the *Ustaša* because of his influence on Pavelić and the genesis of its ideology in the *Franković* wing of Starčević's Party of Rights.[16] Upon Starčević's death, his son-in-law, Josip Frank, took over and made it into the more extreme Pure Party of Rights, of which Pavelić became an important member. While it might be questionable whether or not Croats accepted the Kingdom of Serbs, Croats and Slovenes as their legitimate state, few supported the reactionary *Frankovci*. Certainly, between the two world wars the more moderate Croatian Peasant Party represented the nationalist views of the majority of Croats. In exile from the growing

Yugoslav dictatorship, Pavelić's outlook hardened, especially when King Alexander placed him under a death sentence in 1929, the year Pavelić organised the *Ustaša* ('Rebel') in Italy with the help of Mussolini and Admiral Niklos Horthy, the fascist dictator of Hungary.[17] It was in the pronouncements of the *Ustaša* that extreme racist tendencies crystallised, eventually leading to the emergence of Croatian Aryanism. Thus, on 1 June 1933, Pavelić publicly proclaimed the Principles of the *Ustaša* Movement. The Eleventh principle declared that in the national state of affairs of Croatia "nobody who is not by birth and blood a member of the Croatian people can make any decisions ... no foreign people or state."[18]

Aryanism in Pavelić's Croatia was quickly defined in law as well as official propaganda, and it served as the major justification for the Croatian Holocaust. Croatia began replicating and strengthening the Nazi racial laws as its own on 29 April 1941, only nineteen days after its founding. By decree, all such laws took effect once they were published in the official press, usually in the major newspapers *Narodne Novine* (National News) and/or *Hrvatski Narod* (Croatian Nation). The basis for this anti-Romani legislation was that they were once again erroneously being designated as nomads and aliens outside of the [Croatian] national community. Yet ironically, since the Gypsies' origins were in India, they were more Aryan than the Bosnian Muslims, Croats, and even the Germans. This thought at times seems to have even struck members of the Nazi leadership, like Heinrich Himmler.

In Article 1 of the Croatian Decree Regarding Race Membership of 30 April, Roma were identified as having at least two Romani grandparents, a more inclusive formalization than in Nazi Germany. By contrast, Jews in Croatia were still defined as having at least three Jewish grandparents. Similarly, Article 2 required special permission from the Ministry of the Interior under Andrija Artuković for marriages between Aryans and anyone having one second-lineage ancestor who was Romani or two who were Jews. Proof of racial origins was established by birth/baptismal and marriage certificates of the parents and grandparents, often very rare documents for Gypsies to possess. The Ministry of Interior decided all questionable cases based upon the recommendations of the Race Political Committee.[19] Furthermore, under Decree Number 13–542 of the Ministry of Interior, all Gypsies had to register themselves and their property with the police on 22–23 July. Gypsy enterprises and other property were then to be turned over to individuals of Aryan origin (i.e.

the *Ustaše* and their collaborators) under the Croatian Office of Nationalized Property.[20]

Shortly thereafter and throughout 1941–3, along with the Jews and numerous Serbs and others, most of Croatia's Roma were put in *Ustaša*-manned concentration camps like Jasenovac, Tenje, and Stara Gradiška where they were humiliated and slaughtered. Gestapo agents in Croatia and Serbia commented in their reports to Berlin on the brutality of the *Ustaša* and the Croatian Holocaust. They commented that this excessive viciousness lessened efficiency and was detrimental to achieving the desired outcomes. These reports undoubtedly contributed to the eventual replacement of the *Ustaša* with more SS guards in the Serbian camps, like Semlin.[21]

By the summer of 1942, like their counterparts from occupied Serbia, numbers of Croatian Roma and Sinti were being ordered to be transported to the Third Reich for medical experimentation and more systematic extermination at Auschwitz, Ravensbrück, and other camps.[22] Although some Roma and Sinti were Catholic they received little or no protection from the Church under Bishop Alojzije Stepinac in Zagreb or from Rome. At his war crimes trial in Zagreb in 1986, Artuković was remembered by a witness as having bragged in a speech at Sremka Mitrovica Prison in 1943, shortly before he became Minister of Justice, that the *Ustaša* "had killed the black Gypsies, and all that was left was to kill the white Gypsies [i.e. the Serbs]."[23]

Conclusion

Of the over 300,000 pre-war Yugoslav Gypsies, approximately two-thirds of them were exterminated. Although they were sometimes wrongly associated with the Jews, the Gypsies usually were considered even lowlier, less human, and suffered commensurately. Even the Allied intelligence reports of the time either failed to mention them or just categorized them as others.[24] They truly were a forgotten people. Among others, the Bulgarian Gypsy poet, Dimiter Golemanov, has poignantly mourned the passing of the Romani victims and the historic atrocities against them:

> The upright stone stares angrily
> With clenched fists and a great curse.
> From within a hidden voice
> Tries to send out a song.

> The roads we still travel
> wait to hear
> The Gypsies await the call
> Together with their horses.
>
> But they are quiet, all are asleep.
> Our brothers lie among the flowers
> And no one knows who they are
> Or on which road the victims fell.
>
> Hush, Gypsies! Let them sleep
> beneath the flowers.
> Halt, Gypsies!
> May all our children have their strength.[25]

Moreover, that strength Golemanov wrote about is still needed. Despite their severe losses in Serbia and Croatia, the Romani populations of Yugoslavia rebounded. Today, there are perhaps as many as 800,000 of them in the Yugoslav lands.[26] But the Gypsies are still among the least understood and most vulnerable peoples of Eurasia, and their persecution continues. They endure as the eternal other and suffer continued marginalization, discrimination, and violence.

Hence, mindfulness of significant events of the Gypsies' past, like their genocide during the Second World War, will hopefully lead to a clearer discernment of their present. But, as for example the case of the late Croatian President Franjo Tudjman's revisionist book *Horrors of War* (1996), the current reinterpreting/rewriting of twentieth century Balkan history to create linkages to a mythical-historical past often leads to less understanding of the agony of the Roma and other Holocaust victims. Tudjman diluted the Croatian Holocaust and did not even mention the fate of the Roma. Historians must seek to tell the story of the Gypsies better, and we must all listen to what then is told.

Norway[1] – The final solution is planned

Ted Hanisch

There were no Romanies in Norway when the Germans invaded in 1940. There were, however, several thousand Travellers. These are generally thought to be descended from Romany Gypsies who went underground in the 1600s because of the anti-Gypsy legislation and intermarried with Norwegians who travelled from village to village. [Ed.]

The initiative to address the Gypsy question in 1943 seems to have come from an official in the Department of Social Affairs for Oslo district N.N. In a letter to the Chief of the Security Police on 6 March that year he spoke of internment and education of Travellers. The proposed solution is to collect them in a place designed for that purpose, "so they can eventually be removed from the country".

The official suggested that he himself could take an active part in the work and suggested an annual salary of 6,500 crowns. In the journal *Fritt Folk* he published an article with the title 'The itinerant problem must be solved.' It seems that N.N. got no answer. But the police chief must have taken some notice of it for, in an unsigned memorandum of 31 March 1943 to the chief of the Police Department, the Minister Jonas Liewe, we find:

> *The simplest solution of course is that suggested by the Chief of the Security Police; to collect all Gypsies and Itinerants and get them exported to Poland. But this solution depends on whether the Germans will accept them down there. Even if it was only for the real Gypsies I personally have little faith in this solution and we must prepare ourselves to solve the problem here at home.*

Vidkun Quisling, the fascist Prime Minister, wrote to the Minister of Justice Riisnaes on 22 June.

During my travels I continually notice that there are still some bands of Gypsies to be found on the roads. There is every reason to take up the Gypsy question in all its aspects, including from a race hygiene point of view.

A proposal for the special compulsory regulation of itinerants was put forward in a memorandum dated 30 June.

The Social Affairs official N.N. wrote to Jonas Lie on 9 July and suggested a special internment camp. The following day Lie wrote to the Security Police, drawing attention to a discussion of the question of the Travellers in the country that had [already] taken place on 8 July. He had received the Prime Minister's assent to the following:

Setting up a special guarded work camp.
Interning in this camp all itinerants of Gypsy blood who can be classed as regular criminals.
Confiscation of the Travellers' horses and houseboats.
Racial investigation of the Travellers.
Sterilising Gypsies with criminal inheritance.

Lie continues:

The first part of the campaign will therefore be directed to the professional criminals among them. But the aim is, as soon as we get a clearer picture, to get a final solution of the Gypsy plague, so we can be finished with this question and get it solved in roughly the same way as the Jewish question has been [*i.e. by deportation to a concentration camp.* Ed.].

The General Secretary of the Norwegian Mission to the Homeless, Oscar Lyngstad, wrote to the Police Department on 3 September that he did not believe that regulations to forbid the Travellers from keeping horses would have any purpose. Lyngstad further stated that the number of Travellers was going down, but that there could be some point in further strengthening the Vagabond Law, the Child Welfare Law and the Trading Law (the regulations on peddling).

A note from the Police Department makes it clear that the Mission had given its consent to the card index of Travellers (set up on the basis of the 1935 count and brought up to date) being put at the disposal of the Department.

In a letter to Minister Lie on 5 November 1943, N.N. set out a more detailed plan for a camp. The camp would be in the neighbourhood of the Grong or Skorovas quarries and take in 300 of the 'worst' families. The budget would be balanced by the income earned from hiring out the inmates for compulsory work. N.N. reckoned on an income of some 240,000 crowns for children put out to work as day labourers on the farms around the camp. The regime would be strict, for example, the men would march in a body to the quarry each day. The women would be taken by car. According to a draft of the rules there might be leave and freedom for those who showed good behaviour, while any new breach of Norwegian law would mean their being sent back to the camp for life.

N.N.'s suggestion did not meet Minister Lie's approval. "This is too easy" he noted on the letter. There were no further plans put forward for a work camp. In the first instance, the aim was to stop any nomadism through police control. A new proposal for a Law on Compulsory Registration [of nomads] was put forward on 26 January 1944. Meanwhile Lie had some reservations about this and the question was put aside for a while.

It was not until a meeting of ministers on 12 October that a small committee was set up with representatives from the Police, the Interior Ministry and the Social Services Department. The first meeting took place on 3 November and by 22 December it had met fourteen times. Its proposals were put forward before Christmas. The committee expressed the opinion that the treatment of the question should have two main strands:

1. Regulations to render nomadism difficult for those who were travelling around or to prevent it.
2. Through sexual intervention to stop the travelling families propagating themselves.

In accordance with these proposals, the committee presented drafts of two laws, one with special regulations for itinerants and the other to change the 1943 Law for Protection of the Nation's Stock.

The first draft law set out in its first paragraph that there should be a register of all the nomads in the country. Anyone who in the previous five years before the law came into force had travelled regularly or occasionally in Gypsy fashion had to report to the police within a month with information about themselves. The next paragraph forbade such persons from keeping a horse, a boat or a car. The third paragraph stated that the Law against Vagabondage would apply to anyone who nomadised in Gypsy fashion, regardless of whether he supported himself by unlawful means or not. A breach of the law or its requirements would bring a prison sentence of one year.

There was no direct prohibition of nomadism. The committee was of the opinion that this would not work when there were not the means needed to carry it out. From the point of view of society, it was not desirable, they said, that a large number of people should come to fall on the state as a burden by their internment in work camps.

However, they said that setting up a work camp for men and one for women was inevitable. The men's camp would take 200 people and be situated in Ostland. With regard to the desirability of internment as well as sexual intervention, the committee referred to articles by Scharfenberg, written in 1930. These had been copied and put in the same folder as the committee documents.

The legal authority for sterilisation was established by an amendment to the Law on the Protection of the Nation's Stock. According to the proposal, the paragraph would be as follows:

> Anyone who is condemned to a prison sentence will be investigated with a view to sexual intervention to the extent that he shows pronounced asocial tendencies. The same applies to anyone against whom the authorities decide to take action in accordance with the Law on Vagabondage, Begging or Misuse of drugs.
>
> In the same way anyone who is found nomadising in Gypsy fashion will be investigated with a view to sexual intervention.

The sexual intervention the law proposed was castration for persons with abnormal sexual desires and sterilisation for people with a less dangerous criminal inheritance.

None of the two proposals for laws were put into effect. The last note in the documents of the affair is dated 10 March 1945. The Police Department was waiting for a statement from the Interior Ministry, which was presumably preparing several alterations to the Law on the Preservation of the Nation's Stock. These preparations were never completed.

In May 1945 the German army in Norway surrendered to the Allies. [Ed.]

CHAPTER FIVE

Resistance

Donald Kenrick

"Just to survive one day in the camp without losing one's dignity as a human being was resistance" Esther Braun, a Jewish survivor, at the opening ceremony of the London Holocaust Museum 2000.

Many Gypsies did just that, preserving their dignity by helping others and, in Auschwitz in particular, keeping their children's spirits alive amid scenes of disease and death. Amongst these we may count Stella who killed her own children rather than watch them suffer following an experiment by Dr Mengele. Her twins, Tigo and Nina, had some of their veins sewn together by the Nazi physician and were in great pain. Their mother managed to steal some morphine and killed her own children.[1] Josefine Steinbach was offered a place with other adults to transfer from Auschwitz to Ravensbruck before the liquidation of the Gypsy Camp. She refused, saying she would not leave her children and accompanied them to the gas chamber.[2] She was not alone in this sacrifice. Barbara Richter's mother came voluntarily to Auschwitz to join her fourteen-year-old daughter.[3]

In many countries, Gypsies also took part in the armed resistance, but, in most cases, we know little more than a name and a hint of a story. Henri Roussin, a basket maker born about 1923, joined the maquis in France in 1940 and was arrested and sent to Buchenwald where he spent the rest of the war.[4] Elsewhere in France, Armand Stenegry, later President of the Manouche Gypsy organisation, and well known as a singer and guitarist, became a guerilla officer under the code name Archange. He and other Gypsies in his unit assisted in partisan attacks timed to coincide with the landing of the Allies in Normandy.[5] Another French partisan, known as Petit Jean, was part of an action killing a large number of German soldiers on the Atlantic coast.[6] In Macedonia,

Abdullah Kopilj was a leader in Tito's partisan army,[7] while Enrichetta Stefanin fought in the Partisan Battalion G.Zol. Born in Muggia (Trieste) she was killed in Tomenizza in March 1944.[8] Many Gypsies who had escaped to the forest had to use knives to attack the Germans, as they had no other weapons.

In the prisons in Karzew and in the Warsaw Ghetto, Romany prisoners revolted and attacked their guards. A second group in Warsaw fought with railway guards and escaped while waiting to be loaded on a train to Treblinka. Also in Poland, some young Gypsies fought with a partisan group in the forest of Nieswicz.[9]

In France, the Gypsies imprisoned in Mulsanne camp demonstrated on 2 May 1942 to get the food rations raised. They broke out of the gate and some were able to escape.[10]

One Gypsy at Mitrovica, in Kosovo, Hasani Brahim, then aged 36, joined the resistance from 1943. He worked as a mechanic in a garage being run by the military for repairing vehicles and storing petrol. He would get petrol and made petrol bombs for the partisans.

After supplying bombs for a time, the partisans suggested he should blow up the garage and stores. He set to work and, using more petrol bombs, succeeded in setting fire to the whole garage, destroying many military vehicles and petrol supplies and quantities of other stores.

Hasani Brahim was arrested and held in prison. There was no proof against him and, after a week, he was released and continued to work at the depot. He went on making petrol bombs and later set fire to the military food stores in the town. Then he helped to steal arms and passed them on to the partisans. In 1944, Hasani Brahim went to the mountains with the partisans and remained with them until the end of the war. He received many decorations in recognition for his service and went back to live in Mitrovica doing his old job.

Ljatif Sucuri, a 35-year-old Kosovan Gypsy, knew the Albanian chief of police, a general. When an order came through for the police to round up Gypsies Ljatif Sucuri told him that if any were killed he would personally kill the police chief and the rest of his family and would burn down the houses of the Albanians. He told the police chief to inform his superiors over the telephone that there were no Gypsies at Mitrovica, which he did. Ljatif Sucuri went on with his efforts to save his people, using his influence with the Albanian police chief. The day the police chief came with a paper from higher authorities ordering him to kill all Gypsies, Ljatif Sucuri got him to hand over the paper – and then burned it. Again, he got him to telephone his superiors and say there were no Gypsies in the town, only Muslims. This was about August or September 1943. As a result of his intervention, no Gypsies were murdered in Mitrovica itself. But many people were hanged for helping partisans.

When Ljatif Sucuri heard about their deaths he again went to the police chief, demanding an explanation. This time he succeeded in persuading the chief to have the remaining Gypsies from Mitrovica released from the labour brigade, himself going to Greece to see that this was done. His death was tragic. At the end of the war, collaborators trying to cover up their own activities denounced Ljatif Sucuri and said he had co-operated with the occupiers. Without checking the allegations, the partisans took him away in the night and shot him.[11]

Josef Serinek was arrested in the village of Bohy in the Czech lands and transferred to the concentration camp at Lety. He escaped from there together with Karel Serinek. They found some guns by robbing a hunting lodge, but Karel was later shot by a forest ranger. Josef escaped to the mountains where he met three escaped Soviet prisoners of war and made contact with the partisan organisation R3. He then recruited other escaped prisoners into the Chapayev Unit, also known as the Black Unit, which soon reached the strength of 150 members and worked with Soviet parachutists and other partisan groups. A major operation was an attack on the police in Pribyslav, after the latter had killed General Luzi, head of the R3 organisation. Towards the end of the war, Serinek took part in disarming German soldiers.[12]

Escape

In most camps a failed escape meant certain death. Nevertheless, Gypsies tried to flee. For some reason, Czech Romanies were the most determined. The records of Auschwitz show many attempts from the main camp and some from the Gypsy Camp itself. Vincenc Daniel was a nomadic Romany from Czechoslovakia. He was arrested and sent to the main Auschwitz camp in 1942 and was given the number 33804. He escaped from a working party at the Bina works and returned to Moravia. Unfortunately, he was caught stealing food and sentenced to six months in prison. He was still serving the sentence when the order came that all Gypsy prisoners were to be transferred to the Gypsy camp in Auschwitz-Birkenau. He managed to escape from Auschwitz while the prisoners were being deloused and returned to his homeland, where Czechs fed him while he hid in the woods until the liberation. After the war, he married twice and died in Brno at the age of 51.[13]

A few Gypsies escaped from the Jasenovac extermination camp in Croatia. Josip Nikolić and some other men fled when they heard the group who had gone ahead of them being shot. He jumped into the Sava River and swam away from the Ustashi who were firing their rifles at him. After hiding on the riverbank overnight, he saw the newly dug graves of his companions. He walked back to his home village of Predavec and then joined the partisans. Another escapee from Jasenovac, Janko Gomen, was also in the partisans, but was killed in battle in 1943.[14]

The violinist Franz Josef and three fellow Gypsies fled from a group that was being taken to Lille station to be deported to the east. His three companions were killed but he managed to escape with just a wound in the arm. He was hidden by a barber who looked after him and he remained free until the end of the war. His arm was not treated properly as he did not dare to go to a hospital. Later, a plate was put in his arm but he could not play the violin again.[15]

Righteous Gadje

The Righteous Gadje are the equivalent of the Righteous *Goyim*, a term used to describe those Gentiles who helped to save Jews. Janina Sadowska many years later told how she hid in the forests of Poland near Kielce and Radom. In the winter they stayed with villagers who gave them food for free, or in exchange for a blouse or scarf. One day their tents were surrounded by German soldiers and Polish policemen. The men were taken away and were not seen again. They lined up the women and children, fired some shots in the air and then told them to run away – which they did. Janina continued to live in the woods until the end of the war.[16]

Adolf Frans Petalo (born 1911) fled as the police were escorting his family to Westerbork transit camp in May 1944. He was then hidden by Dutch people but he gives no details. The sixteen-year-old Edi Georg was not picked up with the rest of his family because he was sleeping in the stable looking after the horses. A Dutchman, Hendrik Bethlehem, helped Edi to get a false identity and a place to hide until the end of the war. Many other survivors were helped in Holland. The Guatemalan and Italian consuls managed to free some Lovari families, who had passports from their countries, from Westerbork before the train set off for

Auschwitz. Inspector Knol in Amsterdam saved a small group by telling the Germans they were Dutch musicians while some local police warned Gypsies of the coming arrests. The musician Tata Mirando was saved by a German officer who was also a violinist.[17]

Rosa Metterich described how, after escaping from Lackenbach for the second time, she was protected on a train by a Hungarian officer who stopped the train inspector asking for her papers and gave her food before wishing her "Good luck, Gypsy girl."[18]

Anna S. was born in Pankrac prison in Prague. Her mother was killed but a friendly guard smuggled her out in a sack and she survived.[19]

In Austria, Baron Rochunozy helped the families who were working on his estate to flee across the border to Hungary. Later, he himself had to escape from the Nazis by the same route.[20] In the town of Krasni Yerchi in the Crimea, local Tartars hid a ten-year-old Romani child in their quarter after the rest of his family had been shot.[21]

Zekia A. was eight years old when the Germans occupied Nish. She lived with her family in Stochni, the Gypsy quarter. Left alone when her five brothers, and soon afterwards her parents, were arrested by the Germans and taken to the concentration camp at Crveni Krst, she first stayed with some women whose menfolk had also been taken by the Nazis. Her sister Dudija was shot by a guard when she was pushing some food through the barbed wire at Crveni Krst for her brothers One day in the market she was seen by a Serb called Milan from a neighbouring villager. He knew her as her parents had helped with the harvest on his farm. When he learnt that all her family had been arrested he took her to his village, Chamrlija. He and his wife Lepa dressed her like a Serbian girl. As Germans came to the house daily to take hens and eggs, she had to spend the day in the fields looking after the sheep. Only at night did she dare return to the farm. The Germans also came to the village and searched the farms looking for Jews and Gypsies. Warned by the village headman Zekia was hidden under a haystack. She had to lie there all day without moving or coughing. Only Zekia and one brother survived the war.[22]

In the districts of Talsen and Daugawpils in Latvia, the local administrators stopped the killing of Gypsies in contrast to elsewhere in the country. After the war, the Gypsies from the town of Sabile erected a monument on the grave of Kruminsch, the administrator of Talsen in gratitude for his protection during the fascist period.[23]

There is no reason to doubt that there were many other villagers and officials, especially in Eastern Europe, who helped to save local sedentary Gypsies, although the nomads were less fortunate. But with neither the saviour nor the saved being able or willing to put their story in print after 1945, most of these deeds remain unrecorded.

Roma in the Resistance in the Soviet Union

Valdemar Kalinin

Little is known about the participation of Gypsies in the Red Army. As a paratrooper officer (1969–71) in the Army of the then Soviet state, I got to know quite a few Romani officers and soldiers. During 1999 and 2000, I researched in Moscow, Minsk, Vitebsk, Tolochin and Polotsk about Romani people in the Soviet military.

In 1926 the census of the Soviet Union gave as many as 62,000 Roma, and in 1939 89,000 were counted. Provisionally we should multiply roughly by 2.2: For example the census in Moldova in 1841 gave 17,000 Roma but a census run by scrupulous military officers gave 41,000 in Moldova in the same area. It is difficult to calculate how many Roma took part in the Soviet Army or Navy, in partisan movements, underground activities, or in the battles against facism on the territory of the Soviet state temporarily occupied by Nazis. But notable Romani scholars in Moscow, Y. Druc and V. Gessler indicated that there were thousands of Roma in the Resistance against the Wehrmacht. This might be the result of the new policy towards Roma when the former Soviet government recognised Roma as a national minority in 1925 with the fruitful outburst of the Romani culture which followed. Let us pay homage to all those Roma who fought like heroes and gave their lives for the freedom of mankind from the Nazi plague.

I will deal only with those who identify themselves as Romanies and for whom there is official information (encyclopaedias on war, books and archives).

- **Timofey Ilyich Prokofiev**, born 2/2/13, killed 27/3/44, is the only official Romani Hero of the USSR, the bearer of the Order of Lenin. He was born in the village of Lukyanovo, in Ostashkov County, into a peasant Romani family.[1] He had worked as a sailor on the Moscow

canal and fought in the Navy as early as January 1942. He was a
rifleman in the Special Parachute Battalion No. 384 of the Navy
Mobile Infantry Detachment. On the night of 26 March 1944
Prokofiev was dropped out of the plane, together with others, under
the leadership of Lt. Olshanski, into the rear of the enemy near the
important port of Nikolayev (Ukraine). They were violently attacked
for two days and managed to beat off the Germans 18 times. Prokofiev
perished during these battles. He was rewarded with the title of the
Hero of the USSR posthumously, and on 20 April 1945 he was
awarded the Order of Lenin (the two highest awards of the Soviet
State). He was buried in the Park of Heroes in the town of Nikolayev
in the Ukraine. There is a street there which bears his name and a
monument in the park "to the glory of the perished paratroopers". As
the historian Ivan Dolgov[2] adds, Prokofiev's father took part in the
First World War. Timofey had worked as a high ranking engineer
serving canal vessels and, therefore, he was exempt from being called
up to the front, but when he learned that his two other brothers had
perished at the front he volunteered. From this large family of six
children only one sister survived.

- Another Romani who came to fame during the Sandomerz operation
  in 1944 was a pilot – Captain **Alexander Murachkovski** (1916–77).
  When the Commander of the Regiment, Lt. Colonel V. Obukhov, was
  shot down, Alexander Murachkovski landed his plane next to the
  place where Obukhov was being surrounded by Nazi soldiers.
  Alexander helped his wounded Commander to get out of the plane
  and, using a pistol to fend off the enemy, he managed to drag him to
  his own plane and successfully took off. For this deed he was awarded
  the Order of the Red Banner which he added to the two Medals of
  Glory he had already earned.

- **Nikolai A. Menshikov** (1915–96) graduated from the Romani
  Teachers Training College in 1938. When the War started he finished
  the intensive Infantry Officers College in Oriol and, in 1943, was sent
  to the Front as a Commander of a platoon to fight around Stalingrad.
  The brave Lieutenant was promoted and advanced with his soldiers as
  the Company Commander and his Battalion liberated Ukraine,
  Poland, Czechoslovakia and Germany. During the last four days of the
  War, near Dresden, he was severely wounded and became a military
  invalid with the five highest military honours.

- Captain **Alexander Vasilyev** (1920–42) was the best graduate of the

Romani Teachers Training College in 1938 and a teacher, poet and translator of Romani books. In 1941 he was called up and finished Tank School with a Sergeant's rank. On his way to the battlefield he visited his former teacher's family, Romani leader, poet and translator Nikolai Pankov (1895–1959) who was still in a deep depression following the closure of the Romani Schools in 1938. Vasilyev, a well-loved and good-hearted intellectual, gave all his military rations and money to the Pankov family as Muscovites were starving because of the War. This kind young Romani man turned out to be a brave commander and soon was promoted to Tank Company Commander. He underwent a dreadful death in 1942, being burned with his team inside their tank during bloody fighting defending Leningrad. He was posthumously awarded the Order for Bravery and the Red Banner.

- A talented actor of the Romen Theatre, **Alexander Vasilkov** (1917–43) also graduated from the Romani Teachers Training College in 1938. When the War broke out he volunteered to fight the Nazis and was trained as a pilot. Defending the sky over Stalingrad during the fierce historic operation in 1943, Senior Lieutenant Vasilkov died during an airfight and was posthumously awarded the Red Banner Order.

- The bass singer and actor of the Romen Theatre, **Ilya Sorochinski** (1897–1954), originated from Belarus and served as a Sergeant in the Second World War. During fierce fighting he was wounded. After his recovery he sang as a soloist in the Railworkers' Professional Choir.

- The notable Romani academician poet and co-author of the *Kalderash-Russian-English dictionary* (1989) **Roman S. Demeter** (1920–89) was called up in 1943 to the Red Army. During the military induction course he was immediately singled out as a good physical instructor and was sent to Novosibirsk to prepare fighters of the special forces against the Nazis and Japan.

- Staff-Sergeant **Fyodor Kozlovski** (born 1922), a graduate of the Vitebsk Primary School No. 28 and the Serebryanka Seventh-Class Boarding School near Smolensk, was called up in 1940 and trained as an operator of the famous Katyusha bazooka – an anti-tank gun. He defended besieged Leningrad and finished his military service in Germany. He was awarded the Order of the Second World War Grade II, and medals 'For Bravery', 'For Military Credit', 'For the Liberation of Prague', 'For the Capture of Berlin' and others. From 1947–80 he worked as a fire officer before he retired.

- One of the youngest fighters in the Partisan Brigade 'Death to Fascism', was **Fyodor Klimovich** (born 1927), now residing in Seattle, USA. He spent his youth armed with a rifle. He spent 1943–4 planting mines on the route where the Germans were sending military deliveries to the Eastern Front.
- Two former pupils of the Vitebsk Romani Primary School No. 28, brothers **Ivan Mitnikov** (1920–62) and **Alexander Mitnikov** (1926–78) also fought against Facism. The elder Ivan (a Non-Commissioned Officer) defended Moscow. The brothers were awarded many medals.
- Senior Lieutenant **Ivan (Lavreno) Povarevich** (1920–91) led his company against Nazi troops while liberating his Belarus homeland, Poland and Germany. He was decorated with many medals and Orders. After demobilisation he returned to his Romani way of life as a horse-dealer, but took an active part in talking to school children about the atrocities of Fascism. I had the privilege of meeting the former Commander of an Infantry Company, Captain **Ivan Pasevich** (1921–93), a relative of above-mentioned Ivan Povarevich. He, too, was awarded many medals for his military deeds.
- **Tosia Timchenkova** (born 1924) volunteered to go the Front, was trained as a Field Nurse and was later promoted to officer rank. She received many medals for bravery from the Soviet State and later lived in retirement in Moscow.
- Another young Romani woman, **Polina Morazevskaya** (1926–43), was a secret agent near Vitebsk in the famous partisan brigade of Alexei; she used to come to the military German garrisons pretending to carry a baby in her arms and passed on information to the Moscow headquarters of the security services. Sadly an agent of the German secret field police unit No. 336 discovered her activities and the Ukrainian SS executed her by throwing her into a factory oven. She was awarded the Red Banner Order posthumously in 1944.
- As we know there were three Romani collective farms around Smolensk with the notable Serebryanka Boarding School, whose graduates and teachers fought against fascism. Most of these Romani people were executed near Rudnia. In August 1982, in the village of Aleksandrovka (where there is still a surviving Romani collective farm), a monument was unveiled in the honour of 176 Roma former collective farmers who were shot dead or buried alive in 1942.
- The former Director of the above-mentioned Serebryanka Boarding

School and later the Chairman of the Romani Collective Farm 'Freedom' in Kardymovo (1931–41) was the legendary Romani woman **Jefrosinja (Ruzha) Tumarshevic** (1909–93). She served as the intelligence officer of the Partisan Detachment No. 7 under the leadership of Grishin. Her husband and her daughter were executed by the occupying forces. In 1977 she was awarded the title Honoured Partisan. It was through her efforts in 1982 that the monument referred to above was erected in the settlement of Alexandrovka. Her brother Major **Mikhail Tumashevich** (1907–86), a former tank commander, was deputy commandant of occupied Berlin in 1945–6.

- Two tutors of the Serebryanka Boarding School, **Piotr Morazevskiy** (1910–41) and **Alexander Mikholazhin** (1912–42), also perished at the front during the War.
- Two graduates of the Romani Teachers Training College of 1938, the brothers **Ivan Kombovich** (1918–42) and **Dmitri Kombovich** (1916–43) underwent short term training as commanders of tanks and were fighting heroically when both perished. Another two graduates – also brothers – who studied at the Romani Teachers Training College **Ivan Zhuchkov** (1916–42) and **Phyodor Zhuchkov** (1917–42) were trained as gunners in the air force and both perished in the air battle around Krasnodor. They were posthumously decorated with medals and Orders.
- The younger brother of the above-mentioned Captain Nikolai Menshikov, **Alexander Menshikov** (1917–42), went to the Serebryanka Romani Boarding School and graduated from the Romani Teachers Training College. He was working as a primary school teacher when war broke out so he was entitled to be evacuated with his children to the East, but he volunteered to go to the front. He underwent short-term training as a Sergeant, but his small unit got encircled near Vyazma. Alexander managed to flee through the marshes and forests and joined the secret underground resistance. Unfortunately, he was caught by the Gestapo after a former pupil informed on him. He was executed and quartered.
- The former Romani leader, **Ivan Tokmakov** (1888–1942), was born into a travelling Romani family, but educated by his aunt and elder sister and through self-education in the Urals. He was called up into the Tsarist Army during the First World War and became a Cavalry Non-Commissioned Officer. After the Revolution he was a student until 1922, but later on he was invited to work as an instructor in the

Nationalities Section of the Soviet Government. He worked in the Kremlin and met Stalin. He oversaw the Romani collective farms, schools and co-operatives. At the same time, before the War, he became the Director of the Romen Theatre. When war broke out the Communist Party appointed him to monitor the evacuation of the Romani collective farms but the Nazi forces advanced so quickly that he volunteered to go to the Front. The military authorities felt he was too old to go but he insisted. In 1941 his company was captured, but he managed to escape and set up a small partisan group in the area of Smolensk and Eastern Belarus. Ivan Tokmakov was captured again and sent to the Bobruysk Concentration Camp in Belarus. There he managed to build a small resistance group, but was betrayed and died while being tortured on 15 May 1942.

- Some of the other artists of the Romen Theatre who volunteered to go to the Front also perished on the battlefields, including **Vanya Dement, Grafo Silnickij, Vitya Sishkov, Sergy Zolotariov**.
- The notable poet/playwright **Nikolai Satkevich** (1917–91) was an advisor on Romani Affairs to the Soviet Government for many years. When the War broke out he spent four terrible years in the trenches.
- In August 1999 I managed to interview in Polotsk one of the few surviving 1938 graduates of the Grishkovo Romani Boarding School, **Ivan Tumashevich** (born 1924), who in 1942 was trained as a tank commander. He fought on the Ukrainian front and was twice wounded. He was also in the Intelligence Battalion (an ambush group specializing in the capture of German officers). After recovery from his wounds in 1945 he was on his way back to the front as the War ended.

The Military Archives of the Russian Federation (upgraded in April 2000), the Council of War Veterans and the Red Cross confirm that 2,015 Romani soldiers, sergeants and officers perished on the battlefields. We must remember also the contribution of others whose names so far we have not been able to establish.

Captain Alexander Vasilyev taken in 1942 (photograph courtesy of Valdemar Kalinin)

CHAPTER SEVEN

Swiss policy towards Roma and Sinti refugees from National Socialism: Defensive walls instead of asylum

Regula Ludi[1]
Translated from the German by Bill Templer

Introduction

In 1946, the Swiss pastor Hercli Bertogg conjured up the "silent uncanny danger" emanating from the Travellers (*Fahrende*). He prophesized that: "a sedentary people equipped with a solid moral-religious foundation would possibly be destroyed, or at the very least heavily burdened, by the vagrant, with his work-shy attitude, immorality and magic. Beneath a very thin veneer of culture there lurks the beast."[2] Down into the late 1960s, certain research at Swiss universities, schools for social work and in psychiatric clinics served to bolster such views. Many investigations were based on genetic conceptions that the psychiatrist Josef Jörger had published, beginning in 1905, in his psychiatric studies of families dealing with generations of vagrants, or were grounded on racist publications that came out even after 1945.[3] The National Socialist persecution of Roma, Sinti and indigenous Jenische Travellers was generally regarded in the postwar period as having been a legitimate form of crime prevention, and, in keeping with that assessment, was played down.[4] It was not until 1972–73, when a scandal rocked the Swiss public, after it was divulged that the widely respected Relief Society for the Children of the Highway (*Hilfswerk für die Kinder der Landstrasse*) had, for almost 50 years, been engaged in tearing apart Jenische families, forcibly taking children from their parents and placing them in homes and elsewhere.[5] Down to 1972, there was a general prohibition on Gypsies entering Switzerland. Since that time, Jenische, Roma and Sinti have also established associations in the country promoting the interests and the preservation of the culture of Travellers.[6] In 1998, Switzerland officially recognized the non-sedentary (*nicht Sesshafte*) as a national minority. Yet many government offices still find it difficult to provide Travellers with camping sites or to protect them from racism. The most recent studies indicate that subtle, but no less consequential, forms of indirect discrimination continue to restrict and infringe upon the basic rights of Travellers.[7]

Research on the history of the Roma, Sinti and Jenische in Switzerland can build only on a relative paucity of earlier studies.[8] In addition, such inquiry is sometimes faced with a striking absence of sources. It is likely that important documentation was destroyed.[9] The lack of source materials is also reflective of the fact that the Swiss authorities have barely ever dealt with the problem of Roma, Sinti and Jenische refugees. Thus, for example, not even one of the documents that served as a legal basis for asylum policy made any specific reference to Gypsies. In the practice operating at the border, the category of Gypsy was apparently evident, since they were often classified in the same breath with beggars and vagabonds as 'undesirable foreigners'.[10]

The question thus arises: did the Swiss authorities ever actually perceive Roma, Sinti and Jenische to be victims of racial persecution and genocide, and thus possible asylum seekers during the Nazi period? That focuses questions about the current state of knowledge and the perception of 'Gypsies' by the authorities. It makes it necessary to look back at the very beginnings of state 'Gypsy policy' in Switzerland. Over an extended period, its framework was determined by a tradition of preventing the entry of foreign Gypsies and coercive measures against the native Travellers. Both facets render it improbable that Roma, Sinti and Jenische might have found asylum in larger numbers in Switzerland during the era of National Socialism. Rather, well-documented case histories demonstrate that during the period in question, the authorities left no stone unturned to keep Gypsies out of Switzerland. Moreover, continuity after 1945 suggests that the Nazi era did not constitute a rupture in Swiss Gypsy policy but was rather part of a broader fabric of discriminatory treatment.

Internment and Expulsion

Down to around 1900, Switzerland adhered to the liberal principle of freedom of movement. A basic shift occurred in 1906, when the Federal

Council closed the border to Gypsies and prohibited them as passengers on trains and steamers.[11] At the same time, the federal authorities also tried to initiate cross-border coordination of Gypsy policy, but this came to naught due to the lack of readiness on the part of the neighbouring countries to co-operate.[12] The first decade of the twentieth century thus marks a turn in Swiss policy towards foreigners. This was the first time the national government introduced special discriminatory regulations for a specific group of foreigners. The question thus arose: how should the category of persons falling under the ban on entry be best defined? For practical reasons, a sociological concept of Gypsy was chosen. An internal administrative document from 1907 stated that the regulations did not target "members of a specific race or persons otherwise possessing ethnographic or cultural bonds," but rather was directed against individuals whose way of life was incompatible "with the norms of modern well-regulated life in a state."[13] Thus, what was decisive here was the perspective of the police, according to which Travellers who, by dint of their way of life, "break the laws of the land as a matter of habit and place themselves outside the social order,"[14] and whose behaviour is "refractory against any and all civic rule of law and state authority."[15]

In this way, the culture of the Travellers was construed as having in itself the status of a veritable criminal offence. The change in federal Swiss policy was given concrete embodiment in the Gypsy Registry, introduced in 1911. It gathered together data from police records on Travellers and assisted cross-border exchange of information with analogous institutions, such as the Gypsy Central Office in Munich.[16] Finally, in 1912, the competent Federal Justice and Police Department (*Eidgenössisches Justiz- und Polizeidepartement*, EJPD, hereafter: FJPD) decided to generally expel foreign 'Gypsies' from Switzerland.[17] From 1913 on, Travellers were seized and held in custody for fingerprinting and before being expelled over the border: the men in institutions, the women and children in privately run homes. This amounted to 144 individuals down to the outbreak of the First World War in 1914.[18] The police system of surveillance also functioned swiftly and smoothly after that war, thanks to stricter controls at the border, co-ordinated sweeps and intensive exchange of information with the Munich Gypsy Central Office.[19] In October 1932, the Swiss delegate to the Conference of the International Criminal Police Commission (ICPC) noted, with satisfaction, that Switzerland had no "Gypsy problem, because since the war it no longer permits Gypsies to settle in the country, and at the beginning of the war, all Gypsies present on Swiss soil were interned or required to leave Switzerland."[20]

Race discourse and eugenic measures

Switzerland pursued a policy of forced assimilation toward indigenous Travellers. From 1850 on, the state granted homeless Travellers of Swiss extraction communal and cantonal rights as citizens.[21] Since that time, Gypsy policy has been active at the interface of policy on welfare, foreigners and crime. In the late nineteenth century, these spheres of policy came under the influence of the modern human sciences, which provided possible interpretations for social problems and potential avenues for eliminating social ills.[22] At the time, the human sciences were dominated by theories of evolution, which postulated that essential traits were transmitted genetically from one generation to the next. In addition, they provided the basis of ostensibly scientific proof for justifying political exclusion and discrimination.

One discipline that had a substantial influence on the perception and scientific definition of Gypsies was the field of criminal anthropology, where race theory and policy and crime fused into evidence for "inferiority that posed a common danger".[23] Its basic statements on the "congenital inclination to crime" appeared to confirm themselves tautologically, as it were, in respect to the Roma, Sinti and Jenische. Stigmatized as potential criminals – and for that reason restricted in their freedom of action by discriminatory prohibitions – the risk for Travellers to be arrested for an infraction of the law was especially great. This was manifested in statistics on crime; these in turn provided empirical material to fuel theories about the existence of a racially specific inclination toward criminal behaviour. The Gypsy researchers based their assertions on administrative case histories. These investigators, such as the psychiatrist Josef Jörger, found a receptive ear for their work, particularly in Swiss clinics. With his studies published in key journals of race research, beginning in 1905, he founded a current in research on the biology of inheritance, which had a shaping impact on National Socialist Gypsy research. In his methodology, Jörger based his work on family trees of Jenische in an attempt to establish conclusively "a fateful legacy of moral-ethical imbecility, stemming from an early progenitor and passed on in concentrated form by later ancestors." He considered this genetic inheritance responsible for "vagabondism, crime, immorality, feeblemindedness, mental disturbance and pauperism."[24] However, Jörger was more cautious in his interpretation than other medical doctors, who in a sweeping condemnation included all Jenische families in a "class of criminals."[25] In 1944, the legal expert Rudolf Waltisbühl had no doubt that non-sedentary families were distinctively moulded by the "genetic inheritance of mental inferiority," and he demanded the forced sterilisation of "vagrants with congenitally inherited deficiencies."[26]

In the late nineteenth century, patterns of argumentation based on genetic inheritance theory and racial hygiene also gained sway in the practice of social care and welfare.[27] At the same time, demands were voiced for eugenic solutions to social problems. In 1911, the physician Hans W. Maier argued that

> [...] utilizing precautionary measures in racial hygiene, one could take steps to counter the degeneration of our population now threatening on the horizon as a result of the excessive numbers of inferior individuals. [...] If we don't learn how to hold in check the forward advance of this burden now, at least for the benefit of a later generation, then the healthy, vital elements that support culture will diminish among our descendants, heavily encumbered by the responsibility of providing social welfare for the sick and wretched, the useless and harmful.[28]

The Swiss Civil Code (1912) contained an article on prohibition of marriage based on the theory of degeneration; its introduction had been legitimized by arguments about the betterment of the race or the weeding out of individuals who were socially and mentally inferior.[29] However, in most cases eugenic measures were applied without any basis in law. The corresponding suggestions, ranging from unlimited detention and bans on marriage to sterilisation, all had one common goal: to prevent propagation by persons stigmatized as abnormal, suffering from hereditary diseases or inferior. Such recipes found a broad base of support in the inter-war period across the entire spectrum of political parties in Switzerland.[30] Based on psychiatric expert opinions, forced sterilisations were carried out, targeting females in particular. Such operations were often viewed as a measure of social discipline. To a particular degree, members of groups categorized as deviant fell victim to this practice. In Switzerland, right from the start, that category also included the Jenische.

For that reason, the National Socialist policy of sterilisation found support and praise in the pre-war period far beyond the circles of eugenic research.[31] Thus, the Swiss authorities refrained from protesting against the forced sterilisation of male and female Swiss nationals in Germany, and, as a rule, rejected their repatriation. The reason given for this lack of action, namely that the sterilizing of abnormal persons is by no means the most stupid thing the Third Reich is doing these days, was apparently not an isolated opinion.[32]

Measures of coercion motivated by social pedagogy were also concretely implemented in the removal of children from their families by the foundation Pro Juventute and promoted by government agencies. In 1926, it established the Relief Society for the Children of the Highway (*Hilfswerk für die Kinder der Landstrasse*) directed by Alfred Siegfried. Its avowed aim was to eradicate the non-sedentary way of life and to that end to break up and dissolve the families of vagrants. The latter "constitute a dark spot in our Swiss homeland, so proud of its civilized way of life."[33] With its prominent coterie of sponsors, the *Hilfswerk* enjoyed broad support and was able to count on cooperation from offices for social welfare, teachers, men of the church and charitable organisations. Over the course of half a century, it tore asunder and destroyed Jenische families, transferring more than 600 children to children's homes, institutions and foster families.[34] The activity of this relief society led in many instances to the stigmatizing and criminalizing of the children affected, and had traumatic consequences for many.[35] In 1973, after a series of articles on its "work" was published by Hans Caprez in the newspaper *Schweizerischer Beobachter*, it had to cease functioning.

Switzerland and the Internal Criminal Police Commission

In the period between the wars, the situation deteriorated for Roma in Europe. In many places, they were among the very first victims of ethnic homogenization and the expulsion of minorities. However, aside from one single exception there was no international organisation that adopted the Roma in their plight. That exception was the International Criminal Police Commission (ICPC), set up in 1923 in Vienna. It dealt with Gypsies solely in respect to questions of policy on crime, with disastrous consequences for the victims of expulsion. Shortly after the incorporation of Austria into the Third Reich in 1938, the Commission came rapidly under Nazi control. In 1940, its main office and archives were relocated to Berlin, and the SS-Obergruppenführer Reinhard Heydrich, chief of the Security Police and the Security Service in the German Reich, was selected as the new president of the ICPC.[36]

At the beginning of the 1930s, combating the Gypsy nuisance became an ICPC priority. Its conference in 1935, in Copenhagen, passed a resolution to build up an international Gypsy registry in Vienna. It was also to contain genealogical data and information on the networks of relations of the persons included.[37] There was also a positive response at the time to the paper by the Karlsruhe ministerial assistant secretary Kurt Bader, who reported on National Socialist persecution of the 'Gypsies', proclaiming before the international audience:

> The Gypsies, in so far as they are pure-blooded, constitute a race of a special kind. In it, the instinct to wander is congenital and anchored in the blood. If this instinct to wander is forcibly suppressed, then one can expect phenomena of degeneration to occur. These really function to turn the Gypsy into a criminal.[38]

In 1935, the ICPC expressed its unqualified approval of the racist methods of repression introduced by the National Socialists, methods that violated the principles of states grounded on the rule of law. It supported the policy already pursued by the member states; but at this conjuncture, that policy took on a new and fatal significance. In effect, it now became a denial of the right to asylum for the Roma and Sinti, whose lives were under dire threat in the territory under National Socialist control. In 1938, the National Socialist authorities were granted unlimited access to the international Gypsy card catalogue. From 1940 on, the Commission was firmly in the grip of the SS. All the materials of the ICPC were available to those offices and agencies that planned and organized the genocide of the Jews, Roma and Sinti.[39]

Since the mid-1920s, Switzerland had regularly sent delegates to the ICPC conferences, mainly senior officials from cantonal police offices. The later dominance of the National Socialists did nothing to harm Swiss relations with the Commission. The Swiss delegate Werner Müller, together with Arthur Nebe – director of the Reich Criminal Police Office, and from June to November 1941 commandant of SS Einsatzgruppe B – were members of the editorial committee of the ICPC journal. Müller continued in the administrative committee; in his capacity as a "regular reporter", he was considered, according to the ICPC statutes, to be one of the "assistants of the President", Reinhard Heydrich.[40] In the autumn of 1942, Heinrich Rothmund, head of the police section of the FJPD, visited the ICPC central office in Berlin and conducted talks with various SS functionaries who played an important role in the extermination policy of the Third Reich.[41] Apparently, the leading Swiss police authorities did not see any construable connection with racial persecution. By dint of their unwavering loyalty to the Commission, dominated by the National Socialists, they became, of course, involved and complicit in the genocide of the Roma and Sinti.

The victims of the policy of expulsion between the wars

The genesis of a "complex meld of science and police" (as Michael Zimmermann describes it) in the first third of the twentieth century determined the situation of Roma, Sinti and Jenische, who tried to escape persecution by the National Socialists from 1933 onwards. The restrictive entry regulations in the inter-war era were a severe limitation on the mobility of Travellers, blocking the path of refugees into asylum. Contributions by scholars in the human sciences, in the fields of eugenics, criminal anthropology and racial hygiene, provided existing anti-Gypsy stereotypes with the semblance of a scientific basis. Thought patterns grounded on views in racial hygiene and criminal biology obscured the racist character of Gypsy persecution by the National Socialist regime, since the corresponding measures appeared like a prophylactic and legitimate form of crime prevention. Finally, the ICPC endorsed the dominant views and was the forum at which the National Socialists gained international recognition for radicalizing the persecution of the Sinti and Roma. For Roma, the resolutions of the 1935 ICPC conference had a fateful significance similar to the failure of the Evian Conference in 1938 in its meaning for the Jewish refugees: for victims of Nazi persecution, they closed the doors on the last options for escape.

The deportation and expulsion of foreign and stateless Roma by the European countries in the inter-war years resulted in a situation where Traveller families were shunted permanently back and forth between individual states. In the mid-1930s, Gypsies in Switzerland continued to be designated as undesirable foreigners who should, without hesitation, be turned back at the border and denied an entry visa.[42] In the mid-1920s, fascist Italy heightened the stringency of its Gypsy policy.[43] Subsequently, entire groups of Sinti and Roma were chased back and forth between Switzerland and Italy. The report of a policeman in Wallis describes the methods used:

> So these people were pushed or rather hounded by the Italian border guards on up to the top of the pass. These homeless souls had to stay out in the snow, starving, without any food whatsoever, as indicated, for the

duration of four full days. Understandably, the Swiss border guards initially did not wish to look after them either. But the Italian border guards stood there, their weapons readied, and in the event of any attempt to return were prepared to open fire. This naturally would have developed into serious violence, had pity for these poor people not prevailed on the Swiss side. And so the family was taken in.[44]

The report expresses a strange admixture of pity and disdain. It also mirrors the contradictory attitude of the authorities. Local border and police officers often found themselves caught up in a moral dilemma when they had to carry out pitiless instructions. By contrast, the representatives of the central administration insisted on adherence to principles so as not to create any unwanted precedents. Ultimately, Switzerland and Italy agreed on a compromise. Italy declared it was ready to halt any further deportation of Sinti and Roma to Switzerland. In a coordinated counter move, Switzerland allowed three Sinti groups to stay.[45]

One of these groups was the M. family.[46] In the mid-1920s, they had been expelled for the first time from Italy, and were arrested in the autumn of 1929 in the canton of Ticino. There were nine family members: the father Carlo, born 1892 in Chur, his mother Anna R. and seven children between the ages of five and eighteen. The six-year-old boy Carlo died the following winter of complications from an accident.[47] In the spring of 1930, the M. family tried to return to Italy, but were soon apprehended and expelled immediately back over the border into Switzerland. However, on the orders of the federal authorities, they had to depart again for Italy. A contingent of three border policemen took the recalcitrant group on a three-hour march on foot in pouring rain over snow-covered mountain paths to the border. There they were received by a waiting troupe of some thirty members of the fascist militia, who threatened to stop them by force. This attempt at deportation sparked protests from the public.

In the meantime, the federal Swiss authorities declared their readiness to accept the M. family into Switzerland. They were granted residence in Wallis, but an application for Swiss citizenship was rejected. Due to a lack of valid identity papers, the freedom of movement of the family was thus severely restricted. The family was unable to travel abroad and had great difficulty earning a living by music and the craft of itinerant menders, since they often were not granted permits for residence and the practice of a trade. In 1936, the authorities contemplated another deportation of the family to Italy or the possible forcible break-up of the family. The officials were angered by the fact that the spouses of the daughter Marie and son Johann had joined the family. In this way, as the federal authorities put it, the group had "developed into a real roving band of Gypsies".[48] In 1937, Carlo M. and his family, together with other Travellers, were arrested and charged with vagrancy. Jacques L., the spouse of Marie M. and the father of their son Tschawo, and Loli R., the pregnant wife of Johann M., were expelled immediately to France.[49] Nothing is known about the subsequent fate of the expellees. There are signs that Roma or Sinti who spoke Swiss German were also imprisoned in the internment camp of Rivesaltes in southern France. Whether these individuals were members of the group deported in 1937 from Switzerland cannot be determined.[50]

In the spring of 1938, the rest of the M. family was also expelled by the police to France. Carlo M. had agreed to this measure in order to be able to reunite the family with the members already expelled. The authorities, in return for travel money, had forced Carlo to promise he would never return to Switzerland. The reunification of the family proved a failure. The relations between Carlo's children had been strained and shattered in the tribulations and chaos of the separation of the family and the expulsions. Moreover, the family found no basis for an economic livelihood in France and was forced to return to Switzerland. Carlo M. then applied for a residence permit in Wallis, which was finally granted to him, after several complications, in the autumn of 1939.

A half year later, the communal council praised the M. family for their behaviour: the family was supporting itself and not competing with local trade; they had always paid their taxes and the bills of their suppliers. But the good will was deceptive. When in the summer of 1940 the family returned to their hut after a trip, they found it had been burned to the ground. In 1941, the situation grew more tense as the federal authorities once again contemplated breaking up the family: "We definitely had a great interest in not allowing the family to continue to wander about in the countryside as a roving band – because they will soon increase their size by adding a new (and probably more numerous) generation." In order "to prevent future Gypsy mischief, the family should now be dissolved by force", and the children should be placed in the foster care of farmers or looked after as wards in state institutions.[51] That intention was not made reality. Instead, Carlo M. and his children finally obtained a secure residence. As refugees, the adult family members were assigned to compulsory labour service. As Tschawo M. recalls, several of his male relatives were forced to work as labourers in construction work on the Susten road. In the 1960s, Johann M. applied for citizenship once again. His application was denied and he died stateless in 1974. Tschawo M., who had spent almost all his life in Switzerland and had married a Swiss Jenische woman, was not granted Swiss citizenship until 1993.

The case history of the M. family typifies the situation of stateless and illiterate persons tolerated in Switzerland. Itinerant families struggled with analogous difficulties in the 1930s and 40s.[52] Moreover, the acceptance of individual groups of Travellers did not constitute a breach in the system of defence, but was rather a reluctant concession granted to Italy by the federal Swiss authorities.

Turning away of Roma, Sinti and Jenische refugees

The National Socialist Gypsy persecution was no secret to the Swiss authorities. In 1941, a Swiss diplomat reported on the so-called May deportation in Cologne, where "a large number of Gypsies have recently been deported to Poland."[53] In 1942, a Swiss private citizen informed the Swiss Consulate in Hamburg about mass murders of the Gypsies in the East.[54] Yet knowledge about the racial persecution by the Nazis does not appear to have influenced Swiss policy toward the Sinti and Roma. The sources suggest that the Swiss authorities also kept the ban on entry for Gypsies operational during the war as well, denying refugees asylum. In June 1939, a few months before the beginning of the war, a family of nomads from France attempting to enter Switzerland were refused entry at the border, dubbed as "*étrangers indésirables*", even though they possessed valid papers.[55] Documented also is the denial of entry to the jazz guitarist Django Reinhardt near Geneva in 1943.[56] On 21 August 1944, likewise near Geneva, a "*famille de 12 romanichels*" was refused entry.[57] Toward the end of 1943, five men designated as "*Tziganes réfugiés*" were deported to France.[58] The formulation "*Tziganes réfugiés*" indicates that at least toward the end of the war, there was no longer any doubt about the refugee status of the Roma and Sinti. The following example shows, however, that even in the final phase of the war, endangered Sinti were refused entry at the border.

On 25 August 1944, the seventeen-year-old Sinto Anton Reinhardt swam at dusk across the Rhine to Switzerland, where he was apprehended and brought to the district jail. Anton Reinhardt applied for asylum as a conscientious objector, and hoped to be accepted into Switzerland as a military refugee.[59] But the police officers did not believe him. His origin, a non-sedentary family, only strengthened their doubts. A report determined that Anton Reinhardt was "a questionable individual" and that "his parents before the war had belonged to the Travellers, i.e. to itinerants who mend umbrellas. The actual motives which caused the aforesaid to flee to Switzerland are unknown, it was impossible to determine them."[60] Moreover, Anton Reinhardt was suspected of having made a false statement, because he had registered using the name of his stepfather. As German sources indicate, he was actually awaiting induction into the armed services. In addition, he had not obeyed an order to appear for forced sterilisation, and was therefore being sought by the Gestapo.[61]

During further interrogation in Switzerland, Reinhardt also mentioned racial persecution as the reason for having fled: he stated that he was a Gypsy and that relatives of his mother had been confined by the Germans in the Auschwitz concentration camp. The Gestapo had also threatened him with deportation to Auschwitz.[62] Nonetheless, the Swiss authorities refused to grant him asylum. The decision was made on the basis of the new guidelines of 12 July 1944, according to which in the case of "all foreigners whose life and limb are truly endangered for political or other reasons" there should be no expulsion.[63] Thus, Anton Reinhardt's entry refusal was contrary to regulations, since his deportation should have been regarded as a potential threat to his life. On 8 September 1944, Anton Reinhardt was deported to Alsace.[64] He was soon arrested there by the German police. In March 1945, he was able to flee from the Rotenfels camp.[65] Seized once more in Schapbach on 30 March 1945 while fleeing from the local Volkssturm, the Sinto was tried, on orders from the SS Hauptsturmführer Karl Hauger, by a summary court and sentenced that same night to death. The next morning, Anton Reinhardt was forced to dig his own grave in the forest, and was then murdered by Hauger with a shot to the back of the neck or the stomach.[66]

Swiss Sinti in Auschwitz

The Swiss national Josef F. was deported to Auschwitz on 19 May 1944. Several weeks prior to that, he had been confined on orders from the Dutch police together with 577 children, women and men classified as ethnic Gypsies in the Westerbork transit camp. The camp commandant is said to have replied to Josef F.'s protests: "The Swiss, they aren't Gypsies."[67] Josef F.'s deportation was not some unfortunate accident. Rather, a history over many years preceded it, the tale of the desperate struggle of several Swiss nationals, men and women, living in Holland to have their citizenship recognized. The history of that struggle began in 1930, when the Dutch government sought to expel foreign Travellers. Among them was the family of musicians B., in the possession of Swiss passports.[68] Nevertheless, the Swiss authorities wanted to prevent a repatriation of the Travellers at any price. They refused to recognize the citizenship of the B. family and tried to thwart their return. Finally, the Dutch authorities suspended the expulsion order.[69] However, the problem of their citizenship had not been resolved. In 1931, Emma B. had attempted in vain to have her passport extended.[70]

By contrast, the nationality of Josef F. was uncontested. He had been born in Switzerland, was able to present a confirmation of his citizenship from his town municipality, and spent most of his childhood there, before venturing abroad as a member of the Circus Krone.[71] But the authorities harboured doubts about whether his documents were genuine. Josef F. was deemed suspect because he had connections with the "roving Gypsy band B." and earned his living as a fiddler.[72] An investigation by the federal police finally discovered that Josef F. was an illegitimate child of Katharina F. and in official documents falsely bore the family name of the former husband of his mother. The confusion this discovery caused had a fateful consequence: after the police had recognized the claim to Swiss citizenship of the family F., it questioned Josef F.'s identity and refused to issue him a passport. He tried in vain in the following years to prove his identity. In the eyes of the Swiss authorities, he remained a "Gypsy who wrongly claims he is Swiss and F."[73]

As can be imagined, Josef's chances of being able to point to his Swiss nationality when he was arrested in 1944 were, thus, quite poor. By contrast, some of his fellow sufferers avoided deportation precisely because they were able to present Italian and Guatemalan passports. They were released by the German police after the relevant diplomats had intervened in their favour.[74] Among them were also Travellers who, in previous years, had struggled in vain to obtain recognition of their claim to Swiss citizenship, such as members of the B. family, of whom several were in the possession of Italian passports.[75] By contrast, Josef F. was deported to Auschwitz. He escaped death in the gas chambers by the skin of his teeth. On 2 August 1944, he was placed in the last transport bringing Roma and Sinti from Auschwitz to the Buchenwald concentration camp.[76] Four days later, he managed to flee, but was apprehended on 6 September 1944 and sent back to Buchenwald, where he was registered as a "work-shy Swiss national".[77] He survived the camp. It is highly probable that his mother Katharina F., accompanied by five children, was deported to Auschwitz.[78] It would have been quite easy for the Swiss authorities to shield Josef and Katharina F. from deportation to Auschwitz. The successful interventions by diplomats from other countries in such cases indicate that this was possible.

However, no such interventions are known in the case of the Swiss authorities. Even during the Nazi period, the Swiss authorities adhered to their strategy of defence vis-à-vis the Roma and Sinti. They continued to treat Travellers within the framework of policy on crime, even in the face of the National Socialist persecution on their doorstep. Consequently, the policy of defence practised in the 1930s continued without a break in the practice of denial of asylum. This finding is given added corroboration by statements of high-ranking federal officials, specialists in the field of policy on foreigners and refugees. In 1951, Oskar Schürch wrote that "there are no longer any Gypsies in the real sense living in Switzerland."[79] That same year, Robert Jezler implicitly stated that no Roma or Sinti were accepted as refugees: "For generations, Switzerland has actually had no problem any longer with how to treat the nomadic travelling peoples ... In recent years, we've really only had to deal with three Gypsy families."[80] The "three Gypsy families" he was referring to were the groups taken in from Italy mentioned above.

Measures of exclusion and criminalization ensured continuity without any break in Swiss Gypsy policy down into the 1970s. Not until 1972 did the Alien Police rescind the ban on entry. Since that time, the same regulations hold for Sinti and Roma as for other foreigners. Yet control and surveillance over individuals and special registration of Gypsies were procedures continued in part up into the 1980s.[81]

PART 2

The Aftermath

The National Socialist persecution of the Jews and Gypsies: Is a comparison possible?

Michael Zimmermann
Translated from the German by Bill Templer

Introduction

The focal point of reference for most historical work on the image of the Gypsies and Gypsy policy in Germany is the National Socialist policy of annihilation.[1] The scholarly and political controversies do not revolve so much around the genesis of the murder of the Gypsies[2] and the course it took, but centre more on where it should properly be placed in history and comparative interpretation. Probably the most heated discussion involves the relation between the murder of the Jews – and the parallel murder of the Gypsies.[3] The spectrum of positions here extends from the equating of these two mass crimes[4] all the way to an equally vehement emphasis on the differences between them.[5] Against this backdrop, I would like to examine the question of what common features and differences can be established overall between the persecution of the Jews and the Gypsies. In this nuanced comparison,[6] it is indeed necessary to detail both similarities and differences. A presentation that chooses to accentuate only the shared features or differences between these two spheres of racial policy of the Third Reich would tend, simply by dint of its lop-sided approach, to beg the question, anticipating the result, and would thus hardly be able to do proper justice to the complexity of this topic.

Shared features of the persecution

Firstly, the murder of both the Jews and the Gypsies targeted groups of individuals whom the National Socialists declared to be members of a 'race', but who did not see themselves either as a unitary people or a nation in the modern sense of the term. In the first half of the twentieth century, the majority of the European Jews did not possess, by any means, an integral sense of national, religious and cultural identity. In Germany, for example, they formed a distinctive group, yet without sharp contours of differentiation toward the broader society. Their most important organization bore the emblematic name Central Association of German Citizens of the Jewish Faith (*Centralverein deutscher Staatsbürger jüdischen Glaubens*). Likewise, there was no unitary consciousness of identity among those persecuted as Gypsies. The concept of nation or nationality played a role only among a miniscule minority in their ranks.

But on the basis of the presence of a "portion of Gypsy blood", National Socialist racism even classified persons as "Gypsies of mixed race" (*Zigeunermischlinge*) who were totally integrated within the majority society, and who did not view themselves in any way as Sinti, Roma or Gypsies. That constituted a clear parallel to the anti-Jewish Nuremberg Laws. Though it did not centre on the so-called *Mischlinge*, or persons of mixed race, the definition of the Jew in this legislation, ultimately based on the religious affiliation of the grandparents, was likewise applied to persons who were indifferent to Jewish tradition, had converted to Christianity or were without any religion. Decisive here for the labeling of an individual as a Jew or Gypsy, and thus crucial for the fate of persecution, was the image rather than the identity of those affected.

Other shared features of the National Socialist policy of annihilation worth emphasizing are the following:

Its fundamental determinants were dictatorship and war. All opposition in Germany oriented to democracy and human rights was suppressed. The overwhelming majority of Germans who were not persecuted as individuals deemed "racially inferior" or "alien to the community" saw themselves as part of a "folk community" which had to stand firm against the military foes of the German state. The imperialist and racist war of conquest waged by the German state in Eastern Europe sought to achieve a comprehensive annihilation of the enemy, death and destruction in the most extreme form.

The primary mental predisposition was a racist view of social questions. This racialist view of the world was not only anchored among the ideological elite of the regime, but wider spread among the people. Utilizing notions such as 'final goal' and 'Final Solution', it paved the road to forced sterilization and systematic murder. Popular racism, coupled with the variants of racial anthropology and race hygiene, provided here a discourse that transposed the traditional behaviour of distancing and differentiation – not only toward the Jews, but towards other groups, such as the Gypsies as well – into a relatively unified image of society. In this conceptual universe, the agents of history were not individuals, social classes or a universal humanity. Rather, it was the individual nation, the *Volk*. The hereditary substance of the German people, to be furthered by means of conscious selection, was considered to be endangered both within and without by groups and persons stigmatized as inferior. This biological approach to the social sphere, conjoined with the concept of racial purity, aggrandized the power and capacity of the German people to the point of invincibility. It became the core of the National Socialist project. Along with a special animosity against the Jews, this project as a central predisposition helped spur the concrete processes of decision-making behind the policy of annihilation. To deviate from this dynamic and utopian aim would have been perceived by the National Socialist leadership and the regime's ideological elite as a kind of self-abandonment. Moreover, in the struggles for dominance that raged within the National Socialist polyarchy, it could have been perceived as treachery and betrayal.

Racial politics also gained in importance after 1933 for another key reason: the National Socialist movement was disunited and irresolute in almost every other relevant field of policy, and came up against substantial resistance from various sectors of German society. That in turn favoured a development that Martin Broszat characterized as "selection of the negative elements in world-view": for the consciousness of power and the asserting of the Party's claim to leadership and control, it was of decisive importance that "at least in a few cases, ideological conceptions were also made concrete reality." In Broszat's view, this was most readily practicable by steps to be taken against the "minorities, who were powerless," since "it did not entail a dangerous challenge to the conservative partners and power brokers in the state and society." These minorities included persons with hereditary or mental disease or asocial tendencies, as well as groups such as the Jehovah's Witnesses, Gypsies and Jews.[7]

The National Security Headquarters (*Reichssicherheitshauptamt*, RSHA) functioned as the institution for persecution at the top of the apex. It saw itself in terms of a primarily racist view of security, and its power of implementation was, in large measure, attributable to this functional reduction of social complexity. During the Second World War, the National Criminal Investigation Department (*Reichskriminalpolizeiamt*, RKPA) was, as Office V, under the jurisdiction of the RSHA. The mobile action squads of the Security Police and the Security Service were also under its aegis.

Essential here was a policy of extermination not planned over the longer term but one that would unfold under the conditions of the war, crystallizing within the dynamics of interaction between regional initiatives on the one hand and central decisions on the other. That policy escalated in a short time to mass murder. Of key importance for this escalation was the attack on the Soviet Union in June 1941, and the fact that it ground to a halt a short time later before the gates of Moscow.

Central was a dictator who legitimized the mass annihilation, the ideological motor driving state policy on the Jewish Question.[8] Yet in the concrete implementation of the mass murder, he was only one factor among many – a factor whose specific importance in the historical discussion declines to the extent that it becomes possible to demonstrate the dynamically radicalizing impact of other central and regional agencies and institutions in the equation. The broad participation in murder, and the multitude of initiatives driving that murder, point out the real dimensions of this crime.

A key, shared common feature between the persecution of the Jews and the Gypsies lay in the mental strategies used to deny and legitimize the murder. In both cases, the police and bureaucracy labelled and euphemized the deportations as 'evacuation', 'resettlement', 'transport', or even, in the case of the Gypsies, as a 'journey'. Specifically, by dint of their semantic openness, these terms masked the preparations for murder. In addition, the deportations were a process based on a division of labour. The resulting array of responsible bodies, the principle of carrying out official instructions and the ostensible self-legitimization of bureaucratic procedure led to a numbing of conscience and denial of one's own personal responsibility.

Other shared patterns were: people were only acting under orders, other institutions were more directly involved in the murders and thus bore greater responsibility; the mass killings a person actually had witnessed or knew about could only be regarded as exceptions or deviations due to the war – they did not reflect the will of the leadership. Moreover, the effort to strip the victims of their humanity also functioned to provide a form of psychological exoneration. Thus, the Jews and Gypsies crammed together in the Lódz ghetto at the end of 1941 or in Auschwitz-Birkenau in 1943–4 were so sick and weak that to those who had indeed been instrumental in causing their condition, they seemed to be nothing but sub-human creatures. Another operative fiction was that the mass murder was even conceptualized as an act of mercy for the victims. A number of those involved actually sought to legitimize these murders by claiming they were a far more humane solution than to let people languish in great torment. Moreover, they helped to prevent epidemics and even to preserve the lives of those Jews and Gypsies who had been spared.

Yet among the men who did the actual shooting, the constellation took on a different physiognomy. In their case, the commandment 'Thou shalt not kill' was not only suppressed via ideological motives but also by means of peer pressure. Consonant with that pressure, the common wisdom in their ranks was that, if possible, every person should take active part at least once in the killings. Careerist thinking, brutalization, alcoholism and the growing lust to kill also played a role, as did an image of masculinity, which transfigured the murder into a form of male prowess and severity. That was compounded by another factor: the comforting knowledge that the killings were sanctioned by the political leaders and would be totally approved by them without reservation. However, among some of the members of the police killing squads, these motives barely played any perceptible role. Nonetheless, they too participated in the slaughter. That induced Jan Philipp Reemtsma to coin the following pointed formulation: "Many did it because they wanted to. Others wanted it because they did it."[9]

The statements with which Task Forces (*Einsatzgruppen*), army units and police sought to justify the killing of Jews or Gypsies placed the customary anti-Semitic and anti-Gypsy clichés within a plan of action linked with the German conduct of the war and the occupation regime. Along with the stigma of "useless mouths to feed", a common cliché mobilized against the victims was that they were enemy agents and partisans. Such stereotypes made it possible for the murderers to account for their murder in a fantasy form as actions undertaken against Jewish Bolshevism or Gypsy espionage, and to legitimize them by projecting imaginary positive consequences for the German war effort. Sometimes the murder itself was constructed to serve as a reason for further murder. When in the spring of 1942, near Vitebsk, Einsatzkommando 9 prepared to shoot 20 Gypsies, an old woman among them begged for her life. The commander rejected her plea, commenting that the execution would not then remain a secret.[10]

Differences in persecution

Despite such common factors, there were also substantial differences in the National Socialist policy of murder directed against the Jews and the Gypsies.

1. First of all, National Socialist racial policy had a hierarchical structure. The central threat was perceived as emanating from the Jews who, unlike the Gypsies, were stylized as the "universal enemy of Aryan culture" and the embodiment of eschatological evil. In terms of National Socialist fantasies, the Gypsies undermined the German nation, eroding it from below, while the Jews were deemed an arch-enemy to the Aryans. The anti-Semites alleged that Jews were disproportionately over-represented among the upper class and the intelligentsia and that they possessed particularly destructive attributes. In addition, that arch-enemy had, like a dangerous virus, supposedly already penetrated deeply into the body of the German people. Outside Germany, it was thought that there was a constant struggle in the Western democracies between indigenous powers of protective resistance and an aggressive Jewish contagion – this had also been the case in Germany prior to 1933. By contrast, in the Soviet Union the process of corrosion at the hands of the Jews had already gained an upper hand in the guise of Bolshevism, which for its part was forcing Germany into a battle for national survival.

Hitler, whose tirades about world Jewry are legion, made only passing remarks about the Gypsies. Characteristic of his views are comments during a conversation on 2 October 1941 with Reinhard Heydrich, the head of the RSHA. The topic was military service by German Gypsies. Heydrich had broached this issue and argued using the racist term "asocial Gypsy *Mischling*". Hitler limited himself to repeating standard clichés. First he called the Gypsies a "nuisance" for the rural population, and then went on to clothe the stereotype of the Gypsy thief in an absurd anecdote about the hundreds of Gypsies from Romania and Hungary who are trained, "as if at school", to become pickpockets. In 1908, on the occasion of Emperor Franz Josef's 60th anniversary as monarch, they had "descended in droves" on Vienna. In closing, he localized the romanticism of the Gypsies in the bars of Budapest, stating that all Hungarians were Gypsies.[11] After that remark, probably meant as a punch line, Hitler and Heydrich changed to another topic.[12]

Hitler's minimal interest in the Gypsy Question is symptomatic. The Gypsies did not play a central role in the racist world view of National Socialism. In 1943, Eva Justin, a senior member of staff of the Race Hygiene Research Centre, a unit within the National Health Office,[13] that dealt with the racial classification of the Gypsies, wrote that the Gypsy problem could not be compared with the Jewish problem, since in contrast with the Jewish intelligentsia, the specific nature of the Gypsies was an element unable to "undermine or endanger [the] German people as a whole."[14]

2. The differing forms of the National Socialist images of the enemy pertaining to Jews and Gypsies cannot be properly grasped without knowledge of the quite different history and social significance of animosity toward Jews as contrasted with hostility toward Gypsies. The authorities in the Middle Ages, before the coming of capitalism, had tended to find ways and means to protect the Jews, especially in view of their financial usefulness. For that reason, they took an unfavourable view of popular manifestations of anti-Jewish violence, regarding them as signs of the weakness of their rule, an eventuality that had to be prevented. In addition, the German Empire, founded in 1871, was a state that officially granted the Jews civil equality, thus promoting their integration, albeit in a limited form, into the majority civil society. Consequently, the Jews were exposed to the threat of possible extreme violence should the state forfeit its protective function, allowing them to fall into the hands of anti-Semites.

By contrast, the situation of the Gypsies had been characterized since the sixteenth century by extreme repression and persecution at the hands of the authorities, and their concomitant marginalized social position.[15] The peripheral nature of the relatively small Gypsy population also led to the consequence that anti-Gypsyism in Germany was at no time able to take on the importance of a central image of the enemy, a political ideology of integration and exclusion, or a cultural code, as was definitely the case when it came to anti-Semitism.[16]

In addition, the subordinate role of animosity toward Gypsies compared with anti-Semitism, was attributable to the fact that the dialectic of attraction and repulsion in the myth of the Gypsy was differently configured than in the myth of the Jews. In the social construction of the Gypsy,[17] the image of the noble savage found its dominant negative correspondence in the cliché of the uncivilized and dangerous barbarian. A mundane earthiness and openness corresponded with the stigma of an instinctive drive for inconstant and aimless wandering; simplicity and an unassuming manner close to primitiveness. A lack of bias and innocence complemented simple-mindedness, and a carefree enjoyment of life's pleasures were equated with being dominated by physical urges and wanton shamelessness.

While these binary opposites should be interpreted primarily against the backdrop of social development as practiced in Europe since the early modern era, the likewise ambivalent image of the Jew was decisively shaped by profound doubts on the part of the Christian world in the certainty of its own salvation. By contrast, the Gypsies were classified in part as heathens, in part as Christians, and, thus, not viewed as religious competitors. But in the envious Christian view, a Jew, even if he or she had personally turned away from the ancestral religion, still epitomized God's chosen people, and at the same time the personification of those rejected in the New Covenant. Yet by their very existence, the Jew as one of the chosen people divested the Christian faith of its semblance of self-explanatory integrity.[18] This ambivalence of being both blessed and rejected lived on in the antagonistic fantasy of the Jewish plutocrat and the Jewish Bolshevik, as well as the backward-looking Orthodox Jew and the corrosive modernizer, which now related to the ills of bourgeois-capitalist society.

3. In contrast with the absolute negative image of the diametrically opposed Jewish arch-enemy, vying with the Aryan race for world domination – an image of the enemy that merged plutocracy and Bolshevism – the National Socialist stereotype of the Gypsy contained variants whose differences had considerable consequences for National Socialist persecution of the Gypsies in German-occupied Eastern and Southeastern Europe, and within the Empire. External to the Empire, especially in Eastern Europe, the anti-Gypsy fantasy was directed primarily against nomadic Gypsies whose constant wandering only served to mask their imputed espionage for the Jewish-Bolshevik world enemy. Inside the German Empire, the part-Gypsies were deemed the primary threat. As partially or fully sedentary Gypsies, they maintained close contact with non-Gypsies, and in this way had presumably

penetrated the body of the German people. In contrast, the regime viewed the nomadic indigenous Sinti as 'ethnically genuine' or 'racially pure', as Himmler and the SS office Ancestral Heritage (*"Ahnenerbe"*) termed them in a racist twist on the traditional Gypsy romanticism. Finally, since they stemmed from India, it declared them to be Aryan. By contrast, the National Socialists categorically denied the Jews any Aryan-ness whatsoever.

4. A fixation on the negative image of Gypsies of mixed race was characteristic of the policies in the countries where the Germans themselves were in power. This was connected with the special role played by the concept of 'race hygiene', and the associated Race Hygiene Research Centre, in the National Socialist persecution of the Gypsies. This 'race hygiene' existed alongside traditional anthropology, which classified alien races as inferior, as a second variant of a racism grounded on the concept of genetic make-up. According to its principles, certain groups within a race or people were to be excluded as biologically inferior. Within National Socialism, that encompassed groups that did not appear to satisfy the norms of the German community, such as homosexuals and those stigmatized as asocial elements.

Persons classified as part-Gypsy bore a dual stigma, caught in the intersection of these two variants of racism. They were branded both as persons of alien race and asocial. In this way, the double Gypsy cliché, which viewed them as disturbing aliens and work-shy parasites, was linked to the ideological grid of socio-biological racism. The aim of racial purity was projected not only onto the German national community but also onto ethnically pure Gypsies. The latter, likewise, should be protected from any admixture of blood. In this manner, at least the race hygiene specialists may have legitimated their actions by advancing the fiction, which they believed was supported by scientific evidence, that they were even doing genuine Gypsies a service by a process of culling aimed at enhancing purity and a higher level of racial quality.

The instruments mobilized in the National Socialist persecution of the Gypsies were in harmony with the link-up between racial anthropology and race hygiene. In part, they were identical with the means used in the murder of the Jews: deportation to the east, concentration in ghettos, mass shootings and suffocation by gas. Other measures, such as the prohibition on marriage, forced sterilization and abortion, were lifted from the arsenal of race hygiene.

5. Inside the National Socialist police bureaucracy, the Gestapo was

responsible for the persecution of the Jews. By contrast, the Criminal Police, in the institutional tradition of the Empire and the Weimar Republic, had responsibility for the fight against the Gypsy plague, as the totally pejorative customary formulation expressed it. In keeping with this division of labour, the section dealing with Jews in Office IV (Gestapo) was based in the National Security Headquarters (RSHA), while the National Centre for the Fight against the Gypsy Menace[19] – a name in which the stigmatizing of those persecuted was expressly included – was under the umbrella of Office V, the National Criminal Investigation Department, headed by an SS Brigadier General, Arthur Nebe, and operated there within the Crime Prevention section.[20] Placing persecution of the Jews under the control of the Gestapo reflected the National Socialist fantasy of an extreme threat posed by world Jewry, while the danger presumably emanating from the Gypsies was considered less menacing. As a consequence, even under National Socialism, the oppression and persecution of the Gypsies remained where it had been placed toward the end of the nineteenth century as a result of increasing centralization, professionalism and specialization of the German police: – namely in the hands of the Criminal Police.[21]

6. Unlike in German-occupied Eastern Europe,[22] the persecutors of the Jews in Greater Germany itself insisted on precise definitions, which did not exist in reference to persons stigmatized as Gypsies and part-Gypsies. At the heart of the persecution of the Jews was a strict definition of who was a Jew as spelled out by the Nuremberg Laws and the subsequent decrees. This definition called for exceptions only in respect to "persons of mixed race of the first degree and those living in a so-called privileged mixed marriage." The latter and those of mixed race, who did not belong to the Jewish religious community and who did not maintain any other relations to Jews or persons of Jewish stock, were exempted from the measures of the radical persecution of the Jews. That was instituted as a precaution in order to keep possible friction with and protest from the German population to a minimum. However, in practice, the Gestapo often sought to get around these regulations when carrying out the deportations.[23]

By contrast, the focus on Gypsy persecution in Germany was on the part-Gypsy, estimated by the race hygiene experts to constitute more than 90 percent of the Gypsy population in the state.[24] There was no legally precise formulation of this concept. Genealogy in a comparatively vague form was used alongside criteria of social adaptation. That gave rise to complications, since the priority given to each of these two criteria was open to controversy. In addition, the concept of part-Gypsy (*Zigeunermischling*) had to be demarcated from two sides: in regard to the racially pure Gypsies on the one hand, and members of non-Gypsy families with a small amount of Gypsy blood on the other. The definitions of Gypsy and Gypsy of mixed race were imprecise, a factor compounded by the dispute between various institutions, associated at times with controversial reductions in the scope of the groups of persons persecuted. Another difficulty involved how to classify properly the individuals in the various categories.

7. That particular problem made it possible for local persecutors to interpret central instructions on their own, in a manner differing from the common practice in Jewish persecution. That became especially important in 1943-4 in the selection of persons deported to Auschwitz-Birkenau as part-Gypsies. The Special Express Letter, headed Internment of Gypsies of Mixed Race, Rom-Gypsies and Balkan Gypsies in a Concentration Camp, sent out by the National Criminal Investigation Department at the end of January 1943 to implement Himmler's deportation order of 16 December 1942 excluded "racially pure" Sinti and Lalleri and "good part-Gypsies in a Gypsy sense" from deportation to Auschwitz-Birkenau. This regulation was also valid for several categories of Gypsies of mixed race, for whom forced sterilization was considered as an alternative to deportation. Among them were persons (along with their wives and children) regarded as essential personnel in the armaments industry; persons who on the orders of the Investigation Department were exempted from the regulations on Gypsies;[25] foreign nationals; persons married to individuals of German blood; men serving in the military, war-disabled ex-servicemen and those discharged from the army with a special commendation; finally, those who had adapted socially and who, before the war, had regular work, and could now boast of a permanent domicile. Of those who pursued an itinerant trade, individuals who sold "products that could be shown to be of their own manufacture" would not be deported.[26]

The local branch of the Criminal Investigation Department was assigned the task of identifying these "socially adapted Gypsies of mixed race" who were to be excluded from deportation. In making a decision, it could consult the district leadership of the National Socialist Party, the National Socialist People's Welfare, the Office for Racial Policy of the Nazi party, employers and the compulsory health insurance offices, garnering their advice. The latitude of the Criminal Police for taking action on its own was expanded by Sec. IV.8. in the Express Letter of January 1943. That section empowered them, in the case of Gypsy individuals where no documented opinions from the Race Hygiene Research Centre were available, and who, thus, could not be classified as Gypsies of mixed race, to determine by themselves whether these Gypsies should be sent to Auschwitz. At least inside Germany itself, the Criminal Investigation Department and municipal authorities often employed this ample discretionary latitude to render a town completely or substantially free of Gypsies.[27]

8. As a whole, however, the Jews were persecuted in a far more radical way than the Gypsies, who fortunately were not threatened with possible murder in all the states occupied by or allied with Nazi Germany. In the case of the German state in the borders of 1937,[28] Austria,[29] the Protectorate of Bohemia and Moravia,[30] as well as Estonia,[31] it is difficult to determine which persecution took on more extreme dimensions there – that of the Jews or the Gypsies. This determination depends on what years are chosen as the basis for calculating the proportion of those murdered. However, in the Western European countries of France, Belgium and the Netherlands, there is no doubt that the German police and occupation authorities carried out the deportation of the Jews in a far more systematic manner, devoting substantially more time to the endeavour, than in the case of the arrest and deportation of those classified as Gypsies.[32] In the parts of Italy under German occupation, there were only isolated instances of the deportation of Gypsies (*Zingari*) from the autumn of 1943 on. Moreover, the destination of these deportations remains unclear, whereas the SS and police were more single-minded: they tried at the very least to systematically deport all Italian Jewry.[33] In the case of Hungary, the deportation of Roma to German camps such as Buchenwald and Ravensbrück cannot be equated, despite all its inherent horror, with the systematic mass deportation of the Hungarian Jews to Auschwitz-Birkenau.[34] The same is true for Lithuania, Latvia, Slovakia, Poland, Serbia and the German-occupied areas of the Soviet Union. In the case of Denmark, Norway, Greece and Bulgaria,[35] according to the present state of research, there were no deportations or mass shootings of Gypsies. By contrast, the lives of European Jews were under dire threat across the continent, from Northern Norway to Rhodes, and from France to the German-occupied territories of the Soviet Union. Solely in Denmark and in Bulgaria itself, due to local resistance, were

there no deportations to the extermination camps or other murder operations.[36]

Data remains uncertain for the Roma victims in the satellite states of Croatia and Romania. For the Croatian camp Jasenovac, estimates of the number of Roma murdered differ considerably; a minimum of 25,000 Roma victims is assumed for the country as a whole. In the case of Romania, recent studies have shown that of the approximately 25,000 Roma transported in 1942 to Transnistria, between 12,500 and 19,000 died as a result of starvation, extreme cold, the total absence of medical care and the generally appalling living conditions that prevailed.[37]

The difference in the degree of threat to life and limb of Jews and Roma was attributable to two main factors: the ideological dominance of anti-Semitism and the way in which the image of the Jewish enemy was translated into reality in the German conduct of the war and German occupation policy. In German-occupied Eastern Europe, the murder of Jews was increasingly accepted as something natural, a tried and tested means to alleviate bottlenecks in the supply of essential necessities, epidemics and a lack of accommodation. Compared with the Jews, who were concentrated in large numbers in the area in south-west Russia where Jews were allowed to live, numerically the Eastern European Roma constituted a small group. For that reason, in a policy of murder driven by racist and utilitarian motives, they had far less importance than the Jewish population, or even the Soviet POWs.

Conclusions

I would like to conclude by supplementing the historical account by two considerations oriented more to the present day. It does not follow from the differences between the murder of the Jews and the Gypsies that Roma and Sinti always and everywhere comprised the less endangered group. Investigating the crimes of the Third Reich should not be utilized for generating schematic analogies because inquiry into history would then run the risk of becoming an instrument for rejecting an independent analysis of the present. In addition, it is neither necessary nor meaningful to seek to equate the fate suffered by the persecuted Gypsies under National Socialist rule with the mass murder of the Jews in every facet and respect. On the contrary: such a problematic equating could even serve over time to delegitimize the necessary memory of the murdered Roma and Sinti. In addition, and above all else, the terrible suffering of these persecuted individuals needs to be remembered – even when the Jews, as another stigmatized group, were subjected to far more extreme and extensive persecution. After all, where would we be if we wish to remember and condemn only those crimes against humanity that in their enormity rival the dimension of the Shoah?

12

גלין, גלין, אַצינד די קאַסטאַניעטן פֿלינק אַהער,
איינס ביי איינס, זיי אויסגעזוכט אויסגעקליבן,
פֿון אונזער געביין, אינם אַש איבערגעבליבן — —
אַז וואָס האָט דען נאָך געקענט איבערבלייבן מער ?

אויף אַ קיזל־שטיין געטריפֿט אַ טרער נאָך אַ טרער,
ווי גלאַנציק־גלאַט געשלייפֿט, קונציק אויסגעריבן ,
מער ווי אין טויזנטער פֿאַרמעטן פֿאַרשריבן,
קנאַלענדיק דעם עכאָ פֿון אונזער שבט כ׳הער — —

דאָס אויירינגל פֿון צאָגאָ טאָטאָ אין אויער !
פֿון אַזאַ גרימיק פֿלאַם־צעפֿלאַטערטן טרויער,
פֿון זיבן פֿורפֿיר־שלייערס אַרומגעקומען — —
דאָס שיכעלע איינציגס געבליבן פֿון מיין קינד !
גלין־גלין ! טיזבי די ווינד־מכשיפֿה כ׳בין אַצינד :
וואָס געוועזן, וואָס איז און וואָס ערשט גייט קומען -

Poem from the sonnet cycle 'Gypsies'

Click-clack, quick, search out the castenets
One by one they are found and salvaged
Among our bones. They have survived among the ashes.
What else could have survived?

Onto a pebble tear upon tear is falling,
Making it gleaming-smooth, artfully polished:
Inscribed on it in many thousand forms
I hear, resounding, the echo of our tribe.

A. Stencl (translated from the Yiddish by Heather Valencia)
From a series of sonnets published in the journal *Loshn un Lebn*,
London, June/July 1962

CHAPTER NINE

Criminal justice following the genocide of the Sinti and Roma

Peter Sandner
Translated from the German by Bill Templer

Introduction

In January 1991, the Siegen District Court (North Rhine-Westphalia) sentenced the former SS guard in the Gypsy Camp at Auschwitz-Birkenau, Ernst-August König, to life imprisonment. Although this judgment never became final, due to the subsequent suicide of the accused, in the German public's eyes the verdict was considered the very first sentencing of one of the perpetrators of National Socialist crimes against the Sinti and Roma. Even the respected newspaper *Frankfurter Allgemeine Zeitung* spoke of the "one and only German court trial to date dealing with the National Socialist genocide of the Sinti and Roma."[1]

It was all too easy for this mistaken impression to arise, since the efforts in German criminal justice to grapple with the genocide of the Sinti and Roma were far more hesitant and ridden with gaps than the pursuit of other crimes by the National Socialists. In reality, the König case was neither the first court proceeding nor the first conviction in this matter. Rather, it represents to date the last in a series of several judgments handed down on Nazi persecution of the Sinti and Roma.

The verdict in Siegen was a return to the arena where confrontation in the justice system with this dimension of the Nazi past had begun: the District Court in Siegen not only handed down what is still the last German verdict in such cases, but in 1949 it had also been responsible for what was probably the first sentence by a German court in such cases. Then, several months before the establishment of the Federal Republic of Germany, the court had heard a case brought against several defendants from the local administration and the Criminal Investigation Department of the Dortmund police, and gave sentences of up to 18 months in prison for organizing the deportation to Auschwitz of March 1943.[2]

The two court proceedings in Siegen are characteristic for the first and last of five identifiable phases in West German[3] prosecution of Nazi crimes. These phases are applicable not only to the efforts to deal in the courts with the crimes against Sinti and Roma, but also for the punishment of National Socialist murders more generally.

The five phases of justice

1. The years immediately after the liberation of Germany down to the establishment of the two German states in 1949 were marked by a sense of new hope: while still under the supervision of the Allied occupation agencies, German courts began to dedicate themselves to investigating and prosecuting Nazi crimes. There were comparatively stiff sentences handed down against the perpetrators. One example is the two trials on 'euthanasia' crimes.[4]

2. The following period, the early and mid-1950s, was marked by an aura of greater silence and suppression than other phases. The Federal Republic devoted itself more to reconstruction and orientation to the present and future than to coming to terms with the past. The committed legal expert Fritz Bauer (1903–68), himself a victim of Nazi persecution, complained about the standstill, which he attributed to the prevailing attitude of the federal government in Bonn. Down to the mid-1950s, state prosecutors and courts believed they could conclude, from statements by the federal German vice-chancellor, "that in the view of the legislative branch (Parliament) and the Executive (government), the process of coming to terms with the past in the sphere of criminal justice had been concluded."[5]

3. The creation in Ludwigsburg, at the end of 1958, of the Central Office of the Judicial Administrations of the States (Länder) for Investigation of Nazi Crimes marked a turning point. The years down to 1970 were characterized by a more intensive effort toward adequate prosecution of Nazi perpetrators. This new line was closely associated with the tenure of Fritz Bauer as Attorney General of the state of Hesse in Frankfurt am Main (1956–68). The major Auschwitz trial in Frankfurt (1963–5), and a number of suits against defendants accused of involvement in crimes in other concentration camps, in 'euthanasia' murder institutions or in the framework of SS Task Forces (Einsatzgruppen), were brought to court in this period.[6] Increasingly, the National Socialist past also became a focal point for the crystallization of

social debates and changes that ultimately came to explosive expression in the extra-parliamentary opposition and the student movement of the late 1960s.

4. In the 1970s, there was a marked decline in the prosecution of Nazi crimes under the chancellorship of Willy Brandt (1969–74), who had emigrated from National Socialist Germany. The more public confession and recognition of German guilt determined official policy, the more the interest in the actual concrete deeds seemed to wane.

5. Only toward the end of the 1970s did the Nazi crimes return to the focus of social attention in West Germany. The airing of the U.S. TV series *Holocaust*, in 1979, generated strong public interest. The crimes now became an ever more frequent topic in the schools. A final phase of prosecution of the perpetrators who were still alive began in the courts. Among important factors, the emerging historical inquiry[7] and the intensified activity in civil rights and consciousness-raising of the Sinti and Roma[8] contributed to pointing out gaps in the way the justice system was dealing with crimes against this population group.

Why were so few tried?

What steps has the German justice system taken during the fifty years to punish Nazi injustice against the Sinti and Roma and prosecute the perpetrators? Where were the state prosecutors and courts successful in attempting to deal juridically with genocide, and where did they fail? The results are few and far between, since only in a small number of individual cases were those guilty actually punished for the murders of the Sinti and Roma. There were various reasons for this deficiency. In part it was due to a lack of will to see justice prevail, and at times one can sense that anti-Gypsy sentiments and bias against the victims were operative as part of the judicial equation. In part, however, it was also due to the basic inability to cope with the sheer enormity of the crime utilizing the means of justice available in a constitutional state. But objective difficulties also emerged, as for example when it was impossible to clearly demonstrate premeditated intent to murder.

The five arms of genocide

An analysis of how the National Socialist genocide of the Sinti and Roma was dealt with in the courts points to the differences evident in the juridical treatment of the various groups of perpetrators involved in these crimes. Each of the following groups had taken on specific tasks in the framework on a genocide based on a strict division of labour:

1. The personnel in the concentration and extermination camps.
2. The members of the Task Forces and the civil administration in the occupied territories.
3. The scientists engaged in race-biological examination and registration of the Roma and Sinti.
4. Those responsible for the deportation in the National Security Headquarters (RSHA).
5. Regional and local individuals in the police and civil administration who bore responsibility.

The present essay will detail for each group in what way its representatives were confronted with possible prosecution after the war.

The personnel in the concentration and extermination camps

The most readily identifiable perpetrators were those who had served as SS personnel in the concentration and extermination camps and committed murders of prisoners there. Initially, it seemed easiest to the courts in many cases to establish individual excessive acts of murder and convict the accused. Thus, in 1960 the Munich District Court I (Bavaria) sentenced the former SS Unterführer (Sergeant) Richard Bugdalle to life imprisonment. As a member of the commandant's staff of the Sachsenhausen concentration camp near Berlin, he had personally murdered several inmates. One of the victims in July 1940 had been a Sinto or Rom, who in Bugdalle's eyes was not marching in a disciplined enough manner. As the court determined, the SS guard "ordered this Gypsy to step forward, and then punched him with all the strength he could muster in the side of his abdomen, so that his ribs snapped and penetrated his lungs." The victim died within the course of a few hours in the washroom of the camp.[9] In the subsequent period as well, German courts handed down individual sentences against former concentration camp guards for individual crimes of murder in cases where Sinti and Roma also figured among the victims.[10]

Not until the major Auschwitz trial in Frankfurt am Main, and a number of parallel and follow-up trials in the 1960s, did the practice become established to prosecute not only the acts of individual perpetrators against individual victims, but also to investigate responsibility for the mass murders in the gas chambers as a whole. In such proceedings, the courts often convicted the defendants from the camps not of the charge of murder but a lesser offence: being an accessory or accomplice to murder. This approach was criticized by Fritz Bauer: "Lurking behind the popular assumption of being a mere accessory is the underlying wishful thought that in the Nazi totalitarian state, in actuality there were only very few who bore full responsibility, just Hitler and a handful of his closest associates."[11] Bauer pressed fundamentally for the notion that the institutionalized mass murder, based on a division of labour, should be viewed as a complex in which all those involved ought to be seen as accomplices, merely by dint of their complicity in the operation of the extermination camps. By contrast, many of his legal colleagues only regarded concrete and intentional premeditated individual action, which led directly to the murder of the victims, as a crime.

Another facet of criminal justice now appeared problematic: namely that the penal code described murder as a punishable crime, but that for obvious reasons genocide organized by the state was not specifically mentioned as a felony. Nonetheless, the trials now resulted in convictions. Thus, for example, the District Court in Bonn, in the trial surrounding the Chelmno (Kulmhof) extermination camp, handed down prison terms against eight defendants for being accessories to murder, including several sentences of up to thirteen years behind bars. In its judgment, the court expressly took into account the murder of some 5,000 Sinti and Roma along with the far more numerous murders of Jews in the Chelmno camp, after a former Jewish staff worker in the ghetto administration in Lodz and a former criminal inspector of the state police department in Lodz had given evidence on these murders of Sinti and Roma prisoners.[12]

The Treblinka trial in Düsseldorf in 1964–5 was the attempt to deal in juridical terms with the gassing of hundreds of thousands of Jews and a far smaller number of Sinti and Roma in the extermination camp where the so-called Operation Reinhard (1942–3) was carried out. Just as in all other such proceedings, the justice authorities concentrated on selected main perpetrators whom it had been able to apprehend, and whose responsibility was most readily demonstrable. Ultimately, eight defendants were also convicted here, some receiving life sentences, even though it was incontrovertible that far more persons had been involved in the day-to-day running of the Treblinka camp. Among those convicted was the master tailor Franz Suchomel, who later gained international publicity through his interview in 1985 in Claude Lanzmann's documentary film *Shoah*.

In a trial by jury in Düsseldorf, the court sentenced him "for being an accessory to the mass murder of at least 300,000 persons" to six years imprisonment, but acquitted him of other charges of murderous conduct. These accusations of murder also involved the shooting of Sinti and Roma in Treblinka and were described before the court as follows: "Five or six Gypsy women from the vicinity of Treblinka were brought through the entrance gate into the extermination camp... Suchomel led the Gypsy women, one holding a child in her arms... to the camp sick bay, where the Gypsies and the child were shot." The court concluded that by bringing the victims to where they were murdered, Suchomel had "significantly aided and abetted their murder." However, it "should not be forgotten that he may have been "acting here on orders from a superior", and it was probable "that he had not killed the women and child himself, but rather that they were shot by an SS man on duty in the sick bay." The uncertainties influenced the court to decide in this case in favour of the defendant. The court also considered not proven the accusation of a witness that Suchomel took some fifty Sinti and Roma in groups of two to three persons to the camp sick bay and shot them there.[13] The evaluation of the shootings points to the difficulty the court encountered to clarify beyond any doubt certain circumstances after the lapse of some twenty years on the basis of testimony by witnesses. The principle of 'in dubio pro reo' [in doubt find for the accused] resulted in a situation where, at least in a few cases, the impression of a partisan attitude on the part of the courts in favour of the Nazi perpetrators could arise.

In the major Auschwitz trial in Frankfurt am Main (1963–5), the genocide of the Sinti and Roma was also broached a number of times. Yet, unlike in the Chelmno trial, these murders ultimately had no influence on the outcome and convictions. In particular, the defendant Friedrich Wilhelm Boger, who in the meantime had been employed in a commercial office in Bavaria, was accused in the trial of having participated in the liquidation of the Gypsy Camp in Auschwitz in early August 1944, and, thus, of sharing responsibility for the murder of several thousand Sinti and Roma in the gas chambers of the extermination camp. Although Boger ultimately was sentenced to life imprisonment plus fifteen years as a result of other crimes in Auschwitz, it was not because of the murders of Sinti and Roma of which he had been accused. The court stated that "despite the considerable doubt that the accused Boger had taken part in the liquidation of the Gypsy Camp due to the fact that he belonged to the Political Department, it could not be determined beyond the shadow of a reasonable doubt that the accused had contributed causally to the killing of the Gypsies." For that reason, on this point the court ruled that Boger should be "found not guilty due to the lack of conclusive proof."[14]

A second defendant in the Frankfurt Auschwitz trial, who played a role in the murder of Sinti and Roma, was Pery Broad. The SS man was active in the camp from 1942 to 1945 and was, like Boger, a member of the Political Department, the so-called Camp Gestapo. In the Auschwitz trial he appeared as a "dazzling personality".[15] He was born in 1921 in Rio de Janeiro, had a Brazilian father, and was raised in Berlin. A witness testified in the courtroom that Broad had not been a typical SS man, and had "read books".[16] Due to his knowledge of languages, he also worked in the camp as an interpreter. He demonstrated his adept agility when, after the war, he put his knowledge of the Auschwitz camp as a perpetrator at the disposal of the British occupation authorities. Interned in a camp for POWs, he wrote a 75-page report for the British on Auschwitz. On 7 June 1964, the court in Hamburg had the report read into the record. Broad's text also contained detailed information on the Gypsy Camp in section B II e in Auschwitz-Birkenau. In his apologetic description, he gave the impression of being an objective, seemingly uninvolved historian: "They wanted to destroy the Gypsies... In July 1944, the die was cast. Himmler had ordered that all those able to work should remain in camps. The others should be gassed."[17] Broad was accused like Boger in the Auschwitz trial of having participated in the liquidation of the Gypsy Camp in 1944, but he himself denied this.[18] In the verdict handed down in the Auschwitz trial, that charge was no longer taken into account. The court found Broad guilty of being an accessory to the murder of more than 2,000 Jewish victims, largely due to his involvement in selections at the Auschwitz ramp. He was given a four-year sentence.[19] Half a year later, in February 1966, Broad was again a free man, since his time spent in detention had counted toward the penalty.[20] In the late 1960s, the state prosecutor initiated an investigation of Broad regarding the charge that he had also been involved in the genocide of the Sinti and Roma. Only after the lapse of twenty years was the investigation actually resumed. The *Frankfurter Rundschau* had the distinct impression that the sympathies of the investigative office were slanted all too one-sidedly in favour of the accused. Broad's assertions were given considerable credence, and it ultimately appeared that no one really wanted to get down to brass tacks and deal seriously with this whole matter.

The extensive efforts undertaken by the Central Council of German Sinti and Roma in the 1990s did not result in a new case being brought.

In the meantime, Broad appeared as a witness in the Siegen trial of Ernst-August König.[21] This trial in Siegen against the then seventy-year-old König mentioned at the very beginning of this paper lasted from 1987 to 1991. It clearly differed from earlier trials against suspected perpetrators. For the Siegen trial by jury, the prosecution carefully gathered evidence and interrogated 160 witnesses. Unlike earlier courts, the Siegen tribunal now recognized the statements of surviving Sinti and Roma as credible evidence. Just as a delegation of the Frankfurt court in the Auschwitz trial by jury in 1964 had travelled to Auschwitz, the Siegen court also went to look at the scene of the alleged crimes. After being in session for 177 days, the court regarded it as proven that the concentration camp guard König had himself, in 1943, tormented Sinti and Roma in the Auschwitz extermination camp, resulting in their death. Ultimately, three murders considered proven were sufficient for the court to sentence the accused to life imprisonment. Eight months after sentencing, even before an appeal hearing, Ernst-August König, held in investigative custody, hung himself in his cell.[22]

The personnel of the concentration and extermination camps were the group of perpetrators most frequently prosecuted with success, leading to a conviction. In the population, there was a large consensus that these perpetrators were indeed "really guilty" and should be held accountable. Nonetheless, even in the case of these penalties, it remains doubtful whether they were in proper relation to the gravity of the crimes committed.

The members of the Task Forces and the civil administration in the occupied territories

Large numbers of East European Roma were also murdered outside the extermination and concentration camps. Like tens of thousands of Jewish residents in the occupied territories in the East from 1941 on, they fell victim to the mass shootings of the German Task Forces (and their subsidiary units). These units had been formed from police and SS personnel under the aegis of the National Security Main Headquarters (RSHA). Their primary task, as a court in 1961 summarized it, was the "annihilation of the Jewish population in the East, as well as other population groups deemed racially inferior, along with the functionaries of the Russian Communist Party."[23]

Only in a segment of the trials was the murder of Sinti and Roma expressly raised as an issue. One such example was the 1961 Munich trial against members of Einsatzkommando 8, a sub-unit of Einsatzgruppe B. Several leading persons in the Kommando were found guilty of being accessories to mass murder. But the court acquitted the office worker Karl R. After the war, he had obtained a position in the State Statistics Office in North Rhine-Westphalia, but for two years had been held in investigative detention. The court determined that in Bobruisk, in White Russia, in September-October 1941, members of the Einsatzkommando commanded by R. had carried out two mass shootings. In one of these operations, "30 Gypsies were killed solely because of their race." The court recognized extenuating circumstances to R.'s benefit, stating that he had only carried out these killings against his will and under threat from a superior officer. In view of the reference to the race of the Sinti and Roma, a qualifying remark by the court seems surprising: it stated that it was unable to determine whether the persons shot in Bobruisk were partisans.[24] The court here voiced an argument that was often brought to bear by the defence in the Task Force trials. If the murdered Jews and Roma could be declared to have been partisans, their shooting was then viewed in legal terms as tantamount to a military measure in wartime. Under such conditions, it could not be considered murder, or acting as accessory to murder, so that conviction based on existing criminal law was ruled out.

A few years after this Munich judgment, the Essen District Court (North Rhine-Westphalia) arrived at clear verdicts in two trials against members of Sonderkommando 7a. The former leader of the Kommando, Albert Rapp, was sentenced to life imprisonment, while other members were given shorter sentences behind bars. It is worth noting that, in 1965, Rapp was found guilty not only of being an accessory, but directly of the felony of premeditated murder. The prosecution had accused him, between February and April 1942, in the district of Klincy in White Russia, of ferreting out, apprehending and murdering thousands of persons – "of his own volition, in order to appear as an especially energetic SS leader ready to take action, and to gain new possibilities for personal advancement and distinction, without any consideration of the cost in human lives."

There were also thirty Roma among those for whom there was solid evidence they had been murdered. That knowledge was of especial importance for the argument of the court. It refuted the defendant's claim that the persons shot were Jews, concentrated in the Klincy ghetto. Turning the argument on its head, in the eyes of the court, Rapp's special initiative was proven by the fact "that the victims were rounded up for execution in Klincy on the orders of the defendant."[25]

In 1966, the following year, the same court convicted two other participants in this shooting of being an accessory to the crime, and sentenced them to three and four years in prison. Only one of these sentences came into force, since the other man convicted died before he could be imprisoned. This second trial also involved the sales representative Kurt Matschke, commander of the successor unit of Sonderkommando 7a in Klincy in 1942. When the unit met up by chance with a group of ten to fifteen Roma, Matschke,

> [...] without a moment's hesitation, ordered the shooting of all the Gypsies, including the women and children. In so doing, he was guided by the general order for all Security Service (SD) units, which he was familiar with, to kill all Gypsies in Russia they encountered, without concern for age and sex... The shooting took place at an execution pit on the southern edge of Klincy near a wooded area not far from the stadium. The Gypsies were brought near the pit and then shot one after the next at its edge by a bullet... to the nape of the neck. The victims murdered later could witness what happened with the companions in suffering who preceded them.

The defendant testified in his own defence that he had had the Roma shot as "scouts for the partisans", not for racial reasons. In this case, the court viewed this as a claim to protect himself. It found Matschke guilty of being an accessory to murder and sentenced him to five years behind bars on the basis of this and a second shooting.[26]

The former commander of Einsatzkommando 9, Wilhelm Wiebens, was sentenced in 1966, by the Berlin District Court, to life imprisonment for mass murder. The basis for this judgment were two cases: the premeditated murder of twenty Roma and two Jews. In the first case, Wiebens had received a report around the end of March or early April 1942 that in the vicinity of Vitebsk in White Russia there were a "number of alien elements roving about." Wiebens immediately put together an execution unit and, as the court determined, took the initiative: "Although it was left to his discretion what should be done with these twenty Gypsies – in a conscious and intended act of cooperation with Himmler and Heydrich, according to whose order the racially inferior Gypsies should also be liquidated – he ordered the shooting of these Gypsies, who numbered at least twenty, solely for this reason alone." Based on his initiative, the court considered Wiebens a murderer in his own right, and not simply an accomplice to murder ordered by the regime's elite. Wiebens had rejected the request of an elderly woman to let her go free, remarking: "it's better to kill one more innocent person than to let a guilty one go free." Moreover, the defendant explained, there was another reason why she could not be allowed to go free: in that case, the old woman would be able to report to the other Gypsies about the shooting she had observed.

There were a number of convictions where murders of Roma were mentioned along with members of other groups of victims. The killing of at least 3,000 Jews, Communists, Roma and "mentally ill" persons in Latvia was the object of a trial in 1971 in Hanover (Lower Saxony). Accused were members of Einsatzkommando 2 as well as men from the local German police administration in Libau (Liepaja). In six cases, sentences were handed down with penalties ranging from 18 months to seven years, and were later implemented.[27]

Just as in this trial, two years earlier the Mainz District Court (Rhineland-Palatinate) had heard a case dealing with the alleged crimes of a member of the German civil administration in the occupied territories. Leopold Windisch was sentenced to life imprisonment for his role in the civil administration of the area of Lida (in eastern Poland). In addition to several mass shootings, he was also accused of having been instrumental in connection with the arrest and execution of a group of eighty-six Sinti and Roma.[28]

At the time, the members of the German administration in the occupied territories were also helped by a broadly interpreted principle "in case of doubt, find for the defendant". That was true for example in the case of the former police officer Joseph Viellieber, stationed in 1942 in Gorlice in southern Poland. In a trial before the Karlsruhe District Court (Baden-Württemberg) in 1964, the state prosecutor accused Viellieber inter alia of having led away a Rom in Struce near Gorlice with the words: "This Gypsy's ass is mine." He took him behind some bushes and shot him on the spot. A witness who had observed the incident confirmed both the statement by Viellieber and the subsequent shot. But since the witness had only *heard* the shot and had not been able to see who fired it, the court ruled that this statement had no evidential value. Only on the basis of other acts was the policeman sentenced to forty-two months in prison.[29]

The swift acquittal of Michael Scheftner by the Kassel District Court (Hesse) in 1991 infuriated the Central Council of German Sinti and Roma. The 73-year-old retired police officer was accused of having arrested a group of thirty Roma in May 1942 as a member of the district police, in Sivashi in the Ukraine, supposedly in order to evacuate them. In fact, however, he arranged the transport of these prisoners to a place of execution, where the victims were then shot by men of Einsatzkommando 10a. Scheftner denied the charges, and was quoted in a report on the trial in the *Wiesbadener Tagblatt*: "I was just standing there, that's all." In the trial in Kassel, the prosecution, after a short presentation of evidence, also called for acquittal. The court took the view that it was impossible to prove that the accused had been involved in a crime. In a conversation with the Berlin daily *taz*, the Central Council of German Sinti and Roma protested against the "acquittal by summary trial". The prosecution in particular had made no effort to discover any possible crimes committed by Scheftner. At the time, Romani Rose of the Central Council commented: "Such an approach in court proceedings against participants in an operation involving mass murder is ill-suited to promote trust in the legality of these procedures."[30]

In the cases here mentioned, only the commanders were convicted, while the many subordinates who carried out the orders received no punishment – possibly because they seemed to be "quite normal men."[31] Another conceivable reason was that, in their case, it did not appear possible to demonstrate a will to murder. As in other cases as well, a distinctive tendency in postwar German justice is manifest here: namely to brand individual main perpetrators symbolically as scapegoats, while at the same time sparing others involved in the crimes.

The scientists who carried out the race-biological registration of the Sinti and Roma

Not a single scientist who had taken part in the German Reich in the race-biological examination and registration of the Sinti and Roma was ever convicted and sentenced. The director of this registration scheme under the auspices of the Central Office of Public Health and the National

Security Headquarters, the head for many years of the Research Centre for Racial Hygiene, Dr Robert Ritter, had succeeded in 1947 in being appointed to a post in the Public Health Office of the Frankfurt/Main municipality as a medical officer. The following year he also arranged a job there for his closest associate from the Nazi period, Dr Eva Justin.[32]

From 1948 to 1950, the state prosecutor's office in Frankfurt conducted an investigation of Ritter but did not file charges. The preliminary proceedings were initiated after charges were preferred based on accusations by a number of Sinti and Roma. One charge against Ritter was that he had caused bodily injuries to persons during their race-biological registration. Another charge was that "on the basis of the findings of his investigation and by other measures, he had been instrumental in causing the forced sterilisation of a large number of Gypsies" and had "participated in the forced transport of many thousands of Gypsies to concentration camps during the war, and in part bore blame for their deaths." In the preliminary proceedings, sixty-two witnesses were questioned along with the accused. Ritter tried very hard to contest the credibility of the Sinti and Roma among the witnesses.

The state prosecutor's office was apparently quite receptive to Ritter's racist arguments, stating: "The fundamental question at issue here is whether and to what extent statements by Gypsies can be made the basis for a judge's convictions." At the same time, Ritter's own assertions regarding his role were accepted. He was "quite credible in arguing that he... had had nothing to do with these measures of forced sterilisation and deportation to the concentration camps." They even accepted his false statement that he had known nothing about the Auschwitz deportations until after the end of the war. Ritter only admitted that in the course of his race-biological examinations, he had "on some six occasions" struck the persons being examined. But it was impossible, due to the statute of limitations and amnesty, to enter a charge of bodily harm. The state prosecutor's office even condoned the fact that Ritter continued to endorse the sterilisation of Sinti and Roma several years after the war: in their view, this could not be seen either as "identification with Nazi race ideology" or as a "proclamation of violence" or its incitement. For that reason, the state prosecutor's office finally abandoned the investigation in August 1950, six months before Ritter's death.[33]

Only toward the end of the 1950s, when interest in the Nazi crimes had grown, were new investigations initiated into the race-biological registration scheme. The state prosecutor's office turned its attention first in 1958–9 to Ritter's former assistant Eva Justin, who was still employed in the social services of the Frankfurt municipality, as an educational counsellor. In a departure from the way the investigation had been conducted against Ritter a decade before, the prosecutor's office went public, characterizing its new work as a pilot procedure. The chief state prosecutor announced the ambitious aim of trying to "gain a clear picture of the National Socialist measures of annihilation against Gypsies", and he placed the investigation in a series together with the Auschwitz trial which was then coming up.[34] The investigation into Justin was gradually extended to other persons, including thirteen former staff members of the Research Centre for Racial Hygiene. On the one hand, the Frankfurt prosecutor's office was seriously engaged in trying to shed light on the accusations: hundreds of National Socialist registration files for Sinti and Roma were studied and numerous witnesses interrogated. In the course of this inquiry, the prosecutor's office reached a level of knowledge concerning the genocide of the Sinti and Roma that remained exemplary and unsurpassed by historical research in the following decade. On the other hand, a number of assessments continued to be marred by various deficiencies. Thus, National Socialist coercive measures against Sinti and Roma were classified as "preventive measures" on the part of the criminal police, and various descriptions of the accused that played down their actions were accepted without criticism.

In any event, they were now able to prove that the "Auschwitz Express Letter" sent by the National Security Headquarters in January 1943, which led to the deportation of more than 20,000 German Sinti and Roma to the extermination camp, had been known to personnel in the Research Centre for Racial Hygiene. It turned out that the mass death of the deportees in Auschwitz had not remained a secret. However, the state prosecutor's office decided on this basis that all measures for profiling and registration *before* January 1943 were inadmissible as evidence in the framework of the investigation of the crimes committed. When it became possible to prove that Eva Justin had issued a "race-biological certificate" for a Sinto after January 1943, this did not lead to a charge because the man had not been deported to Auschwitz. In December 1960, the state prosecutor's office finally halted the investigative proceedings against Eva Justin.[35] She continued to work for the Frankfurt municipality until shortly before her death. For a time, the municipality even assigned her the task of gathering social data on Sinti and Roma at a Frankfurt caravan site. But, public attention in Germany had now been aroused and sharpened to the point that her work at the municipality was permanently in the crossfire of journalistic criticism.[36]

The other staff members of the Research Centre for Racial Hygiene were also spared conviction and were able to build their careers in postwar Germany unhindered. Dr Gerhart Stein practiced as a doctor in Wiesbaden, where he died in 1979.[37] Dr Sophie Erhardt was professor of anthropology at Tübingen University. Dr Adolf Würth was employed at the State Statistics Office of Baden-Württemberg in Stuttgart.[38] Renewed investigative proceedings against Würth and Erhardt were halted by the Stuttgart prosecutor's office in 1982: they argued that especially since the accused had left the staff of Ritter's centre in 1940 and 1942, they could not be held responsible for the later Auschwitz deportations and murders on the basis of their race-biological examinations.[39] More than in the case of any other category of persons involved, scientists were able to claim that their actions had served a non-political purpose of research, and that the *consequences* of their work in connection with measures of registration, namely the genocide, was something they had neither desired nor anticipated. In no single case was the legal system successfully able to refute this assertion in a way that would have sufficed for a conviction.

Those responsible for the deportations in the National Security Headquarters

In the course of the investigation against Eva Justin, the Frankfurt state prosecutor's team had also dealt with actions by various police officials and SS members who had been on the staff of the Central Criminal Police Office (RKPA) in the National Security Headquarters and who might be potentially considered as persons responsible for ordering and implementing the deportations to Auschwitz. At issue was involvement in the "Auschwitz Express Letter" of January 1943 and later deportations to the camp ordered directly by the RKPA. After closing the files on Justin, the Frankfurt state prosecutor's office passed them on to colleagues in Cologne. There, in 1964, a major trial was opened against Dr Hans Maly. In addition, they were also taking steps against other police officials. In 1943, Maly had been active as a police official in the National Security Headquarters and later advanced to chief of the Criminal Police in Bonn. The charge against him of sending Sinti and Roma to the concentration camp in 1943 (deprivation of freedom leading to death) did not result in a conviction in the 1960s. Due to the defendant not being able to participate, for reasons of health, the Maly trial was suspended; he died a year later.

In its investigations into various top-ranking police officials, the Cologne state prosecutor's team also ran up against difficulties because the accused, by dint of their important positions, had significant evidence at their disposal. That circumstance hindered for example the investigation against the Munich official Supp. Thus, the state prosecutor's team conducting the Supp investigation in Cologne thought it was problematic "that the accused, the former detective inspector Karl Wilhelm Supp, formerly employed in the Reich Criminal Investigation Department Berlin, Central Office for Gypsy Affairs, is now head of the Section for Wanted Criminals, to which the Office for Itinerants and Travellers is subordinated." Research by the historians Fings and Sparing has shown that the Munich office dragged its feet or even thwarted the transfer of the requested files to the Cologne state prosecutor's office. Ultimately, the Cologne proceedings also ended without a conviction. If the defendant had not passed away in the meantime, the proceeding was halted due to the statute of limitation or insufficient suspicion of having committed a criminal act.[40]

Accountability and officials in the local and regional police and administration

In conclusion, I will briefly return to the first trial in Germany for the genocide of the Sinti and Roma mentioned at the beginning. This trial, before the Siegen District Court, was also the only one in which persons responsible from the regional and local administrations were convicted of participation in the deportations to Auschwitz in 1943. The Dortmund detective Josef Iking was on the staff of the Criminal Police, as an expert in the Section for Gypsy Affairs. In this capacity, in February 1943 he passed on the "Auschwitz Express Letter" to the local offices in Berleburg (near Siegen). The deputy mayor Karl Schneider consulted the responsible district official, District Administrator Otto Marloh, who, in co-ordination with the district chief of the National Socialist Party, Norbert Roters, approved a comprehensive deportation of the Sinti from the Wittgenstein district. At a meeting in the office of the District Administrator, those involved, including a municipal official, city inspector Hermann Fischer, put together a list of Sinti to be deported. Of the 132 then deported from Berleburg, 125 did not survive the Auschwitz camp. In 1949, the court sentenced all those mentioned to prison sentences, mainly for one year to eighteen months. But Marloh, who as a senior official had played a primary role, was given a four-year sentence. Two high-ranking officials from the criminal police in Dortmund, on the other hand, were acquitted. The conviction of the others was based on a law of the Allied Control Council. The deportation was seen as "deprivation of freedom and forced deportation", and "at the same time, persecution for racist reasons" and, thus, a "crime against humanity". The court emphasized that the judgment would have been the same even if all the deportees had survived and returned in good health after the war. Decisive for the conviction was that the defendants were unable to avoid accountability and pass responsibility on to those above them. Why in this instance? Because in the neighbouring town of Laasphe, in the same district, the mayor there had flatly refused to put the name of even one of the Sinti and Roma resident in the town on the list of deportees. For that reason, no one was deported from Laasphe. The mayor was not prosecuted by the National Socialist state for this decision.[41] The behaviour of Mayor Bald from Laasphe constituted a rare expression of solidarity with, and protection for, the persecuted Sinti and Roma in the Third Reich.

As far as is known, no other police official from a regional office of the criminal police, no mayor and no district administrator was ever convicted for having participated in the deportation of the Sinti and Roma to Auschwitz in 1943. Investigative proceedings against various officials were halted, such as a procedure in 1958 against officials of the Criminal Investigation Department in Frankfurt am Main[42] and in 1960 against members of the criminal police in Berlin.[43]

Conclusion

The way in which the criminal justice system dealt with the Nazi genocide of the Sinti and Roma remained rudimentary in (West) Germany. Most convictions involved perpetrators who had committed crimes as members of the SS in the extermination camps or in the framework of the Task Forces. Even there, the courts in numerous instances contented themselves with prosecuting the main perpetrators who had given the orders, or those who had committed excessive atrocities. By contrast, individuals who had contributed their share to the persecution of the Sinti and Roma within the borders of the German Reich – as normal officials of the police and municipal administrations, or as scientists – were, aside from a very few exceptions, able to pursue their career in postwar Germany without ever having been called to justice for their acts.

13 April 1946

One day in the Trial of one of the Major War Criminals in Nuremberg 1945-6

Defendant: Franz Kaltenbrunner

Kaltenbrunner was head of the Central Security Office (RSHA) from 1943 and responsible for the administration of the concentration camp system and the programme for the extermination of the Jews.

He was in the witness box from 11 April to 13 April. On the final morning evidence against him included the shooting by the Task Forces of 1,000 Jews and Gypsies in the occupied Soviet Union*.

Kaltenbrunner accepted all the evidence as true but denied that he had any knowledge of or responsibility for the day to day activities of his department.

Together with eleven other defendants he was sentenced by the Tribunal to death by hanging.

* See Volume 2 of this series

CHAPTER TEN

Compensation withheld: The denial of reparations to the Sinti and Roma

Wolfgang Wippermann
Translated from the German by Bill Templer

"It's just like with the Jews, the same thing. There was no difference between the Jews and the Gypsies."[1] That was the answer given by the commander of Task Force D, Otto Ohlendorf, to the question of the Nuremberg Trial prosecutors: why did his subordinates murder Gypsies too?

The notorious SS Obergruppenführer (Lt. Gen.) Erich von dem Bach-Zelewski was curt in describing the work of the Task Force B that he commanded: "The main task was the annihilation of the Jews, Gypsies and political commissars."[2]

Neglect in the immediate postwar period: A web of continuity

It was already known at that early juncture that genocide had been committed against the Sinti and Roma. Nonetheless, there were never any consultations at Nuremberg or any other international conference as to whether the Sinti and Roma were entitled like the Jews to reparations (Wiedergutmachung). Reparations for Sinti and Roma, proper compensation, were not a topic of discourse in 1945 – not for the victorious powers, and most certainly not for the defeated Germans.[3]

Nonetheless, some Sinti and Roma did call attention right after the end of the war to their ordeal.[4] A few even succeeded in being recognized as "victims of fascism".[5] Yet that came about largely through the assistance and pressure of the victims' organizations. Of these, the Association for the Victims of Persecution by the Nazi Regime (Vereinigung für die Verfolgten des Naziregimes, VVN) soon acquired the reputation of being a communist front organization. After the outbreak of the Cold War, that was scarcely a good recommendation, especially in West Germany, for any group. So, it transpired that the Sinti and Roma, who had, along with the Jews, been prime victims of the National Socialist race war, now had to suffer from the consequences of the Cold War.

In any event, the functionaries of the VVN, most of them communists, showed very little interest in helping the Sinti and Roma to gain their proper rights. But that was not the only reason why many Sinti and Roma once again soon lost the status of being seen as bona fide victims of persecution. Another factor was the remarkable circumstance that their persecutors in the ranks of the Gypsy police offices – personnel who were not punished for their crimes but rather kept on in their jobs, most of them at their old desks – left few stones unturned in their efforts to prevent the Sinti and Roma from obtaining compensation for injustices suffered, and to perpetuate the persecution.[6]

The officials of these former Gypsy police offices, which after 1945 were renamed "Vagrancy police offices" (Landfahrerpolizeistellen), intensified the contacts among themselves, which in any case were largely still intact. In this network, they exchanged information about the Sinti and Roma, unashamedly making use of the card catalogues and data that had been assembled before and during the Nazi period, and which had served for the registration, race-biological evaluation and deportation of the German Sinti and Roma. This also holds true, as has been clearly proved,[7] for the race certificates issued by the Research Centre for Racial Hygiene and Hereditary Biology in the National Office of Public Health. Under the direction of Robert Ritter, it was built up into the central institution for the registration, race-biological classification and ultimate deportation of the German Sinti and Roma.[8]

This web of co-operation among the perpetrators, which also took on mafia-like proportions,[9] had serious consequences for the Roma and Sinti survivors. State offices refused to issue them licences as itinerant craftsmen and sellers, arguing that the applicants were, after all, asocial Gypsies. In this they relied in their profiling on information from the Vagrancy offices. Some Sinti and Roma were even refused repatriation and restoration of their German citizenship, of which they had been stripped before deportation to the East. Here, too, the officials utilized the expert opinions of officers of the Gypsy police who were, either, still in active service or retired.[10] That fact should be regarded as more than scandalous – it was indeed a flagrant violation of the West German Basic

Law, since art. 16 sec. 1 states that a German citizen cannot be deprived of German citizenship.

Race biology and its lingering impact on defining entitlement to compensation

In the 1950s, courts rejected claims of Sinti and Roma survivors for reparations arguing that these Gypsies were "asocial individuals" bereft of any entitlement. Since the "Gypsies and Gypsies of mixed race [...] had not been persecuted and imprisoned for racist reasons, but rather because of their asocial and criminal attitude", the Baden-Württemberg interior minister issued a decree on 22 February 1950: it ordered all "applications for compensation from Gypsies and Gypsies of mixed race" to be channeled, "first of all to the State Police Records Office in Stuttgart to be checked."[11] In this way, the former perpetrators ultimately decided who had been a victim and who was eligible for compensation.

However, the legislators were also to blame for the fact that things could have gone so far. Even before the establishment of the Federal Republic in 1949, various state parliaments in the Zones of Occupation had introduced laws on compensation for National Socialist injustice. That legislation specified that only those persons were eligible for compensation who had been persecuted for reasons of political convictions, religious or philosophical beliefs or for reasons of race.[12] This formulation was taken over almost verbatim in the Federal Supplementary Indemnification Law for the Victims of National Socialist Persecution of 18 September 1953,[13] which was subsequently amended several times. However, the definition of the status of persons deemed victims of persecution remained unchanged.[14]

Although some Sinti and Roma certainly actively resisted persecution,[15] instances of persecution for political convictions were rare. Since all the Sinti and Roma living in Germany were Christians, there could be no talk of having been persecuted due to their faith or philosophy of life. So that the determination remained: they had been persecuted for "reasons of race," and race alone. It is well established that there are no human 'races', nor are there races of differing human quality. It is clear that we are all different and, of course, basically the same, a single species. Hence, any attempt to categorize human beings according to physical or mental features runs up against insurmountable difficulties.[16] This notwithstanding, Africans, Jews and other peoples,

and also the Sinti and Roma, have been regarded as an alien and inferior
race. The animosity against Sinti and Roma since the end of the
eighteenth century has been racially motivated. Along with a racist anti-
Semitism, there was, and is, a racist anti-Gypsyism.[17] The history of this
Romanophobia reached its highpoint in the racist persecution of the Sinti
and Roma by the National Socialists.

Racial stock "Pure" and "Mixed"

The German judges could easily have recognized that fact had they but
looked at the basic decree by Himmler of 8 December 1938. It stated
unambiguously that policy was aimed at "resolving the Gypsy Question,
proceeding from the basic nature of this race."[18] In this final solution of
the Gypsy Question, the "racially pure Gypsies and the Gypsies of mixed
race [Mischlinge]" were to be dealt with separately. What was meant by
this distinction between "racially pure Gypsies" and "Gypsies of mixed
race", at first glance rather strange? That could have been readily
understood by consulting the Implementation Ordinance, of 1 March
1939, to Himmler's earlier decree,[19] likewise readily available in print, as
well as the various publications of Robert Ritter.[20] On 8 December 1938,
Himmler had expressly referred to Ritter's race-biological research.

In Ritter's view, which Himmler made his own, the Sinti and Roma
were primitive Aryans, and to that extent comparable both to the Aryan
peoples and likewise to the inferior Slavic peoples. Yet in Ritter's view,
most of the Sinti and Roma living in Germany were not racially pure (his
estimate was 90 per cent), because their ancestors had mixed and mingled
with criminal and asocial elements in the German population. Since
according to the widespread thesis in criminal biology at the time, asocial
and criminal behaviour could be passed on from generation to generation,
these Gypsies of mixed race were born criminals and Gypsies at the same
time, their blood doubly tainted. They were thus doubly inferior, because
Gypsy blood was mixed in their veins with asocial blood. That was why
Gypsies of mixed race were persecuted far more severely than Jewish
Mischlinge. Even part-Gypsies, (ZM-) *i.e.* persons with supposedly only
one Gypsy great-grandparent, were in the end also deported to
Auschwitz, just like full-blooded Jews.

This differentiation between racially pure Gypsies and Gypsies of
mixed race seems grotesque, yet is quite logical in terms of the abstruse
theories of the Gypsy researchers and race politicians of the day.

However, the West German judges and commentators on the Federal Indemnification Law did not bother to look at the background to the persecution of the Sinti and Roma. Instead, they embraced uncritically the view of the National Socialist politicians and officers of the Gypsy police, which lumped together all Sinti and Roma, stigmatizing them as asocial and criminal. To designate all members of a national minority as asocial and criminal is purely prejudicial, and in this case a racist, or more precisely criminal-biological bias, underpinned by racialist criminological theory. In addition, it cannot be emphasized too strongly that it is fully incompatible with legal norms to confine people in concentration camps and to murder them, without any trial, solely because they have been abstractly classified as congenitally asocial.

Living in denial: Court rulings and qualifying dates for persecution

The Sinti and Roma were the victims of a racist injustice. However, this evident and unambiguous fact was denied by the (West) German judges and jurists. Thus, writing in 1955, Otto Küster advanced the thesis, in his commentary on the Federal Indemnification Law, that all measures against the Sinti and Roma down to 1943 had been undertaken "in conjunction with policy on crime".[21] In his view, the National Socialist agencies had restricted themselves to combatting those Gypsies who had proven themselves to be asocial. It was not until 1943 that Sinti and Roma who were personally unobjectionable had been deported to Auschwitz. Küster left unanswered how he knew this, and why the other Sinti and Roma were all seen in aggregate as asocial.

Yet Küster's thesis was adopted by the Federal High Court, which officially ruled that the persecution of the Sinti and Roma by the Nazi regime down to 1943 had not been guided by race-ideological views. Rather, it had been determined by the asocial characteristics of the Gypsies. That had been the reason for subjecting the members of this people to restrictions.[22] Even in Himmler's decree of 8 December 1938, the planned measures it referred to were viewed by the High Court as "not, by their nature, specifically geared to racial persecution, but within the scope of standard police and security measures."[23]

Yet, since other courts, led by the Appeal Court in Frankfurt am Main, reached different conclusions and final judgments, the High Court finally found itself forced on 18 December 1963 to backtrack and, at least in part, revise its ruling of 1956.[24] The judges conceded that race-political motives "may have been a contributing factor" in the measures associated with Himmler's. For that reason, Sinti and Roma were now permitted to enter claims for compensation as victims of measures of persecution that occurred after 8 December 1938.

To proclaim such a qualifying date may make sense in some spheres of civil law, such as in actions to vacate certain premises, but in the persecution of the Sinti and Roma it was total nonsense. No one would have come up with the idea, for example, to regard all the anti-Jewish measures of the Nazi regime as legal down to the pogrom of 9–10 November 1938. After all, the Nuremberg Race Laws of 15 September 1935 had been applied to the Sinti and Roma effectively from 26 November 1935 onwards, if not before.[25] Some measures of persecution had been introduced from the very beginning of the National Socialist regime. And the Sinti and Roma had in fact been discriminated against before 1933 by the Gypsy laws on the statute books in all the German states. These were in basic violation of the Weimar constitution, since they denied the Sinti and Roma equal treatment under the law.[26] Strictly speaking, the Sinti and Roma should have been entitled to compensation even for the injustice they had suffered in the Weimar Republic.

But no one has even considered that prospect. In any event, the Sinti and Roma were accorded the possibility, pursuant to a resolution of the Federal Parliament of 14 December 1979, to file for a one-time financial support of 5,000 DM maximum.[27] However, the period for filing a claim was strictly limited, and came to an end on 31 December 1982. Many of the Sinti and Roma survivors who had been denied their rights in the 1950s had, in the meantime, died. For that reason, there is a resounding ring of cynicism in the final report of the Federal Government dated 31 October 1986 on compensation and indemnification for National Social injustice and the situation of the Sinti, Roma and related groups. There it is expressly stated that the effects of the mistaken judgment of 1956 had in practical terms, been relatively minor.[28]

Present and future prospects: The struggle for justice continues

Yet the story is not over. As a result of German unification and new lawsuits threatened by former victims against the Federal Republic and individual companies, a new situation has arisen that affects not only the negotiations about compensation for former forced labourers, still not concluded, and the other victims of National Socialist racism as yet uncompensated (an aspect often overlooked). In addition, there are a number of German Sinti and Roma who, for whatever reasons, have not currently received any compensation. This category also includes almost all foreign Sinti and Roma. They were denied what was granted to the Jews in the Luxembourg Agreement of 1952 – namely that all Jews, not only German Jews, have a right to compensation. In the case of foreign Jews, the stated reason for this concession was that they did belong, after all, to the circle of German language and culture.[29] That cannot readily be applied to Roma in Eastern Europe. To date, there have been no negotiations between representatives of the Sinti and Roma people on the question of compensation. There is need for a second Luxembourg Agreement.

Another reason why that is necessary is that the Federal Republic in 1953, in the London Debt Agreement, put off compensating all other victims of National Socialist racist murder, delaying claims settlement until a time after a final peace treaty with a unified Germany. That time has come, or would appear to be at the gate: Germany is reunified, and the two-plus-four negotiations of 1990 (the four victorious powers and the two German states), which made reunification possible, are regarded by many experts on international law as the legal equivalent to the non-existent final peace treaty.[30] The Federal Government in Berlin and the German corporations also appear to see things this way, otherwise they would not be insisting so emphatically – and, as far as the victims are concerned, so cold-heartedly – on assurance of absolute legal guarantees.

This is improper: Justice must remain justice for the Sinti and Roma too. They were, and are not, simply Gypsies. They have a clear entitlement to compensation. Our task as historians is to bolster that right by presenting historically grounded arguments in which we lay out in clear and unambiguous terms – and prove through documentary evidence – that the persecution of all Sinti and Roma throughout German-occupied Europe was driven by racist motives. Historians who continue to deny this should be confronted and their views rejected.[31] They are spreading untruths and serve, even if they deny this, the aims of the negators, revisionists and deniers of the Holocaust.[32] That sounds like a harsh judgment. It is meant to be so. The denial of the Porrajmos, the racist genocide of the Sinti and Roma, should be condemned just as emphatically as the denial of the Shoah.

CHAPTER ELEVEN

History and memory: The genocide of the Romanies

Susan Tebbutt

Introduction

The boundaries between nations and cultures are fluid.[1] This concept is particularly relevant to the history of the genocide of the Romanies, the largest ethnic minority group in the whole of Europe, but the least understood and most maligned, the group least likely to be seen as a nation. As Thomas Acton argues: "Romani nationalism saw itself as combating Gypsylorist racism in much the same way as anti-colonial movements had combated European imperialism, and thus being under the same necessity of 'nation-building', or bringing together the diverse Gypsy groups of different countries into a common Romani identity based on culture."[2]

Most of Europe's states are characterised today by cultural plurality and hybridity,[3] yet the discourse of historians tended to move within the established national and political boundaries and the cultural identity of the dominant group or groups in society. This thinly disguised cultural imperialism had particular repercussions for the Romanies, who were doubly disadvantaged, first because they belong to a minority culture, and secondly because it was only in 1979 that the International Romani Union was officially recognised by the UN.[4] Even then, internal factionalisms marked the debates between Romanies from different countries, reducing their potential strength in rescuing the Gypsies from their situation in the diaspora.

The culmination of centuries of discrimination, the genocide of the Romanies whose "proportional losses to the Nazi murder programme approximated that of the Jews"[5] is mediated through different perspectives. I would like to argue that it is difficult to draw a line between the work of 'historians' in the traditional sense, who are almost all Gadje, and survivors, who depict history from their own experience, since the former rely heavily on the evidence of the latter. Any division into the perspective of the historians and the Romanies would implicitly undervalue the importance of the latter's contribution.

Conversely, when members of the Romani community become empowered and represent the history of their own fate through autobiographical accounts, in the form of prose or artwork, they often reach a wider public through the help and endeavours of Gadje. Therefore, there is not a clear-cut dichotomy between the Gadjo and the Romani perspective, but this is more helpful than the historian/survivor dichotomy.

The Gadjo perspective – from omission to inclusion

For many years after the fall of the Third Reich, it was rare to find more than a passing reference to the Gypsies, and the Holocaust was seen exclusively in terms of the genocide of the Jews.

Since 1945, as the years and decades passed it gradually became more common for the fate of Gypsies to be included in accounts of the Holocaust. Kenrick and Puxon's *The Destiny of Europe's Gypsies* (1972) was the first study to bring the genocide of Europe's Romanies to light. It has been translated into six languages, including Romani, and remained, for many years, the authoritative work in the field. At the start of the new millennium, the two most extensive studies are Michael Zimmermann's 574-page *Rassenutopie und Genozid* (1996), which goes into far more depth than American historian Guenter Lewy's 306-page *The Nazi Persecution of the Gypsies* (2000).

Zimmerman devotes the whole of his second chapter to the historiography of the National Socialist persecution of the Gypsies. He gives a detailed account of the trend from legal studies and Hermann Arnold's efforts to exonerate Robert Ritter and his Research Centre in Berlin from blame for mass annihilation, and Lukrezia Jochimsen's emphasis[6] on the Gypsies as a marginalized social group, to what Zimmermann describes as a new politicised 'awareness' at the end of 1970s and start of the 1980s.

In *Auschwitz vergast, bis heute verfolgt: Zur Situation der Roma (Zigeuner) in Deutschland und Europa* (Gassed in Auschwitz, still persecuted today...) (1979), edited by Tilman Zülch, Chairman of the Association of Threatened Nations, highlights the role of the Romani civil rights movement against a continuing background of discrimination. In the 1980s, the trend was towards increased emphasis on oral history, particularly since Romani is primarily an oral language. Yet Zimmermann urges caution, since most interviews are conducted in the language of the country in question, and not in the survivor's native Romani. There have been a number of monographs on the regional and local dimension, but, as yet, the only studies of the fate of Gypsies in concentration camps have been on Bergen-Belsen and Dachau. For studies of German-occupied Europe, the national museum in Auschwitz-Birkenau has contributed greatly to research by listing the names and details of over 22,000 Sinti and Roma forcibly taken to Auschwitz and some 20,000 who died there. Zimmermann points out the pioneering US research of Ian Hancock, himself of Romani origin, who sees the term Holocaust as a collective term for the genocide of the Jews and the Gypsies, but introduces his own term, 'Porrajmos',[7] in his article 'Responses to the Porrajmos (The Romani Holocaust)'.[8]

Having surveyed existing research, Zimmermann proceeds to give a lucid, immaculately documented, meticulously structured comprehensive account of the persecution of the Gypsies, first in Germany itself from 1933–9, then in the Greater German Reich and in Europe under German occupation from 1939–45. He devotes a whole chapter to the Gypsy camp in Auschwitz-Birkenau and the persecution of the Gypsies in the last years of the war. There are almost 200 pages of closely typed notes, bibliography, sources and indexes.

In *The Nazi Persecution of the Gypsies* (2000) Lewy uses a wide range of documentary materials gathered from German and Austrian, federal, state, local and police archives. He concludes by welcoming the erection of memorials to Romanies who were deported or murdered, but warns against what he terms the paranoia of the Central Council for German Sinti and Roma.

Any attempt to impede the exploration of all aspects of Gypsy history, in particular, is self-defeating in the long run. The examination of the role of the Criminal Police, the Kripo, in the persecution of the Gypsies, for example, should not be shunned because Gypsies worry about being stigmatised as criminals, since they were dealt with by the Kripo rather than the Gestapo. Terms employed by the Nazis such as 'asocial' and 'preventive crime fighting' cannot be ignored; they must be put into their proper context rather than declared taboo. As Michael Zimmermann has correctly stressed, failure to confront the past honestly can only perpetuate the trauma of the victims and their descendants.

Lewy's position, that the acts of murder were not part of a plan to destroy the Gypsy people as such,[9] and that the persecution of the Gypsies was not on biological grounds, is highly controversial.

Lewy explicitly rejects what he terms "the vulgar exercise of comparative victimization",[10] but it is unclear whether he is alluding here to Wolfgang Wippermann's *Wie die Zigeuner: Antisemitismus und Antiziganismus im Vergleich* (Like the Gypsies: A Comparison of Anti-Gypsyism and Anti-Semitism) (1997), the first historical study to trace the parallels with the fate of the Jews from the Middle Ages to the present day. Wippermann's third section, on the Final Solution,[11] deals with the similarities between the persecution on racial grounds, subsequent exclusion from schooling and intermarriage with Germans, and arrest and incarceration of both Jews and Gypsies. He also treats differences, such as the fact that whereas Jews were not enlisted, Gypsies had to serve in the army up until 1943, and the treatment of the two groups in terms of restitution after 1945. Unlike Lewy's study, Wippermann's powerful analysis never sinks to cheap jibes.

The European dimension is clear in the philosophy behind the Interface Collection, developed by the Gypsy Research Centre in Paris, and responsible for *Gypsies under the Swastika* (1995) and the previous two volumes in this series entitled *From 'Race Science' to the Camps* (1997) and *In the Shadow of the Swastika* (1999). The second covered measures adopted in Italy, Austria, France, Bulgaria, Romania, the Soviet Union and the Baltic States and occupied Czechoslovakia and concluded with an ambitious and, of necessity, highly selective synoptic chronology of the persecution of the Gypsies under National Socialism (1933–45) by writer Reimar Gilsenbach, in the form of two columns, the left entitled 'The suffering of the Romanies', the right 'The Violent World'.[12]

By the 1990s, it had become more common to find the Romanies included in studies of the Holocaust. One of Martin Gilbert's 26 maps in *The Holocaust: Maps and Photographs* (1994), for example, represents the fate of the Gypsies under Nazi rule.[13] Michail Krausnick, however, in *Wo sind sie hingekommen? Der unterschlagene Volkermord an den Sinti und Roma* (Where did they get to? The genocide of the Sinti and Roma they omitted to mention) (1995) draws attention in the first part of his study to the widespread failure to register the survivors' stories. It is worth noting that even historians who have written persuasively about the genocide of the Romanies elsewhere may relegate it to a subordinate role. Neither Fulbrook in *German National Identity after the Holocaust* (1999) nor Burleigh in *Ethics and extermination: Reflections on Nazi genocide* (1997) devote much space to the Romani perspective.

Without a doubt, the person who has done most to popularise the Romani Holocaust is Isabel Fonseca in *Bury me Standing: The Gypsies and their Journey* (1995), which achieved prominence not least thanks to aggressive media marketing. Despite the romanticised, journalistic travelogue-style, the penultimate chapter, 'The Devouring',[14] paints a powerful picture of the significance (or perceived lack of it) of the Romani genocide in the late twentieth century. Fonseca comments:

> The Nazi genocide against Sinti and Roma was officially acknowledged only in 1982 by [German Chancellor] Helmut Schmidt. But little has changed. The few Gypsy survivors who are able to navigate the bureaucratic obstacles may find that it isn't worth the trouble. For example, all social-security payments received by the successful claimant since 1945 are automatically deducted from any reparations, as if they were the same thing.[15]

The regional and local perspective

The 1990s saw the publication of a number of studies of individual regions or towns, bringing to light much evidence from police reports and official municipal documents as well as newspaper and eyewitness accounts. Difficulties in locating sources, which may have gone missing or been destroyed, are common to all studies, and survivors may not feel able to describe the full horror of their experiences. As survivor Bernhard Steinbach from Worms says: *What I describe is only scraping the surface.*[16]

It is important to disentangle officialese and individual experiences. In her article on entries on Romanies in reference works and encyclopaedias (1998), Anja Lobenstein-Reichmann analyses the use of generalisations, lack of differentiation and downright prejudice. This potential for manipulation of language is particularly relevant to the contrasts often made between officialese and survivors perceptions. Engbring-Romang in his study of Marburg (1998) points out that the archives mention 'voluntary' sterilisation, whereas for the survivor, faced with threats of deportation, agreement was the only choice.[17]

Local history studies of Gypsies in the Third Reich

City/Region	Author/Editor	Publication year
Berlin (Marzahn)	Benz	1996*
Cologne	Fings & Sparing	1991*
Darmstadt	Heuss	1995
Dusseldorf	Fings & Sparing	1992
Frankfurt am Main	Hase-Mihalik & Kreuzkamp	1990
Frankfurt am Main	Sandner	1998
Hamm	Brand	1994*
Karlsruhe	Krausnick	1990
Mainz/Rheinhessen	Heuss	1996
Marburg	Engbring-Romang	1998
Munich	Eiber	1993

*article

Although there are obvious similarities between all the local reports, each gives fresh insights into the diversity of experiences, whether it is Benz's account of Marzahn camp and its insanitary conditions, with two toilet blocks for up to a thousand people, and the site itself adjacent to a cemetery, a taboo site for the Romanies, Fings and Sparing's studies of Cologne (1991) and Dusseldorf (1992), or Hase-Mihalik and Kreuzkamp's work on Frankfurt (1990).

The studies are characterised by the focus on the individual, revealing the reality behind the statistics, moving away from an undifferentiated picture. Benz quotes a fourteen-year-old girl's memories of Marzahn: *We all got a Gypsy identification card, which was different to all other ID cards and passes. There was a large Z stamped on it and next to the passport photo was the fingerprint of the right index finger. Our food ration cards and household goods cards which we received later were also marked with a Z.*[18] As well as describing the liberation by the Red Army in April 1945, Benz reports on the long-drawn-out fight for restitution, and the efforts of Reimar Gilsenbach on behalf of the Berlin Gypsies.

The aftermath of the genocide is an important part of the studies. Fings brings to our attention that in Cologne where only 100, of some 500, Sinti and Roma returned, every family had some members missing.[19] Mechtild Brand points out that Romani Holocaust survivors do not automatically originally come from the region where they now reside, and that those living in Hamm were originally from the Sudetenland.

Why were the volumes produced? Eiber's volume *Ich wusste, es wird schlimm* (I knew it would get bad) (1993) was the catalogue that accompanied an exhibition mounted in Munich town hall on the occasion of the 50th anniversary of the deportation of Sinti and Roma to Auschwitz, and includes many photographs and individual accounts, with references to individuals and families anonymised out of respect. Of necessity, disproportionate weight is given to the survivors, since only they can tell their story, whether it be of their life prior to 1938, deportation, slave labour, or the concentration camp universe.

The publication of studies of Gypsies during the Nazi period may serve to strengthen the role of the official regional organisations of Sinti and Roma. In the 1990s, works were published, for example, by the Rhineland-Palatinate and Hessen organisations. These were Engbring-Romang's study of Marburg (1998) and Sandner's study (1998) of Frankfurt in which the Romani perspective is at the fore. In his study (1998) of Darmstadt (1995) and Mainz and Rheinhessen (1996) Heuss, for example, makes extensive use of accounts by survivors to argue that Goldhagen's analysis of the question of collective guilt, Hitler's willing helpers and the predisposition of the Germans to genocide, was misguided: "The mentality of the murderers was based on these images which dated back generations. In order to emphasise the cold gruesomeness of the mass crimes committed by the National Socialists, more was definitely needed than prejudices."[20]

Sandner's 364-page study of the persecution of Sinti and Roma in Frankfurt is, by far, the largest single study of one city. It deals with the early history of Romanies in Frankfurt, the communal and police initiatives taken to implement the policy of persecution, the compulsory labour camps in Dieselstraße and Kruppstraße, racial science, the systematic genocide of the Romanies and the lives of the perpetrators after 1945. Sandner appends a list of 357 Sinti and Roma (largely anonymised) who were born in Frankfurt, and/or lived in Frankfurt during the Nazi period, and/or were interned in one of the work camps, and/or were compulsorily sterilised in 1943–4 in Frankfurt and/or were deported to Auschwitz from Frankfurt. The overwhelming impression is of the extent of the devastation caused to individual families.

The Gadjo perspective – Accounts of the experience of children

Accounts of the treatments of innocent Romani children are particularly poignant. Johannes Meister's article on the deportation of Gypsy children from the St Josefspflege children's home in Mulfingen (1987) includes minutiae recorded by the Nazis such as the number of buckets of potatoes picked by various children. Karola Fings and Frank Sparing's article '"tunlichst als erziehungsunfähig hinzustellen". Zigeunerkinder und jugendliche: Aus der Fursorge in die Vernichtung' ('"as far as possible to be put down as ineducable". Gypsy children and young people: From being in care to destruction') in the periodical *Dachauer Hefte* (1993) deals in more detail with this same case, which was later made into a documentary film by Michail Krausnick.

Like the books on local history mentioned above, the volume edited by Bamberger and Ehmann on children and young people as victims of the Holocaust was published in a series by the Documentation Centre of German Sinti and Roma. It attempts to redress the balance by empowering survivors, such as Sinto Herbert Adler and part-Gypsy Else Baker from Hamburg, to tell their story. Themes such as the exclusion of Sinti children from school and exploitation at work are highlighted. W. Lehmann remembers how he and other children were used as slave labour: *I, too, was used for slave labour as a child. For example, moving stones which were needed for road building, but sometimes we had to do totally pointless work, simply taking the stones to and fro. We ate nettles and grass in order to survive.*[21]

The volume is uncompromising in its insistence on portraying the inhumanity that the children faced. An account of children being deported to the ghetto in Lodz is described in gruelling detail. When boxes containing corpses were opened, whimpering signalled the presence of a Romani child, which had a rope round its neck and later died in hospital. The massacre of Sinti and Roma including children near to the extermination camp in Treblinka is described by a survivor, describing the separation of women and children from the men and how the men were shot and the women and children then murdered in a bestial fashion. Some 180 sites were the scene of such execution of families, including the village of Szczurowa in the south of Poland, where all the Sinti and Roma were taken from their homes and shot, and their homes then burnt. The shooting of some 50 Soviet Roma from the village of Walniera in April 1942, the internment and then gassing of Romani women with their children in Sajmište concentration camp in Yugoslavia, children as victims of medical experiments, the existence of youth concentration camps in Moringen and Uckermark, the low life expectancy of children born in Auschwitz (all of the 371 children born in the camp died)[22] are just some of the atrocities outlined.

A survivor relates how children being sterilised screamed so loudly he had to hold his ears:

The worst thing was that many girls were much younger than they claimed to be. They believed that if they claimed to be older they would have a better chance of surviving. We were after all living in constant fear that the children would once again be 'selected' and sent back to Auschwitz. I knew of one child who was sterilised who was only seven years old.

Not only are the horrific extremes of barbarism highlighted. It is the contrast of the normality of everyday life and its sudden interruption that comes up repeatedly. Herbert Adler (1995) reports literally being taken out of the schoolroom to the Dieselstrabe camp in Frankfurt:

One day there was a knock on the classroom door, and two men in black leather coats came in and talked quietly to my teacher. Two Gestapo men wanted to speak to me. I thought to myself, what trouble am I in this time? I was always part of a gang. We played football, broke the odd window pane from time to time or played cops and robbers – just boyish pranks. Of course we also helped ourselves to the odd apple or pear. But my teacher said, 'Take your satchel, you'll be back here tomorrow.' He wanted to comfort me, although he knew it was a lie – but he couldn't help me.[23]

Later he was taken to the Kruppstraße camp in Frankfurt and then to Auschwitz, Sachsenhausen, Buchenwald and Ravensbrück.

Persecution at work and maltreatment in the name of medicine and science

Benno Müller-Hill's *Tödliche Wissenschaft: Die Aussonderung von Juden, Zigeunern und Geisteskranken 1933–1945* (1988) (Murderous science: Elimination by Scientific selection of Jews, Gypsies and others. 1988) presents a chronology of the misuse of science in the supposed name of the well-being of the nation. He illustrates how anthropologists and psychiatrists identified and segregated supposedly inferior Germans, which finally led to the 'Final Solution'. In interviews with professors and assistants he establishes a web of complicity.

Romani Rose and Walter Weiß edited a volume published by the

Central Council of German Sinti and Roma in Heidelberg, *Sinti und Roma im Dritten Reich: Das Programm des Vernichtung durch Arbeit*, (Sinti and Roma in the Third Reich: The Programme of Annihilation through Work) (1991). They detail the work carried out by Sinti and Roma women for the SS, in concentration camps as slave labour, building roads, digging canals, quarrying, working in agriculture, forestry, munitions firms, and other firms such as Siemens, Daimler-Benz and BMW.

In *Im Schatten von Auschwitz: Die nationalsozialistische Sterilisationpolitik gegenüber Sinti und Roma* (In the shadow of Auschwitz: The National Socialist Sterilisation Policy towards Sinti and Roma) (1995) Hansjörg Riechert looks at the background to the programme of sterilisation of the Gypsies from 1933 onwards. This programme was based on the grounds of supposed mental deficiency of the Gypsies, the compulsory sterilisation of those deported to Poland, as well as sterilisation of those in the concentration camps, and finally the question of the restitution awarded to the victims. Riechert estimates that between 1934 and 1935 ten per cent of all Sinti and Roma were compulsorily sterilised.[24]

The educational perspective

How is the genocide of the Romanies made accessible to school-children? The following three instances illustrate different approaches.

Holocaust historian Sybil Milton produced the first catalogue to deal with the representation in art of the genocide of the Romanies, *The Story of Karl Stojka: My Childhood in Birkenau* (1992) about an Austrian Romani who was deported first to Auschwitz-Birkenau, then to Buchenwald and Flossenbürg. It includes suggestions for its use as a classroom resource. Milton explains that the case study "helps students examine various aspects of the Nazi killing operations: segregation, incarceration, deportation, and murder." She points out the problems associated with studying the treatment of Gypsies by the Nazis: "Educators are all too familiar with the fact that students often reveal a wealth of negative stereotypes and misinformation about various groups, and Gypsies are no exceptions... Students need to be reminded that all groups have diversity and teachers may need to caution against portraying Gypsies as one-dimensional."[25]

In *From Prejudice to Genocide: Learning about the Holocaust* (1993), marketed for 15-16-year-old pupils studying history, Carrie Supple devotes one of the twelve chapters to the history of the Gypsies in Europe from 1400–1928 and includes a number of short documents and excerpts relating to the Gypsies. She encourages an interactive approach and invites readers to ponder on the "Forgotten Holocaust".[26]

The final example is Michael Leapman's highly accessible *Witnesses to War* (1998), which won the Times Educational Supplement Senior Information Book Award in 1999. It is a paperback aimed at schoolchildren, which contains eight true stories of persecution during the Nazi period, of which one is the story of a Gypsy who survived Auschwitz, Czech–born Barbara Richter. Leapman based this section on an interview with Richter published in the journal *Lacio Drom* (1974/5) in Rome. The fact that the account of a Gypsy is one of only eight accounts gives the report more prominence than that normally accorded to the Romani Holocaust.

The genocide in literature and film

Crossing (1971), Jan Yoors' rather exotic and somewhat melodramatic account of limited co-operation between the French resistance movement and the Romanies in fighting the Nazi regime, is written from the point of view of one fascinated by the Romanies. As he himself puts it: "like the insect fatally drawn to the flame that will devour him."[27] Yet his Gadjocentric perspective grates at times: "Whereas many aspects of the Jewish persecution and genocide are well-known, the persecution and the extermination of the Gypsies has remained mostly undocumented. This is largely due to the Gypsies' own lack of a sense of history. Even though over half a million of them were massacred, they are content to remain forgotten and unnoticed."[28]

Erich Hackl's short novel *Abschied von Sidonie* (Farewell Sidonie) (1989), based on the true story of Sidonie Adlersburg, an abandoned Gypsy baby adopted by the Breirathers, an Austrian family in the town of Steyr, has been widely acclaimed, and the film version has won awards. It combines a vivid evocation of the brutal racism of the Nazis with a sharp indictment of the contemporary Austrian government and its failure to acknowledge its complicity in the deportation of Austrian Gypsies. The Breirathers' last image of Sidonie is of her clutching her doll as she leaves in the train, yet the farewell has not been taken, and Hackl concludes the work by drawing attention to the continuity of anti-Gypsyism.

Other accounts, such as that in this volume by Katalin Katz, herself an Israeli Jew of Hungarian origin, describe the trauma of memory and the public indifference to the film *The Unburied Dead* (1996), by Director Jancso Miklos and the Gypsy journalist Agnes Daróczi, which dealt with the murder of some 20 Gypsy villagers in January 1945 in the village of Lajoskomárom.

The Romani perspective

Any analysis of representations of the genocide of the Romanies must include the Romani perspective. Yet this is no more monolithic than is the Gadjo perspective. Said challenges the cultural map of imperialism:

> No one today is purely one thing. Labels like Indian, woman, or Muslim, or American are not more than starting-points, which if followed into actual experience for only a moment are quickly left behind. Imperialism consolidated the mixture of cultures and identities on a global scale. But its worst and most paradoxical gift was to allow people to believe that they were only, mainly, exclusively, white, or Black, or Western, or Oriental. Yet just as human beings make their own history, they also make their cultures and ethnic identities.[29]

As Said points out, the label is just the starting point. Each Romani writer and artist is a Holocaust survivor and a Romani. However, first and foremost, they are an individual with multiple identities, and it is the richness of these interconnections that shines out.

Up to now I have looked at the historiography of the genocide of the Romanies from the Gadjocentric point of view. The volume *Den Rauch hatten wir täglich vor Augen: Der nationalsozialistische Völkermord an den Sinti und Roma* (1999), a 379-page catalogue to accompany the permanent exhibition in the GSR headquarters in Heidelberg, forms a bridge between two sections of this chapter. Like many of the works discussed above, it combines personal eyewitness accounts and commentary with photos and facsimiles of official documents. Those able to visit the exhibition can also see archive footage. The catalogue forms a landmark in that its editor, Romani Rose, is himself a Romani and head of the Zentralrat Deutscher Sinti und Roma (Central Council of German Sinti and Roma).

Autobiographies

Unusually, the publisher of the first substantial accounts by Romanies of their experiences during the Nazi period was Beltz, specialising in children's books. The editor of *Da wollten wir frei sein! Eine Sinti-Familie erzählt* (Then we wanted to be free! A Sinti family tells its story) (1983), Michael Krausnick, himself a successful author of children's books, recorded four generations of a German Sinti family talking about themselves and their experiences over the whole century. They range from 85-year-old Elizabeth Kreutz and those born in the 1910s and 1920s, to members of the postwar generation like Dronja Peter (born 1946), his wife Janet Maria Peter (born 1948), and Elizabeth Kreutz's granddaughter Jacqueline Lagrenne (born 1964), who have grown up with the accounts of their parents and grandparents. The volume offers insights into the confiscation of the family fairground business, typhoid, starvation, transportation to Auschwitz, and the persecution, hard labour and physical abuse suffered at the hands of the Nazis, and the aftermath with the failure of the German government to provide appropriate restitution. The volume was reprinted in the 1990s, when the upsurge of the neo-Nazi racist attacks meant that, regrettably, it had lost little of its immediacy.

From the end of the 1980s to the end of the 1990s a dozen autobiographical works appeared, written by Romanies from Germany, Austria and Slovakia, yet it is rare to find even one of them in bookshops. The majority are hardbacks. Sometimes the exact dates and place names have been added by the editor, and occasionally names have been omitted or altered to preserve the anonymity of other survivors. In almost all cases a third party, often a historian, journalist or activist, has helped with publication, and some works contain an introduction or afterword by a historian or prominent figure. All the authors express their wish that their book should contribute towards preventing such events ever being repeated.

Four works, two by Ceija and one by each of her brothers Karl and Mongo, all including a number of photographs, taken as a group give insights into the history of the members of one Austrian Romani family, the Stojkas. Ceija was the first Romani woman to write an autobiographical account.[30] In her first volume, *Wir leben im Verborgenen: Erinnerungen einer Rom-Zigeunerin* (We live hidden away: Memories of a Rom-Gypsy) (1988) written with the help of journalist

Karin Berger, Ceija (born 1933) sets her suffering in Auschwitz, Ravensbrück and Bergen-Belsen in its context, contrasting it with the freedom she knew as a young child. Even when describing the darkness and despair of the concentration camp she still finds space to comment on the beauty of nature around her and the love and affection that emanated from her mother.

Yet her account is not idealised. She is particularly critical of the women's camp in Ravensbrück, where the SS-women were worse than Satan.[31] In an interview with Karin Berger, she says about her time in concentration camps: *Every day in there was a year, every hour was an eternity*.[32] In her second volume, *Reisende auf dieser Welt: Aus dem Leben einer Rom-Zigeunerin* (Travelling in this world: From the life of a Rom-Gypsy) (1992) the emphasis is more on the postwar period and her work to promote the Romani culture, but the shadow of the Holocaust is still very much visible.

Karl Stojka (born 1931) emphasizes the importance of travelling in his life. In *Auf der ganzen Welt zu Hause: Das Leben und Wandern des Zigeuners Karl Stojka* (At home in the whole world: The life and travels of the Gypsy K.S.) (1994), he writes:

> When I look back at my life today, the war years and the time in the concentration camp were definitely the formative elements. I was only a child, but nobody should think that a child is not capable of taking in impressions and storing them up in their mind [...] in later years people often asked me; 'Aren't you angry with the Germans who did that to you?' But I always say in response; 'I'm not angry with the Germans because it wasn't this or that nation which robbed me of my childhood and my health, it was human beings who did that to me, and if there is one thing I can't understand, it's how human beings can do such a thing to other human beings'.[33]

Stojka describes his early childhood, his recollections of learning of the murder of his father in Dachau, his own memories of hard labour, hunger and disease, and his impressions of America after the war and his later return to Vienna. Yet, as he himself says, the whole of his life is inextricably linked to his experiences of the Nazi period.

For Mongo Stojka, *Papierene Kinder: Glück, Zerstörung und Neubeginn einer Roma Familie in Österreich* (Children on paper: Happiness, destruction and the fresh start of a Romani family in Austria) (2000), the closeness of his family is important, yet this is to end. In the section entitled *E Romengi Luma Pabol: Die Welt der Roma steht in*

Flammen (The world of the Romanies burns) (2000)[34] the family begins to be decimated. The style of writing is strikingly simple, yet never simplistic. The atmosphere of Birkenau after queues of people have entered the gas chamber, for example, is poignantly portrayed:

> *Die Menschenschlange geht hinein*
> The queue of people goes in,
> shortly after: Screaming.
> Silence. From the chimney smoke rises.
> A dreadful sweetish smell spreads around.
> The queue of people has been gassed and cremated.
> This gruesome drama is presented to us almost every day.[35]

There are a number of works written by German Roma and Sinti; each of the works has its own individual character. Alfred Lessing's *Mein Leben in Versteck: Wie ein deutscher Sinti den Holocaust überlebte* (My life in hiding: How a German Sinto survived the Holocaust) (1993) is a tale of escape, subterfuge and strategic actions taken to avoid the Nazis finding out that he is a Sinto. Lessing (born in 1921) even performs in a band for the German troops in Buchenwald concentration camp.

Is there a distinctive women's style? Arguably, as in Ceija Stojka's work, there is a marked lack of bitterness.[36] Philomena Franz' *Zwischen Liebe und Haß: Ein Zigeunerleben* (Between love and hatred: A Gypsy life) (1992) is in three main parts, *Meine Kindheit* (My childhood), *Mein Holocaust* (My Holocaust) and *Weiterleben nach dem Nullpunkt* (Carrying on living after the zero point). She describes her route from Dresden to Auschwitz, Ravensbrück, Oranienburg (Sachsenhausen), and then back to Auschwitz. Whilst stressing the role of religion in her life and her love of nature and celebrating festivals, Philomena Franz (born 1922) does not shrink from describing horrific details such as the way her sister is strung up on the gallows and tortured, and how she was stripped naked waiting to go into the gas chamber when she and a five or six-year-old girl are among the few spared, but later have to load the ashes onto lorries:

> *The girl was perhaps five or six years old, but small and delicate. And she was such a hard worker she got hold of the human ashes with her bare hands. She obviously didn't want to end up going to the showers and the crematorium. And we threw these human ashes onto lorries with our bare hands, and the child helped us. It all looked like gravel and it still smelled of corpses. And I felt as if I was standing in water and had to hold back the*

river. And at the same time I had the feeling that I was standing right up to my ankles in urine. It was dreadful. But we were standing there the whole night. Then we were allowed back into the women's camp.[37]

In a number of other autobiographies the diversity of the Sinti experience is underlined. Anna Mettbach (born 1926), in *Wer wird die nächste sein?: Die Leidensgeschichte einer Sintezza, die Auschwitz überlebte* (Who will be next?: The story of the suffering of a Sinti woman who survived Auschwitz) (1999), writes of her childhood and early years in and around Heidelberg, deportation to Auschwitz, then work as one of some 500 prisoners doing slave labour for Siemens in Wolkenburg in Saxony, then liberation from Dachau by the Americans. Otto Rosenberg (born 1927) recounts, in *Das Brennglas* (The Burning-Glass) (1998) (trans. *A Gypsy in Auschwitz*), his youth in Berlin, then time in Marzahn, Auschwitz, then Buchenwald, Bergen-Belsen, where he was liberated, and his return to Berlin, where he found the camp was empty and burnt out. Walter Stanoski Winter – *Winterzeit* (Winter Time) (1999) – was in the navy from January 1940 to March 1942, when he was dismissed as a non-Aryan. One unusual tale is of a football match between the main camp at Auschwitz and the Gypsies, which the Gypsies won 2-1.

Diversity may be visible in terms of language. Lolo Reinhardt (1932-1994), whose mother tongue is Romani, speaks broad Swabian (a dialect found in the south-west of Germany) and his account *Überwintern: Jugenderinnerungen eines Schwäbischen Zigeuners* (Overwintering: Childhood memories of a Swabian Gypsy) (1999) gives a flavour of the dialect.

One work, which is unlike any of the aforementioned in tone, is *A false dawn: My life as a Gypsy woman in Slovakia* (1999). The story of Ilona Lacková, who experienced Auschwitz-Birkenau, Ravensbrück and Bergen-Belsen, was taped and transcribed by Milena Hübschmannová, who translated it from the Romani into Czech. It was then translated into English by Carleton Bulkin and published by the University of Hertfordshire Press as part of their series of books on Romani themes. Even when writing about the Second World War (approximately 10 per cent of the 224 pages) and the forced labour camp, transports, and visits of the hygiene patrol who came to shave everyone so they do not spread typhus, she manages to preserve her sense of humour and her own identity as a Romani. The section on the Second World War closes on a note of optimism:

When the Russians came, old Cibrikana said: *It's the end of the war, we've survived. After every darkness comes the dawn. But after every dawn also comes the darkness. Who knows what's in store for us.*

In reply, my mother said: *After the darkness comes the dawn, and then another darkness, and then another dawn, it's all in God's hands, and we have to have hope.*

Conclusion

From the earlier omission of the Romanies from accounts of the Holocaust there has been a growing recognition on the part of historians that the fate of the Romanies is worthy of attention. From the ground-breaking work of Kenrick and Puxon in 1972 to the detailed studies by Zimmermann and Lewy at the end of the twentieth and start of the twenty-first century, evidence is finally being amassed, the focus being on the implications for individual towns or families of the victims, rather than on the anonymous facts and figures produced by the perpetrators. By investigating the persecution at work and in the name of science, researchers have also underlined the widespread abuse of the ethnic group. Studies of the fate of the children are particularly important in highlighting the innocence of the victims of the misguided racial atrocities. The Gadjo perspective also brings up the issue of the continuity of the persecution in the period after 1945.

Memories written down or painted by the survivors form an important part of the Romani heritage, and need to be taken as testimony, even though they were not created until some forty or fifty years after the events. They chart the inhumanity and the destruction caused by the Nazis.

In the accounts by the Romanies the contrast between the Nazi period and life before persecution are emphasized. They are looking back to a childhood that was stolen from them.

Szálkák a világ szemében

As a splinter in the eyes of the world
and on the margins of history
shine in black
the wide open glances of the children.

A burning, glittering message.

Their faces are still covered by mist,
but they already gather here
on the verge of their acceptance.

The conviction document is laid there cumbersome
on the twentieth century's table.

As a splinter in the eyes of the world
and on the margins of history
shine in black the wide open glances of the children.

György Rostas-Farkas in Murányi Gábor (ed.) *Egyszer karolj át egy fát!, Ciganyalmanach*, 1986, Budapest: A TIT Országos Kozpontja, Cigány Ismeretterjeszto Bizottsága (translated from the Hungarian by Katalin Katz)

Leni Riefenstahl's failure of memory: The Gypsy extras in *Tiefland*

Susan Tegel

Leni Riefenstahl, who was the Third Reich's most privileged film director, always suffered from a failure of memory regarding the Gypsy extras she used in her feature film, Tiefland *(1954). Shortly before her one-hundredth birthday she was finally forced to acknowledge their fate, though she made it seem as though she had only just learned of this. Until her death the following year she never admitted to the circumstances in which they worked.*

Introduction

Leni Riefenstahl (1902–2003) made very few films. They include four documentaries produced during the Third Reich, three of which were on the annual Nazi party rallies and were commissioned by Hitler. The fourth was on the 1936 Olympic Games, and ostensibly made by her own production company, but was secretly funded by the state.[1] Riefenstahl also made two feature films, which she not only directed and co-scripted, but also starred in. *Das blaue Licht* (The Blue Light) (1932) appeared ten months before Hitler came to power. It was at this time that she first made contact with him, possibly spurred on because of the negative response to her film by critics of Jewish origin.[2]

The second feature film was *Tiefland* (The Lowlands), which was made during the war, but was not released until 1954. In that film, Riefenstahl used more than one hundred Gypsy extras taken from two Gypsy internment camps, Salzburg Maxglan and Berlin Marzahn. The latter had been set up in 1936 to 'cleanse' Berlin prior to the Olympic games and the former was set up shortly after the outbreak of war in response to a Reinhard Heydrich decree, later rescinded, calling for the deportation of Gypsies to Poland.

Riefenstahl's privileged position

Riefenstahl was a very privileged film director. Her position was unlike that of any other Third Reich film director. She had her own company, Riefenstahl-Film GmbH, which came into existence shortly before she commenced work on *Tiefland* in January 1940 and is likely to have been funded by Hitler from his cultural fund, itself the recipient of royalties from *Mein Kampf*.[3] Moreover, she was in negotiations with Albert Speer and would have had her own gigantic studio on land donated by the state, near to her Berlin-Dahlem home, but for the outbreak of war.[4] When things went wrong with *Tiefland*, and a great deal did, she could always call on Hitler to intervene, if only indirectly because of the war. His deputy, Martin Bormann, always obliged, as when in 1942 she was in dispute with the National Economics Minister, Walther Funk, about obtaining foreign currency for filming on location outside Germany – in the Italian Tyrol and in Spain.[5] In August 1942, Bormann sent an urgent letter to the Chief of the Reich Chancellery in which he claimed that, after having presented the papers to Hitler, the Führer himself had decided that Riefenstahl should be allowed foreign currency, and emphasized the status of her company:

> As you know, Riefenstahl-Film GmbH was founded with the active support of the Führer; the costs of the *Tiefland* film which has been in production for over two years is, on the Führer's instructions, to be borne by funds administered by me... I am requesting that you urgently and most speedily transmit this Führer decision to... Funk.[6]

The Minister of Economics, who believed that foreign currency should be used for the purchase of militarily essential raw materials, was forced to comply though grumbled to Goebbels afterwards.[7] When she made another request following Stalingrad in February 1943, nine days after Goebbels Total War speech – unfortunate timing one might think – she was refused and again turned to Bormann, who again intervened:

> This situation has been presented to the Führer; this film is made with the approval and corresponding support of the Führer, and he has today emphasized that after completion the film should gross considerable foreign currency abroad. For these reasons the Führer wishes that the 240,000 pesetas be paid to Frau Riefenstahl.[8]

In late 1944 she was demanding technicians to complete her film, with the grandiose claim that it was so optically advanced that it could not be compared to any other German film.[9] She managed again, against opposition, to obtain the services of one of her cameramen, who was pulled from another production, thus jeopardising the production of one of the few colour films made during the Third Reich.[10] In April 1945, she was cabling the Propaganda Ministry to intervene and locate some of her actors for synchronisation.[11] In her postwar recollections, Riefenstahl has never alluded to her privileged position.

Tiefland became the Third Reich's third most expensive film – the first two being in colour – though it was not essential to the war effort. Goebbels, as Propaganda Minister, controlled the film industry but not Riefenstahl and was grateful not to be directly involved. In late 1942, after a visit from Riefenstahl, he recorded in his diary:

> Leni Riefenstahl has told me about her *Tiefland* film. It has become involved in a whole series of complications. A total of over five million has already been frittered away on this film, and it will still take another year before it is ready. Frau Riefenstahl has become quite ill due to work and the burden of responsibility and I urged her first to go on vacation before taking on additional work. I am glad that I have nothing to do with this unpleasant affair, and thus also carry no responsibility.[12]

Tiefland

Based on an opera by Eugen d'Albert, *Tiefland,* which was set in Spain, had its first performance in 1903 and was a Hitler favourite.[13] Riefenstahl not only directed and scripted the film but also took the lead of Martha, described in the titles as a 'beggar dancer'. She plays her as a Gypsy though in the opera the character had not been one. Living in a caravan – in the opera she had lived in a mill – she wears large gold earrings, is dressed in Gypsy costume, and dances with castanets in a pastiche flamenco. Martha is the waif-like mistress of Don Sebastian (played by Bernhard Minetti) who lives in the Lowland. In financial difficulties, he plans to marry the daughter of the wealthy mayor, while simultaneously marrying off Martha to a shepherd, though still retaining her services.

Riefenstahl had first wanted to make this film in Spain in 1934, but fell ill and was then called on to make *Triumph of the Will.*[14] Now she hoped to film on location in Spain but, in April 1940, Hitler and Goebbels withheld approval.[15] This forced her to look elsewhere for her Spanish villagers. She found them mainly in Gypsy holding camps or collection

camps (*Sammellager*): from Salzburg Maxglan for the outdoor filming –
most of them were children – and from Berlin-Marzahn for the indoor
filming at the Berlin-Babelsberg studios. Such camps were run by the
Criminal Police, rather than by the SS, and have never been classified as
concentration camps, though in the case of Salzburg the head of the
Criminal Police was also a member of the SS. For the Salzburg Maxglan
extras, we know the terms of their use because a contract was drawn up
between the Salzburg Criminal Police and Riefenstahl's company.[16] For
Berlin-Marzahn we have a less detailed list, compiled for the purposes of
proof of payment for a recently introduced surtax on income for
Gypsies.[17] By the time that list was drafted, most of the extras were in
Auschwitz.

The Maxglan extras

In August 1940 Riefenstahl or her assistants, Dr Harald Reinl and Hugo
Lehner, or all three – though this is disputed – came to Maxglan to
handpick the extras.[18] Her appearance at Maxglan, which she always
strenuously denied, is not actually mentioned in the documents.[19]
However, it is likely to have taken place, given her need for total control
and her interest in physiognomy. Those chosen were used in the autumn
of 1940 and again in the summer of 1941. They were sent to Krün, near
Mittenwald in the Bavarian Alps, supervised by two reserve police
officers, for no more than a few weeks on each occasion.

The name, sex and age of every Maxglan extra was listed, for
permission for their use had to be given, and these lists were then
circulated by the Salzburg Criminal Police.[20] On 23 September 1940 they
confirmed the names of nineteen Gypsies whom the Salzburg Labour
Office had arranged for film work. Sixteen were children; the others were
one adult male, and two adult females, one of whom was seventeen.
Sixteen of these nineteen Gypsies came from three families.[21] The
statement 'None were related to Jews' appears at the bottom of this and
subsequent lists.

On 4 October, the Riefenstahl company telephoned for an additional
four Gypsies, all female adults. On 17-18 October four Gypsies were
returned to Maxglan, including two adult females, one of whom had
arrived with the small group on 4 October, and two children who had
come with the larger group on 23 September.[22] On 19 October another
fourteen were recruited: eleven children including two babies (one nine

months old and one three months old). Of the three adults – one male and two females – the two females were the babies' mothers. On 14 November 1940 it was noted that, due to bad weather, filming in Krün had ended, with all Gypsies having been returned to camp the previous day.[23] In August 1941 filming resumed and another request for extras was made.[24] The total number of Maxglan extras has been estimated at between forty and sixty men, women and children, though the actual number according to the extant list is 51. 37 were used in autumn 1940, and 48 the following summer of who 14 were new to filming, while 3 previously used were not used again. This brings the total to 51.[25]

A contract dated 23 September 1940 was drawn up between the Labour Office (with the approval of the Criminal Police) and the Riefenstahl film company. It stipulated a number of points:

1. Only Gypsies approved by the Criminal Police could be used. This Gypsy group was to be kept isolated from others, especially from prisoners of war, and would be at the cost of the film company.
2. Food and sanitation (for what was envisioned as a ten to fourteen day period) were also to be at the cost of the film company.
3. The Criminal Police would place at the disposal of the film company, again at their cost two reserve policemen.
4. Each adult extra was to be paid seven Reichsmarks per day and the same amount for every three children. [An English pound was then worth twelve Reichsmarks or five US dollars.] Payment was higher than for the adults sent for working on regulating the River Glan as they got only one and a half Reichsmarks per day.[26] The money was not to be handed directly to the Gypsies but was to be paid direct to the Mayor of the District of Salzburg, Dr Schmidt, for the Gypsy *Gemeinschaftskasse* (communal fund).
5. The Riefenstahl Film Company was to be responsible for all transportation costs.
6. Any illness or attempt at escape was to be reported immediately to the Salzburg Criminal Police by telephone and in writing.
7. Any extension or shortening of the ten to fourteen-day filming period was to be reported immediately and with at least two days advance notice given. At least one day's notice was to be given to the Criminal Police prior to the Gypsies' return to camp, so as to ensure that the return went 'without friction'.

8. The required food cards were taken from the camp kitchen and handed to a representative of the film company against a receipt.[27]

This contract makes clear that the Maxglan Gypsies were compelled to work on the film. Though work for Gypsies was compulsory, it was not for children. The agreed wages for this, as for other work, went into a communal fund to support those unable to work. As the extras never saw this money, it is not surprising that some survivors believed that they had never been paid. Some were given clothing, shoes, and pocket-money. Work on a film was, of course, less arduous than work on the road, but many children were used – indeed a majority of these extras were children – and it is unlikely that they were given special consideration. Furthermore, it was alleged that some sequences were shot by the perfectionist Riefenstahl twenty-five to thirty times.[28] Some survivors, however, who were then child extras, later refer to "Tante Leni" suggesting an amicable relationship. They also mention rewards of chocolate.[29] Doubtless the conditions for filming during this short period were better than in the camp.[30] Filming also took place in summer and autumn. As the farmers in the district had refused to take them in, the extras – with the exception of one family, the Winters – were housed in a large barn, which was locked at night.[31] According to a Salzburg Criminal Police report, Riefenstahl, who had "personally directed the filming", was so pleased with the good work of two Gypsy families (Winter and Reinhardt), that she requested they be given exceptional support. The police suggested she pay for the purchase of clothing.[32]

Survivors' accounts

Two survivors, who were not children at the time, provide harsh accounts. Rosa Winter published her story in 1987.[33] Fearing that her family was to be deported, she had run away from the film set, was arrested and kept in a Salzburg prison, where Riefenstahl visited her. She refused to go back to the set and was sent to Ravensbrück, which she miraculously survived. Riefenstahl never challenged this story. Another story came to light in 2002. It concerns a certain Anna who wished to remain anonymous. Riefenstahl had been injured and the then twenty-year-old Anna had doubled for her in a riding scene. Wanting to reward her for doing so well, Riefenstahl granted her a wish. At a loss, the girl consulted her mother who suggested that she ask that her two brothers be released from Dachau and Buchenwald and her sisters from Ravensbrück. However, Riefenstahl replied that she could only arrange for one release. The mother decided on the one son, Matthias Krems, who had a heart condition. Approximately two weeks later he appeared in Salzburg. He never worked as an extra. Brother and sister were later deported to Auschwitz; only the latter survived.[34]

Erika Groth-Schmachtenberger's photographs

Fifty photographs, including some of Riefenstahl directing, were taken in Krün in September 1941 by Erika Schmachtenberger (later Groth-Schmachtenberger). A fine nature and ethnographic photographer during the Weimar period, she also worked as a press photographer and produced stills for the film industry – she worked for the Tobis film company between 1941 and 1944. (Riefenstahl's own company had links with another film company, Terra.) She was not employed by Riefenstahl, but apparently came across the film-set in September 1941 while out walking in the Alps. She stayed to take a number of stills, especially of the Gypsy extras in Spanish costume.[35] After the war (whether for personal, financial or political reasons) she offered the notes she had taken on the set to a magazine publisher as evidence that Riefenstahl had treated the extras harshly.[36] Riefenstahl insisted that the extras were well fed, well housed and well cared for.[37] She never alluded to the fact that the extras had been taken from a camp under guard, and that they remained under guard, which is clear from one of the photographs.[38] In March or early April 1943 Maxglan was liquidated. Most of the inmates went to Auschwitz and some to Lackenbach, another collection camp.[39]

The Marzahn extras

Eight months after filming had ended in Krün, the interior sequences were shot in the Berlin-Babelsberg studios in the spring and summer of 1942. The eminent director Georg Wilhelm Pabst, having returned to Germany in 1939, directed some of the actors, including Riefenstahl, though an ungrateful Riefenstahl claims to have had to redo some of the sequences.[40] Extras were needed mainly for the tavern sequence, when Riefenstahl performs her flamenco pastiche with castanets.[41] Recruited from Berlin-Marzahn they form the male audience who observe her dancing. Riefenstahl had to apply to the Criminal Police to obtain travel permits, since during the war Gypsies were forbidden to use public transport.[42] Filming lasted into the summer; some extras were used for as many as fifty-seven days.[43]

On 26 March 1942 the National Minister of Finance introduced a special tax *(Sozialausgleichsabgabe)* for Gypsies. Like the Jews and the Poles previously, the Gypsies were now expected to pay a fifteen per cent surtax on their income tax on the grounds that they did not pay dues to the German Labour Front.[44] A list from Riefenstahl's film company, compiled for this purpose and dated 6 April 1943, provides the names of sixty-six extras, taken the previous year from Marzahn, for whom this tax had been paid from 27 April 1942 onwards. The total amount was RM 3060.45 – that is fifteen per cent for sixty-six adult Gypsies, taken out of their earnings and indicating the number of days worked. All were paid more than double the daily rate for the Maxglan extras of seven Reichsmarks – approximately seventeen or eighteen Reichsmarks – though for the former the company also bore the costs for food and lodging.[45] Some were also paid more than others. One particular extra was paid double the rate of others who worked a similar number of days – doubtless because he had a small speaking part, which technically makes him not an extra. He is the character who brings Martha to her master.[46] No children's names appear on this list as they were not liable to the tax, but it is unlikely that children were used for the indoor shots. Gender is not indicated. Five weeks before this list was produced in March 1943 – that is six months after filming had ended – Marzahn was cleared. Almost all the inmates were sent to Auschwitz.[47]

Auschwitz

Once the extras reached Auschwitz it is not difficult to establish their fate. The detailed lists (names, dates and places of birth) of the Maxglan extras are available, thanks to the fastidiousness of the Criminal Police, and the Marzahn list, compiled for the social equalisation tax, though less detailed, is still useful. Both can be matched against the published Auschwitz death lists.[48] So far this has been done for forty-eight.[49] Not every name has been traced, but this is no reason to assume a higher survival rate for the 117 extras whose names appear on either list.

The released film

When finally released *Tiefland* was ninety-nine minutes long.[50] It included several sequences involving the Gypsy extras: two shot outdoors involve the Maxglan extras; two shot indoors involve the Marzahn extras; and two involve the Gypsy extra with a small speaking part. The Maxglan extras are mainly children, though one woman holding a baby appears in both outdoor sequences. In the first outdoor ninety-second sequence, which occurs early in the film, the children follow Riefenstahl through the village-street to her caravan. In medium close-up we see them peer at her through a curtain; they smile shyly. In the second outdoor sequence, which lasts over two minutes, the children follow the shepherd down the same village-street on the way to his church wedding. Other adult Gypsies (mainly female) mill about. The indoor sequences show forty or more males observing Riefenstahl's tavern dance (just under three minutes) and later seven or eight women sitting in a balcony observing the wedding party (fifteen seconds), after which the camera pans down to the wedding celebration below. The sequence involving the extra with the small speaking part lasts just under four minutes: it shows him delivering Riefenstahl to Don Sebastian, then having a drink and playing cards, and finally being thrown out by Don Sebastian. Other sequences involving 'Spanish' peasants are performed by South Tyrolean villagers whom she had used in *Das blaue Licht*, or by professional actors, or by Spanish horsemen as in the Spanish location sequence.[51]

Riefenstahl's denazification

In 1948, Riefenstahl's two denazification hearings resulted in her complete clearance. On the insistence of the French occupation authorities, it was revised (13 January 1950) and she was placed in Category IV (fellow traveller). A further hearing in Berlin, in April 1952, upheld the first decision, which enabled the return of her architect-designed Berlin-Dahlem home.[52] Her earlier clearance had caused surprise, as had that of Veit Harlan, the director of the anti-semitic *Jud Süss* (1940) and *Kolberg* (1945). He had been put in Category V (exonerated) in December 1947, which led to a media outcry and the intervention of the Hamburg State Prosecutor, who charged him with crimes against humanity, the only film director to be so tried. Acquitted twice (in 1949 and 1950), Harlan, in contrast to Riefenstahl, was able to

resume filmmaking in West Germany in the 1950s. He too had used
extras: Jewish ones to play Jews in *Jud Süss*, one of whom survived to
provide sworn testimony.[53]

The *Revue* case (1949)

One week after Harlan's first acquittal, on 1 May 1949 a Munich
illustrated mass circulation weekly, *Revue,* published a one-page spread
entitled 'The "Unfinished" of Riefenstahl: What is happening with
Tiefland?' It included five photographs taken by Groth-
Schmachtenberger – three of the extras – and a small amount of text on
Tiefland. Focusing on her use of Gypsy extras, it also mentioned that the
French had confiscated *Tiefland,* and rejected her request to be allowed to
complete the film. The sixty (sic) extras were described as "film slaves"
taken from:

> [...] concentration camps in Berlin and Salzburg, who initially were
> excited at the prospect of exchanging work in munitions factories with film
> work. Yet Leni did not let them off easily. Scenes, which other directors
> would shoot six or seven times, were repeated twenty-five to thirty times.
> Also her treatment lacked a feminine tenderness. In the evening the
> Gypsies were escorted by police back to their camp. How many will have
> survived the concentration camps?[54]

Revue did not actually claim that many extras had died in Auschwitz; it
merely posed the question as to whether they had survived. With legal aid
Riefenstahl took the publisher, Helmut Kindler, to court, one of many
occasions when she would seek judicial intervention to protect her
reputation. In her memoirs she claimed to have won over fifty times.[55]
She objected to several statements: firstly, that the film had cost over
seven million Reichmarks, when normally a film cost 200,000; secondly,
that she only had to ask for money for it to be given; thirdly, that for the
role of the shepherd she had selected a Viennese bank teller from two
thousand Mitterwalder mountain troops who had filed past her several
times. Finally, and most damaging, that the sixty Gypsy extras from
Berlin and Salzburg were "film slaves" taken from a concentration
camp.[56]

Riefenstahl's case was heard in the Munich District Court
(*Landesgerichthof*) and, on 30 November 1949, the judge found in her
favour. *Revue* had been wrong about the film's finances and the casting of
the shepherd. The film's soaring cost was attributed to Riefenstahl's

illness and to the outbreak of war, which prevented her from covering film costs through the sales of *Olympia* (the subterfuge concerning the funding of *Olympia* was not yet public).[57] The cost was put at between four and five million Reichmarks rather than over seven million. Riefenstahl had not sought the shepherd from mountain troops but had found him "accidentally".[58] We now know, however, that *Revue* was closer to the truth. Kindler was criticised for not checking Groth-Schmachtenberger's notes, but the judge accepted that he had taken them in good faith. Fined DM600 plus costs, Kindler was required to publish a retraction in several Bavarian papers and in a forthcoming issue of *Revue*. The article's "sarcastic" and "ironic" tone, however, was deemed not to have infringed press law.[59]

Mainly concerned with Maxglan, rather than with Marzahn, the court had tried to establish whether it had been a concentration camp and, thus, whether the extras could be considered "film slaves". Evidence was heard from Riefenstahl, some members of her crew, surviving camp inmates and some Austrian officials, including SS *Sturmbannführer* (Battalion leader) Dr Anton Böhmer, director of the Salzburg Criminal Police (January 1940–May 1944) and, hence, of Maxglan, who had also visited Krün on three occasions. Maxglan, Böhmer maintained, was not a concentration camp but a "welfare camp" with its own character, under the control of the Criminal Police and the welfare administration.[60] In the last year of the war, Böhmer had lost his post, was charged with disobeying orders and, for a brief period, even became a concentration camp inmate himself.[61] This may have lent his testimony an element of credibility. The judge decided that "the Berlin and Salzburg camps were much more collection or reception camps." Maxglan was not a concentration camp in the sense that Eugen Kogon had described in his recently published book, *The SS State*, since at the time of its creation it was not yet part of a plan for the racial persecution of Gypsies. Despite the barbed wire, Maxglan lacked the character of a concentration camp and, thus, was an exception. It was also not under the rule of the SS but of the police. Moreover, in some areas Gypsies could still roam freely. Some witnesses even maintained that to 1943 such camps contained only asocial and criminal elements, and that the reason for the barn being kept locked at night was to prevent the Gypsies from stealing.[62]

Gypsy witnesses – and there were few – faced difficulty. Johanna Kurz, who had declared that "all the Reinhardt family had been gassed" and that giving children chocolate as bait constituted torture, was accused of providing false information.[63] When witnesses contradicted themselves there was laughter in court.[64] The *Revue* article appeared shortly before the establishment of the Federal Republic and the trial took place during the first six months of its existence. The response of the spectators, the nature of the questions asked, and the verdict itself reflect that context. Nevertheless, it is significant that already in 1949 Riefenstahl was deemed vulnerable for having used Gypsy extras and that this could be used in a media campaign directed against her rehabilitation.

Revue and the Konskie photographs (1952)

Three years later *Revue* returned to the fray. Two days before Riefenstahl's final denazification appeal they published a photograph of her taken in the second week of the war, while witnessing one of the first atrocities of the war in the Polish village of Konskie. She is standing amongst a crowd of uniformed onlookers, but her face is the only one to register horror.[65] Though seemingly to her credit, *Revue* used this as further proof that she could not plead ignorance to German atrocities. Uncharacteristically, she reached a settlement out of court, possibly because she did not want to bring German soldiers into disrepute.[66]

The Nina Gladitz documentary, *Zeit des Schweigens und der Dunkelheit* (1982)

In 1982, the filmmaker Nina Gladitz (born 1946), produced a documentary in collaboration with Josef Reinhardt, a surviving extra, called *Zeit des Schweigens und der Dunkelheit* (Time of Silence, Time of Darkness) and gave her reason for doing this: "Riefenstahl has been portrayed as a misguided, myopic artist. When I began to pursue this, everyone said, 'Let's forget all this.' Well, I feel we must not forget anything so tragic."[67] Broadcast by Westdeutsche Rundfunk (Cologne) on 3 September 1982, and by Channel 4 in Britain, it was subsequently shown at a film festival in Baden-Württemberg. The documentary concluded with sequences of Riefenstahl, in 1980, giving a lecture on the Nuba, in Freiburg, at the invitation of the *Badische Zeitung* (with Reinhardt seated in the audience) and at a book signing the following day. Gladitz, according to Riefenstahl, acted under a false name, when obtaining her permission to film her in Freiburg.[68]

Most of the sixty-minute film is concerned with the Gypsy extras recruited from Maxglan. Reinhardt, thirteen in 1940, interviewed the survivors – mainly his relatives. Referred to as Tante Leni, they were adamant that Riefenstahl had appeared at the collection camp to select the extras. Survivors also insisted that they had been compelled to work on the film, that they had not been properly paid, and finally, and most seriously, that she had known that they would be sent to Auschwitz. When there were plans to screen the documentary for a second time at a film festival, Riefenstahl decided to go to court.[69] Failing to interest the Munich State Prosecutor in pressing criminal charges,[70] she turned to the civil courts, for an injunction forbidding further screenings and sued on grounds of "monstrous defamation".[71]

Riefenstahl's civil action against Nina Gladitz (1985–7)

The civil case was first heard in the Freiburg District Court (*Landgericht*) in November 1985 – Gladitz lived in the area – but was adjourned for several months. The judge stated that he was concerned with ascertaining whether the film's accusations were based on provable facts and whether any assertions could be construed as libellous to Riefenstahl. He sought clarification to several questions. Was the camp a concentration camp? Did Riefenstahl come to the camp in person to select the extras? Were the Gypsies paid for their work? Were they compelled to work? Did she know that they would soon go to Auschwitz?[72]

In June 1985, the court decided mainly in Gladitz's favour. Riefenstahl appealed. The Superior District Court (*Oberlandesgericht*) in Karlsruhe reached a similar decision in March 1987. Riefenstahl's libel action failed mainly on two counts: namely on her claims to having never set foot in Maxglan to personally select the extras and to having paid them a hefty thirty marks a day. It particularly incensed her that it could not be proved conclusively whether she had been at the camp, given that there was no reference to this in the Salzburg documents. That she had not paid them thirty marks a day is, however, apparent from the Salzburg documents. The adults were paid seven marks per day, not directly but into a fund, though pocket money was given directly: fifty Reichspfennigs per day per adult and twenty-five per day per child. (The Berlin extras received more – approximately seventeen to eighteen marks, which was still well under Riefenstahl's claim.)[73] Moreover, the extras were compelled to work since labour was compulsory, even if film work was less onerous than other forms.[74]

Riefenstahl won on only one count, namely that at the time of filming she could not have known that the extras were destined for Auschwitz – in any case, she would not have been privy to that decision. Some survivors believed that she could have interceded on their behalf, and that she had even promised to do so. Such comments had to be cut from the film, if it were to be shown again; non-compliance resulting in a fine of DM500,000 or six months detention.[75] The film was withdrawn.

Riefenstahl's memoirs (1987)

In the same year, 1987, Riefenstahl published her memoirs, in which she discussed both court cases and claimed that after the war she had bumped into many of the *Tiefland* Gypsies. Some had expressed gratitude.[76] Nevertheless, the issue rankled. In October 2000, when asked at the Frankfurt Book Fair what was the greatest lie perpetrated against her, she replied: "That I was in a concentration camp and there engaged Gypsies for my film." She even had letters from the Gypsies recalling that this had been the greatest time of their lives.[77]

Riefenstahl's admirers

Riefenstahl has had her cinematic admirers, adept at separating style from content, concerned with art rather than politics.[78] Even feminists have been able to overlook a female director's service to a patriarchal ideology. Many believed she was harshly dealt with because she was unable to make another film. Since unification in 1990 Riefenstahl has been accorded a more favourable reception in Germany. A filmmaker could even describe *Tiefland* as an anti-Hitler film:

> *Tiefland* however, more still than *Das blaue Licht* is no Nazi film, although Hitler appears in it, only here he is called Don Sebastian…. *Tiefland* is Leni's dispute with the Nazis, with Hitler, and with the criminals whom she has served and for whom she now wishes nothing less than death.[79]

Overlooked is the fact that Riefenstahl was first drawn to *Tiefland* in 1934, shortly before making *Triumph of the Will*, and that neither then nor later, when filming during the years 1940-1944, is there evidence that she had wavered in her commitment to the Third Reich. That she added a scene about a peasant uprising[80] was for dramatic rather than political reasons. Ultimately, *Tiefland* was not dissimilar to *Das blaue Licht* and allowed her to work again within the same genre.[81] True, the tyrannical lord is overthrown, but that hardly constitutes resistance to fascism. Just as it is difficult to believe that Riefenstahl was unpolitical when making *Triumph of the Will*, similarly it is difficult to accept that she was political when making *Tiefland*. Indeed, her memoirs indicate the opposite: *Tiefland*'s advantage, she claimed, was that it had nothing to do with politics or war.[82] Unfortunately, this was not the only attempt to suggest that *Tiefland* was a work of resistance.[83]

The Rom e V case (2002)

Several months before her one-hundredth birthday, doubtless emboldened by the increasingly favourable media attention, Riefenstahl gave an interview in which she went further on the subject of the Gypsy extras: "After the war we have seen again all the Gypsies who worked on *Tiefland*. Nothing has happened to a single one."[84] For this remark she faced the possibility of civil action, appearing now in a new role as defendant rather than plaintiff. Supported by Rom e V, a Cologne-based local Gypsy association, Zäzilia Reinhardt, aged 76, one of the last surviving Gypsy extras who was sent from Maxglan to Lackenbach, was prepared to take Riefenstahl to court. Riefenstahl's production company issued a press statement on 7 August 2002 to the effect that she had never said these words; her partner, Horst Kettner, suggested that it had been a misunderstanding. Moreover, it was only now that Riefenstahl had learned of the terrible fate of her extras. A press conference was called in Cologne for 16 August 2002 to announce a planned civil action. A deadline was set for noon the previous day for receipt of a written retraction. That retraction (dated 14 August) arrived by fax, in which Riefenstahl gave an undertaking never to assert again or allow to be asserted again that all the extras had survived. She had received good legal advice, for she was in no position to deny her words: they had been taped, she had authorised the interview, and signed the transcription as a true record.[85]

In view of this retraction, it was announced at the press conference that the civil action had been dropped. However, Rom e V made several demands: the names of all the extras should be added to the video and should be described as minor actors *(Kleine Darsteller)* rather than extras. Moreover, the surviving extras should be compensated not only for their labour, but also for the suffering to which Riefenstahl contributed in denying the fate of their murdered relatives.

Rom e V also sent the papers to the Frankfurt State Prosecutor, since in Germany it is a citizen's right to request an investigation into Holocaust Denial (§130/3). A few days after the press conference (on Riefenstahl's centenary) the Prosecutor's Office informed Rom e V that they would begin the preliminary investigation. One month later they decided not to proceed due to lack of evidence, partly because Riefenstahl had issued a retraction. However, the Prosecutor had considered charging Riefenstahl with another offence, Maligning the Memory of the Dead (§189/1), but thought it not in the public interest to proceed, given her age. That decision was subsequently made public on 18 October 2002. One year later Riefenstahl died at the age of 101. None of Rom e V's demands have been met.

Filming Tiefland on location in Krün, summer 1941 (photograph by Erika Groth-Schmachtenberger). Copyright: Bildarchiv Preussischer Kulturbesitz, Berlin

The effect of persecution on the German Sinti

Heike Krokowski
Translated from the German by Bill Templer

Summary

The National Socialist policies of persecution and annihilation pursued against the German Sinti and Roma had an immense impact not only on individuals but the ethnic group as a whole. The later traumatic consequences are insurmountable for the survivors of the persecution and the concentration camps. They persist down to the present and have also influenced the life of later generations of Sinti born in Germany after the Second World War.

The survivors of persecution are marked by its searing experience and the extreme conditions to which they were exposed over an extended period of many years. None emerged unscathed from this ordeal, all the victims bear physical and mental scars. Sinti and Roma society suffered profound damage as a result of the persecution, which shook its social and cultural structures to their foundations. The extended family structures and their networks, a primary social foundation for the ethnic group, were, as a rule, destroyed as a result of the war. The older members of the Sinti and Roma community, who had long functioned as bearers and transmitters of social and cultural traditions, had almost all fallen victim to Nazi murder. After the war's end, there were only very limited vocational and economic options open to the Sinti and Roma, since they lacked a basis of continuity with the pre-war period on which to build a new existence: National Socialist policy had denied them education and confiscated their possessions.

Introduction

This paper reports on an investigation of the forms of traumatization following the experience of extreme persecution and the psychological effects on the survivors. The study was conducted using interviews conducted largely with North German Sinti who had lived through the years of National Socialist terror. The study's primary focus can be supplemented by utilizing the extensive research material available on Jewish survivors. That is necessary because there is no comparative scientific material on survivors among the German Sinti and Roma.

The reports of survivors presented in the course of this paper, and on which the later observations are based, stem from a collection of over 65 interviews gathered in the course of three research projects centred at the University of Hanover. The interviewees were born between 1908 and 1934. At the time when measures of National Socialist persecution, such as deportation, and concentration camp internment were initiated, they were between six and 32 years old. At the time of the interviews, their ages ranged from 58 to 82.

Limits of the narrative interview as a research tool

A basic problem in work with interviewees is the nature of memory and its fundamental variability. The reason for this lies in the period of time lapsed between events and their remembrance, as well as the individual forms that working through of experience can assume. For that reason, the reliability of what is said is often limited. The events remembered in the interview frequently have a restricted factual content. Rather, this is the past recollected, which in the years prior to narration has been reshaped, reworked and adapted to memory. Nonetheless, the interviews with survivors of National Socialist persecution provide the possibility of drawing conclusions from the way experiences are described in two dimensions: the significance of the actual experience of persecution and how individuals have worked through these experiences. Basically, every description in these discourses is stamped by dealing with an experience that is extreme. Yet this means that the interviews should not be viewed just as a supplement to the normal documentary sources. Rather, they are a direct expression of the psychological state of the survivors, their post-traumatic responses and individual processing of highly traumatizing experiences.

Ways of dealing with memory

Within an interview with a survivor we can basically learn only about fragments of what the individuals experienced during National Socialist persecution. The preponderant majority of the experiences, and most especially the trauma, lie hidden beneath the pain and grief associated with these experiences. Frequently an attitude of repression is characteristic of the way survivors tend to deal with memory. Only when the tales and reports are read in detail, separated from the factual content on the surface, does a window open onto the extent of persisting trauma. It is far greater than the surface impression of the transcribed texts might suggest. Even when the interviewees attempt to report in a cool and unemotional manner about their experiences, one can still sense how burdensome this memory is and how much they still suffer from it, regardless of the external composure they manage to show. Often questions after interviews were met with an adverse response. Many older Sinti did not want to expose themselves to a discursive situation, where they feared it might bring long repressed memories and pain to the surface once again. But many of the Sinti women and men who were prepared to engage in discussion suffered enormously from recalling and reliving the memory of this traumatic chapter in their lives.

The interviews with German Sinti survivors, on which the study is based, were conducted almost 50 years after the end of the Second World War. This distance in time, as mentioned, has impacted on the extent of the interviewees' memories and the way they are shaped. Some events grow fuzzier and more indistinct in the mirror of memory, and, in several cases, fragments of the experiences are condensed and merged into a unified chain of events. The decades that have passed also provide space for altering the events and experiences in memory so as to make it easier for the individual to deal with thoughts about these terrible experiences. These changes can provide insight into the necessity of constructing a memory in such a way that it is emptied of a portion of its intolerability and pain. The description of the experiences of persecution must be viewed from a temporal distance. On the basis of the way memory of the experience of persecution presents itself, it becomes possible to draw conclusions about the manner in which this experience has been worked through and accepted by the survivors. That points to just how powerfully the National Socialist persecution and resulting post-traumatic responses impact on the Sinti down to the present day.

This article will detail several typical aspects of the problems resulting from the after-effects of trauma. The description of the way individuals grapple with concentration camp experiences and the memory of them provides a possibility for presenting several examples of psychological traumatization and the way Sinti survivors have worked through their experience of victimization.

Trauma and its repercussions

The trauma suffered as a result of experiences of persecution at the hands of the National Socialists was severe and enduring. Thus, for example, the abrupt and lasting dehumanisation of the individual in the situation of the concentration camp was destructive for that person's self-esteem. Being permanently confronted with sickness, suffering and death – both of close relatives and the great mass of fellow prisoners – led to a process of emotional numbing. The cultural code of morals and values of the Sinti also shed its meaning in the daily struggle for survival. In this way, the Sinti lost the stability of their culture. Yet had they adhered to the traditional rules of behaviour, this might have endangered their very lives.

The long-term effects of traumatic experiences became evident after the end of the war and persecution. Along with organic consequences, there were persistent feelings of anxiety, a loss of orientation and heavy depression. It was especially hard for the survivors to endure and overcome the loss of their families. The experiences of the camp and genocide were ever present in their mind, and for the most part still remain so today. Nightmares, insomnia and anxiety make it impossible to forget these experiences.

The survivors are repeatedly confronted anew with the experience of persecution. The Sinti survivors cannot elude the presence of this experience. Recollections of the persecution and concentration camps are present in their thoughts as well as in everyday life. The trigger for memory are the associations that can arise as a result of diverse and often banal trifles. A certain odour or taste, brief impressions and feelings can transport individuals emotionally back in time to the situation in the camp:

Do you still have a memory of the camp?
No... But the feelings of anxiety, I've still got them today... Like sometimes I smell things, when you go selling from door to door, I smell

something somewhere, an old odour, it enters my nostrils. And then I say:
that was the smell in the camp.

Many instances where the traumatic experience is relived were forced on
to survivors by external factors, as, for example, in connection with the
bureaucratic procedures for compensation. These procedures were often
marked by a petty and unfeeling approach by the German authorities in
their dealings with the survivors. Just as often, bias and discriminatory
attitudes influenced behaviour toward the applicants for compensation as
well as the decision in their case. Yet even without such concrete
occasions, the experience of persecution remains ever present and
palpable in the everyday life of the survivors:

Well, I can, er, in any case I can't forget. Not as long as I live. Like when I
go to bed in the evening... but that's always there before my eyes, again
and again, always... No, I won't be able to forget it, not ever, all the stuff I
went through.

For the survivors, the experience of persecution is the dominant
component in their lives. It represented a "break in their lifeline",[1] one
which every one of them was forced to experience. As a result, the effects
of the experience of persecution also had a negative impact on the family
life of the German Sinti. Their children grew up with the psychological
consequences that victimization and its trauma had on their parents,
learning to internalize these as a part of the history of their own family.[2]

In the immediate postwar period

In the personal sphere, the social and psychological effects for the
survivors of National Socialist persecution are huge. In the immediate
postwar period, the life of the Sinti and Roma was strongly marked by the
attempt to reconstruct family structures and to repress the experience of
persecution. But the experiences of the concentration camps and
genocide were, and remain, ever present, and repeatedly erupt into
consciousness in everyday life. They are manifested, as already noted, in
symptoms such as nightmares, insomnia and fears of persecution. The
Sinti and Roma, who had a very closely meshed social and family
network, largely isolated themselves from the German majority society
after the war. This was also a reaction to the continuing social and state
discrimination and exclusion that they had to face after the Second World
War. The reason for this was mainly due to the continuity of personnel in

government offices and agencies, and in the traditional biased, racist patterns of thought prevalent in the German majority population.

All the Sinti who survived the persecution and confinement in concentration camps were physically and psychologically damaged. Though their joy in having survived and now being able to live in freedom once again was great and initially dominated their feelings, that joy was tempered by worry and concern. It was soon submerged by the oppressive realities they had to contend with. Anxiety, despair, depression and an encompassing sense of apathy, indifference and numbness[3] accompanied many Sinti survivors from the end of the war on. Frequently these after-effects, persist down to today.

Fear and anxiety

Feelings of anxiety are among the most lasting and permanent effects of a long period of persecution. During confinement in the concentration camp, anxiety was a striking factor shaping the everyday lives of the prisoners – fear of the guards, fear of the prisoners with responsibilities, fear of hunger and disease, fear of the selections and murder operations. It was also a necessary impulse that guided behaviour, assisting the individual at times to survive in the camp. After liberation from the camp, fear persisted as a determinant feeling: *Once we were outside, we didn't even dare go out onto the road, see, since we were scared that they'd get us... We were afraid, 'cause we were intimidated. I mean we weren't able to think straight.* In the interviews with Sinti survivors, many interviewees tell about the fear that dominated people's behaviour after their liberation. Caution, reserve and the attempt not to be noticed by others shaped the behaviour and demeanour of the Sinti survivors outside the concentration camps as well:

> Q: Did you fellows also take the train to Hamburg?
> A: *No, because we were too scared to.*
> Q: You were scared? Of what? After all, you'd been liberated!
> A: *Right, but the fear was still there, see. So we went off on foot... from Bergen-Belsen we walked all the way to Hamburg.*

The fear was anchored so deeply that even the liberators in the concentration camps were perceived as a threat. A Sintezza reports that in Bergen-Belsen she was afraid of the British soldiers who took over the camp in April 1945:

My mother hid us from the English because they ...

Q: You were afraid of the English?

A: *We were all scared, see. We were all afraid, all of us, about what would happen now. I mean, we weren't normal any longer.*

So terribly afraid they were "no longer normal" is a frequent assessment expressed today, in retrospect, by Sinti survivors about their behaviour at the time. People were unable to abruptly set aside the psychological exhaustion that had persisted for years, the sense of insecurity and the precautionary measures practised and internalized over a long period. Even many years after their liberation, these feelings of fear and anxiety still often shape the lives of the Sinti. These feelings are stubbornly persistent, and can be reactivated by the slightest stimuli. Reports of racist attacks or the appearance of uniformed personnel can trigger memories that erupt onto the surface and feelings of anxiety return again. They are enduring and, in many cases, still have not been overcome today.

Despair and grief

Another psychological manifestation among Sinti survivors after the war was despair and depression. These were often an expression of mental exhaustion in the wake of the dehumanisation they had suffered over many years:

I sat down under a tree, there was this oak tree in the village where I was liberated. And I was no longer able to hold back the tears. I didn't cry, I called out for help. The feeling came back to me again, see, like that we had been liberated.

When survivors became conscious of the magnitude of their loss, then the façade of joy over the fact of their survival could no longer be maintained. They were overcome by grief and they could no longer cope with their life after the persecution and experience in the concentration camp:

So now I was at home, my grandparents were there, and many friends too. And it was like I was there, and yet I wasn't there... Now I noticed for the first time just how alone I was, since my parents and all my brothers and sisters were gone. I all by myself, no, no... I was so depressed that I just couldn't get used to the fact that both my parents were gone... Then I noticed how alone I was, how everything was gone... And then I also thought about the camp and those things, see... I no longer could really feel quiet and at peace. Then one chap came in, and another, and another, and then we started in to drink... Well, and I was almost constantly drinking something, see... Honestly, like I wanted to drink myself to death. Yes. That's how bad it'd become for me.

The extent of the despair that often overwhelmed the survivors after the war becomes clear in the attempt here to drink oneself into a stupor and repress memory. Loss, loneliness, one's own psychological wounds and mental pain were a heavy burden on the survivors after the war. Frequently these after-effects were also enduring and remained dominant in the lives of the Sinti survivors for many years, even decades.

Space here permits the presentation of only a few examples of individual symptoms and after-effects. Along with these typical narratives and the trauma they reflect, other consequences for the survivors were also serious, such as their lack of orientation after the war, their emotional numbing or a tendency to heavy depression. Significantly, the survivors were already troubled by the after-effects of their experiences immediately after the end of their internment in a concentration camp. Later forms of dealing with the experience of persecution emerge that point to a more or less conscious working through of the experiences.

Working through the experiences

In the years following the end of the war, the survivors tried to find a way of dealing with the experience of persecution that was appropriate for them. Often that consisted of denial and repression. The demands that life made on individuals after the war helped survivors to repress their traumatic experiences, and sometimes even to forget them for a period of time. After initial bewilderment and despair, the Sinti directed their main attention to reuniting and regenerating their families, and the job of building a new economic basis for themselves.

Decades after the actual experiences, repression for many Sinti survivors is often a well-learned internal mechanism. But the experience of persecution as such is accepted as a dominant part of their lives. The way they assess this experience is largely characterised by an inability to grasp how the persecution and mass murder in the camps could have happened. Another determining element is the sense of helplessness in the face of the tortures suffered and the loss of family members. Several descriptions by the survivors reflect the sense of unreality which stamps the memory of their experiences in the concentration camps:

The concentration camp is something that's unbelievable. I mean, that seems unbelievable too. That's why I say, when I talk and think about it today, see, that I dreamed the whole thing, that it was all just a dream. It was a bad dream, and I also say, yes, I insist that it was a bad dream I went through in the concentration camp.

The feeling of irrationality that is frequently connected with the memory of the concentration camps demands a way of dealing with the experience of the persecution which makes it possible to tolerate and endure the thoughts that arise about it. Often the memory was unconsciously altered. Experiences were in retrospect made to conform to a picture which the survivors constructed of the time spent in the camp, their role and their behaviour there in an extreme situation. These reconstructed memories were also important for the survivors in order to maintain a certain image of themselves.

Examples of reconstructed memories should be viewed as ways of working through experiences. They make it possible for survivors to grapple with the traumatic experiences of persecution and the concentration camps. In the process, some reconstructed memories take on the function of explaining their own survival. But they also have the job of functioning as defensive mechanisms against the sense of guilt associated with survival. Other such constructs are necessary in order to reinstate and develop the necessary sense of self-esteem.

Constructed memory

The constructed memories which speak to and reflect the experiences and traumata of the majority of Sinti survivors, such as the death of close family members and one's own incomprehensible survival, took on the form of "collective patterns of explanation and identity"[4] among the German Sinti. Other such forms of working through experience are more dependent on the psychological prerequisites of the individual. They mirror individual memory constructs which serve to help rebuild the individual's personality.

The Bergen-Belsen story

I will now look in greater detail at one example for the construction of memory. Central here is an incident often reported by the German Sinti, which supposedly took place shortly before the liberation of the Bergen-

Belsen concentration camp in April 1945. There is no corroborating proof for this incident in the literature or in other oral or written documentary sources. All the more striking then is the regularity with which German Sinti report about this in their interviews. In their memory, there is no doubt that the incident took place. A large number of interviewees tell about an attempt by the SS to murder all the prisoners in Bergen-Belsen shortly before their liberation:

> *The day we were liberated we were supposed to... But we were already sick, we could no longer eat anything. First of all, we didn't get any bread, you see and secondly, there was no longer any real food for meals at the end. And so we were supposed to get some bread, see, and it was poisoned... The English came in two hours earlier. If they'd got there later... we'd all have been dead. But the English got there two hours earlier, and took over the kitchen. Then they (burned down) the kitchen.*

Other interviewees narrate this same story, adding various details. For example, there is variation in the kind of food that is supposed to have been poisoned. Some mention bread, others canned vegetables or even a cooked dinner that was given to the half-starved prisoners. Several Sinti report that the British officers threw the food to the dogs in order to point to the danger:

> *And then we were supposed to, er, this bread, so then we were supposed to get some bread again, see, and it simply was poisoned.*
> Q: Who said so?
> A: *The British threw it to the dogs, and they (started) foaming at the mouth and died.*

There are other diverse deviations in individual narratives. Among other things, the moment for the planned murder of the prisoners in Bergen-Belsen is set weeks before the liberation, or in the moment just after the British soldiers arrived, or shortly after liberation. In some reports, the liberators warn the prisoners about eating the supposedly poisoned food; in other narratives, the German camp guards warn the inmates. Other Sinti narrate that they saw fellow prisoners die after eating food, and had been forewarned by this. In addition, there are also individual interviewees who tell about the incident as having occurred in other camps, such as Ravensbrück or Wolkenburg, the Flossenburg satellite camp.

   Common to all these narratives is that the supposed intent of the SS and the guards to kill the prisoners became known to those telling the story only by accident, and that only in this way were they barely able to escape death. Since the tale of the poisoned food is remembered and claimed by so many Sinti to be an event they experienced, it acquires the character of a metaphor both for the murderous persecution of the Sinti and the unexpected rescue of the individual by pure chance. The attempt by the SS to poison the people in the war situation, already lost for them, stands in this symbolic tale for the merciless persecution of the National Socialists, and their intention to exterminate the prisoners. But the rescue by the British soldiers who warn them embodies survival of the genocide per se. The decisive feature in the metaphor is its sheer fortuitousness, the unexpected fortunate constellation which made survival possible.

Although this incident is narrated, as mentioned, by almost all the Sinti interviewed who were imprisoned in Bergen-Belsen, there is no historical proof that it actually occurred. There is no supporting documentary evidence in any British archives, nor is the incident mentioned in our eyewitness accounts about the Bergen-Belsen camp from the period directly after the war's end. It is not inconceivable that such a murder was indeed planned in the chaos that predominated in the camp shortly before it was handed over to the British army. Moreover, there were indeed countless murder operations against prisoners in other camps or during the evacuation transports.

Nonetheless, such a plan is improbable. The hand-over of the concentration camp in April 1945 had been negotiated several days earlier by German Army officers and a British staff officer, in the framework of a partial cease-fire. Most of the SS guards were withdrawn two days before the camp was handed over to the British. For that reason, only a small fraction of SS male and female guards still remained in the camp at the time of the arrival of the British army. The small number of SS personnel would not have constituted an obstacle in carrying out a murder operation of the kind in the Sinti report. Yet it is doubtful that the attention of the SS guards still in the camp was focused on such a scheme. Their concern was probably to ensure their own safe departure from the camp. The imminent arrival of the British army in Bergen-Belsen could be expected after the conclusion of negotiations, so that one cannot suspect there was any element of surprise for the SS. Shortly before the departure of the SS from the camp, pits for mass graves were dug, reported by many of the interviewees. For them this points to the intention of the SS guards to kill the prisoners. In actuality, however, this more likely was a helpless, cosmetic attempt by the camp authorities to gather together in a few

places the numerous dead bodies lying scattered across the camp grounds
in a bid to mitigate the horrific picture presented by Bergen-Belsen in the
final weeks before liberation.

In connection with the reports by the Sinti about poisoned foodstuff, it
is worth mentioning that the storerooms in the Bergen-Belsen camp were
full of large quantities of food. Some of the prisoners plundered these
edible supplies immediately after the arrival of the liberators. In addition,
it is narrated that the pigsties of the SS were stormed, the animals
slaughtered and then consumed. Several Sinti also report that despite the
warnings by British soldiers, prisoners pounced on the food and gobbled
it down. This is possibly a point that sheds light on the actual events
underlying the incident with the poisoned food as reported by the Sinti.
Because as a result of the fact that the prisoners had gone hungry for
weeks, their bodies were no longer able to digest the heavy fare and large
quantities of food:

> There were some people there, in Bergen-Belsen, where we were. There
> were some who... The British came, see, and they didn't shoot at the
> concentration camp. That was already the liberation. They gave us stuff to
> eat, and everything, and many people got a sick stomach, they died from
> the food.

Another Sinti man also mentions the connection between the excessive
consumption of unaccustomed food and the heavy strain that put on the
organism of starving prisoners:

> And the Americans [...] they came in their jeeps, they threw us some
> corned beef, in big cans. [...] And because the other prisoners had now
> opened up the cans of corned beef and had eaten all they could, you know.
> Why, they were lying there, stretching for many metres in the ditch of the
> road – all dead!

The connection between unaccustomed food and serious illness or even
the death of the prisoners is evident from the above reports. On that basis,
it is also possible to make certain assumptions about the origin of the
incident narrated by the Sinti in the Bergen-Belsen camp. It is likely that
in their narration there was an unconscious linkage in memory between
the consequences of eating the unaccustomed food and the story of the
planned poisoning of the inmates. Its cause lies in the perception of the
survivors that the foodstuffs obtainable after liberation were perceived to
be harmful, in effect poison for the emaciated bodies of the half-starved
inmates. Their system had become so sensitive and susceptible to illness

that even comestibles meant to help people regain their strength had a lethal effect.

This reversal in the everyday experience which the prisoners were familiar with from before their confinement in the camp was very hard for them to comprehend. The construction of the poisoned food entered the memory of the Sinti survivors as an explanation for this experience. In addition, this reshaping at the moment of liberation may even have come to the aid of the prisoners. In the situation at the time of the sudden surplus of provisions where there had long been none, it was necessary to dampen the strong craving for anything edible, stoked by the extreme hunger they had suffered, and to prevent sudden illness by overtaxing their digestive system. Thus, over the course of the years they constructed a memory which serves the Sinti as an explanation for their own incomprehensible survival, and hence is of exceptional power in determining their own self-identity as survivors.

The firm conviction of the Sinti that the reported incident actually occurred points to an important function that this constructed memory has for the survivors in working through their experiences in the concentration camps. To shake their faith in this incident would also mean to take from them this possibility for working through their experience, leaving them with something missing to explain the fact of their own survival. Dismantling the constructed memory of the poisoned foods would also shatter the possibility for the Sinti to live with the memory of their own survival, the recollection of the indescribable phenomenon of mass death in the camps and the death of their loved ones and relatives.

The constructed memory described here functions for the Sinti interviewed as a pattern for explaining the fact of their own incomprehensible survival. At the same time, this explanatory pattern serves to help people deal with the incomprehensible mass death of their fellow prisoners and closest relatives by the consumption of unaccustomed foods. In addition, this construction can be assigned the task of finding a way to grapple with the subconscious feeling of guilt vis-à-vis their dead relatives. By a fortuitous event, which is a determinant element in the narrative of the poisoned food – it was only *by chance* that British soldiers arrived at the last moment and warned them about the poisoned edibles – their own survival becomes fortuitous, accidental, and independent of personal dispositions or ways of behaving. In this way, the feeling that an individual might have survived wrongly, without justification, or at the expense of others is suspended. In addition, the constructed memory of the poisoned provisions can be seen as a metaphor for the persecution and genocide of the Sinti.

Along with this collective constructed memory, which is a part of the recollection of Sinti survivors, there are also individual reconstructions which serve the individual's need to work on their trauma, his or her working through the traumatic experience of persecution and confinement in a concentration camp. Their principal task is to assist in reconstructing the shaken structure of personality. In this connection, one might mention reconstructions that act to eliminate additional discrimination during the persecution. This could be of importance to survivors who, stripped of their rights in the camp situation, were subjected to additional degradations and debasement, since they occupied positions which were very low within the hierarchy of prisoners. That was quite frequently the case when it came to Sinti. Also worth mentioning here are reconstructions which suggest to the survivor that he or she possessed an ability to make decisions and act within the situation of the camp, where the autonomy of the individual person was destroyed. These reconstructions helped people to regenerate and rebuild such an ability to act after the end of the shattering experience of the camps.

Conclusion

This article has only been able to touch on a small number of examples of different forms of the psychological aftereffects and the working through of experience among Sinti survivors. The extent of later consequences of victimization is far greater than indicated here. But all the after-effects are characterised by being long-lasting, with a massive impact on the lives of the Sinti survivors over extended time.

In conclusion, a few points can be summarized. Given the enduring effects of trauma as a result of persecution and genocide, the German Sinti survivors perceived their future after the war as destroyed. Their families had largely been murdered, their social structures shattered, and they themselves had been seriously damaged both physically and psychologically and debilitated by their ordeal. There were barely any possibilities available for them to build a new economic and social existence for themselves, underpinned by an intact family structure. Consequently, the rebuilding of the family and social community required many years, mobilizing the remaining strength they could muster. Their lives were dominated by the memory of persecution and grief over the loss of their closest relatives. After the war ended, the Sinti survivors suffered from depression and despair in the face of the sheer magnitude of their loss. They were helpless and without any orientation.

Down to today, many of them suffer from feelings of anxiety. The memory of their experiences of persecution repeatedly erupts onto the surface of everyday life, and frequently can no longer be repressed. In order to be able to live with that memory, it was necessary to find specific forms of dealing with the experience of persecution. The welding together of isolated fragments of memory served as a pattern of explanation for the experiences, helping them to confront the death of their family members and fellow prisoners, their own survival and the feelings of guilt bound up with it. But the reconstructed memories also helped them to piece together and rebuild their own personality, and to find the strength to go on living. However, none of the various ways of grappling with the experience of persecution were able to remove the extreme weight of their trauma and psychological injuries. All they could do was to aid survivors in tolerating the memories and learning to live with the fact of their survival.

Notes

Editor's note: As in the previous volumes, archive references have been left in the original language to assist researchers. Place names occurring in the Oxford Gazetteer are spelt accordingly.

English translations of German institutions and terminology have been edited to correspond to those used in volumes 1 and 2 of the series. The vocabulary of the National Socialists was so warped that every second word could be put in italics or single quotation marks. In practice, this has been done sparingly while double inverted commas are reserved for direct quotation.

Introduction

1. For Belgium see Vol. 2 of this series, pp.85–7. For Holland see B. Sijes, *Vervolging van Zigeuners in Nederland 1940–1945*. 1979 (English summary).
2. For Poland see D. Kenrick and G. Puxon, *Gypsies under the Swastika*. 1995, pp.73–6.

1. Hübschmannová: Roma in the so-called Slovak State

1. Nečas, Ctibor, *Nad osudem českých a slovenských Cikáni v letech 1939–1945*. 1981; new edition *Českoslovenští Romové v letech 1938–1945*. 1994.
2. A five-year programme in the Romani Language and Studies Department was established at Charles University in 1991.
3. [*Editor's note: In this volume we render all the quotations from Romani interviewees in italics as they form a major part of the texts. In Vol. 2 (in particular the article on Romania) similar extracts were printed in a smaller point, not in italics.*]
4. Josef Tiso (1887–1947), a Catholic priest, was President of the puppet Slovak Republic in 1939–45.
5. According to E. Horváthová (*Cigani na Slovensku*. 1964) only 1,000

Roma out of 80,000 were murdered during the Second World War. This number is probably an underestimate, however not by very much. According to the statistics presented by V. Kladivová (*Konečna stanice Auschwitz-Birkenau.* 1994, p.34) there was only one Rom from Slovakia in the Gypsy camp in Auschwitz-Birkenau II. Roma witnesses relate that some Roma were sent to Nazi concentration camps along with other participants of the Slovak National Uprising after it was suppressed by the German army.

6.   Horvathová, op. cit. pp.137–44.
7.   Each caste in India has its own *dharma* (lit. obligation) and, in the past, Romani clans in Slovakia generally kept to one profession.
8.   Wrought-iron smiths in Podunajské Biskupice had already founded a cooperative in the 1930s. Apart from the sale of wrought-iron artefacts, they worked at restoration of castles, manor houses, etc.
9.   Pivon', R. in *Romano džaniben.* 2001/3–4.
10.   In Slovakia the commonly used term for Gadje (non-Roma) is still 'whites' in contrast to the 'blacks' – the Roma.
11.   Kalal, K., *Slovenska vlastivéda.* 1928, p.151.
12.   Kamenec, I., *Slovenský stát.* 1992, p.38.
13.   Kamenec, I., 'Holocaust na Slovensku' in *Neznámý holocaust.* 1995, pp.64–70.
14.   Nečas. 1981, p.70.
15.   Ibid.
16.   Ibid.
17.   Kamenec. 1992, p.37.
18.   Salner, Peter, *Prežili holokaust.* 1997, passim.
19.   Ibid. p.53.
20.   See her biography trans. from Czech as I. Lacková, *A False Dawn.* Hatfield: University of Hertfordshire Press. 2000.
21.   Salner, op. cit. p.53.
22.   The event Bendik discusses must have occurred before the Czechs were expelled from the fascist Slovak Republic during the Second World War. At the time of the so-called First Czechoslovak Republic many Czech teachers, police, customs officers, and clerks worked in Slovakia. Some Slovaks, who tried to establish an independent Slovak State long before the Second World War, thought of the presence of the Czech intelligentsia in Slovakia as further oppression following the earlier Hungarian oppression.
23.   Hlinkovec: The Catholic priest and politician Andrej Hlinka (1864–1938) was a comparatively restrained propagator of Slovak independence. His Slovak People's Party gradually abandoned its democratic character and leaned towards authoritative nationalism. During the fascist Slovak Republic the Party was numerous and absolutely resolute in its support of the puppet state. The term 'hlinkovec' is still used meaning a rightwing

nationalist.
24. Nečas. See note 2.
25. Nečas. 1981, p.76.
26. Nečas. 1981, p.99.
27. Nečas. 1981, pp.106, 112.
28. Lit. I lick your little soul.
29. Nečas. 1994, p.126.
30. Nečas. 1944, p.124.
31. Nečas. 1994, p.131.
32. Nečas. 1994, p.146.
33. Nečas. 1994, p.132.
34. Nečas. 1994, p.122.
35. Nečas. 1981, pp.74, 77.
36. Gecelovský, V. in *Obzor Gemera.* 1986/3, p.175.
37. Nečas. 1981, p.75.
38. For Lacková's autobiography, see note 20.
39. The play was performed about 800 times from 1947 to 1949. It launched the author's fame and redirected her future life.
40. Gecelovský, op. cit. p.176.
41. A *bastí* is a caste area within traditional Indian villages. A member of an 'upper caste' will not walk into a *bastí* inhabited by members of a 'lower caste' (ascertained during the author's research in Rajasthan in 1969 and 1990).
42. Janotková, Z., *Padli, aby sme žili.* 1975, p.101.
43. Kamenec. 1992, pp.82, 83–4.
44. Nečas. 1981, pp.138–44.
45. Nečas. 1981, p.140.
46. Janotková, op. cit. p.71.
47. Nečas. 1994, pp.156–60.
48. Nečas. 1994, pp.157, 158.
49. Nečas. 1994, pp.159, 160.

2. Katz: The Roma of Hungary in the Second World War

1. Translated by Donald Kenrick from the German version of this article.
2. Fifty-seven interviews were conducted by the author personally in the period 1994–2000, others are taken from published material. The persons who are quoted in the following pages have agreed to their names being published.
3. Orsös, Dr F., *A házassági tőrvény fajvádélmi kiegészitése a Felsőház előtt.* MONE, Budapest: Orvostársadalmi Szemle, 1 August 1941.
4. Cs.23.014/5–1944 szám.
5. Kalman. See B. Mezey et al. (eds.) *A magyarországi cigánykérdés dokumentumokban (1422–1985).* 1986.

6.   Lucidus (pseudonym). See Mezey, above.
7.   Vassanyi, I., *Cigányködex*, Magyar Kőzigazgatás, 1936/44, 1936/46, 1936/47.
8.   Almási, I., In *Fuggetlen Magyarország*, 20 Marc 1937.
9.   Szentkirályi, Z., 'A cigányok arzenobenzol-érzékenysége, Kassa, 1941' in G. Gervai, *Emberkisérletek Kassán*. 1941.
10. Szentkirályi, Z., *A cigánykárdes*. 1942.
11. Orsös. See note 3.
12. Arrow Cross: The Hungarian fascist party. Nyilas: A member of the Arrow Cross party.
13. Lovas, 'Hitler is, Sztálin is deportálta őket' in *Amaro Drom*. 1991/7, p.9.
14. Erdős, I., 'Legalább a szavak' in *Palöcfőld*. 1997/3, pp.332–41.
15. Ibid.
16. Péntek, I., 'Németországba hurcolt zalai cigányok visszaemlékezései' in *Ùj Forrás*. 1978/3.
17. Bársony; Karsai, L.; Puskás (see notes 28, 38 and 18).
18. Puskás, B., 'Adalékok a cigánység II. Világháborús tragédiájához' in *Somogyi Kultúra*. 1995/6, 5, pp.47–50.
19. File 147/Hdm.korm.bizt./1944, Szombathely.
20. Vincze, P., 'Elfelejtett holocaust (2)' in *Ùj Magyarország*, 9 Julius 1997.
21. Schermann, V., 'Emberi Jogok? A cigánység jogvédelme 1945 előtt Magyarországon' in E. Varnagy (ed.) *Tanulmányok*. 1985.
22. See note 19.
23. MK rendőrség kaposvári állomásparancsnoksága SZ: 231/3–1944.
24. A tabi járás főszolgabiraöjatöl.
25. Tolna megye, pécsi IV, Csendőrkerületi parancs, 10 Oktober 1944.
26. Lakatos, M., 'A rettegés évei' in *Magyar Hirlap*, 28 Julius 1984.
27. Karsai, E., *Sostar? Miért?* 1994.
28. Bársony, J., 'Magyarországi cigány Holocaust' in *Phralipe*, Oktober 1996.
29. Puskás. See note 18.
30. Bársony. See note 28.
31. For the march from Mezőkövesd see also D. Kenrick and G. Puxon, *Gypsies under the Swastika*. 1995, p.103.
32. Varga, I., 'A sotet felho tortenete' in *Romano Nyevipe*. 1992/12.
33. Mezey. See note 5.
34. Bársony. See note 28.
35. Puskás. See note 18.
36. Schermann. See note 21.
37. In Péntek. See note 16.
38. Karsai, L., *A cigánykérdés Magyarországon (1919–1945)*. 1992.
39. See the accounts in E. Karsai (note 27) and Puskás (note 18).
40. See note 28.
41. Bari, K., 'Cigányok visszaemlékezései a Soah-ra' in *Múlt és Jővő*. 1978/3.
42. Lakatos, M., *A cigányok sorsa 1944–ben*. 1984.

43. Bársony and Puskás. See notes 28 and 18.
44. Karsai, L. See note 38.
45. In Bernáth, G. (ed.) *Porrajmos*. 2000.
46. Karsai, L., op. cit.
47. See note 27.

3. Reinhartz: The Genocide of the Yugoslav Gypsies

[*The author's historical notes have been omitted.* Ed.]

1. See Marushiakova and Popov, *Gypsies in the Ottoman Empire: A contribution to the history of the Balkans*. Hatfield: University of Hertfordshire Press. 2001.
2. See, however, p.92 of Vol. 2 in this series and D. Kenrick and G. Puxon, *Gypsies under the Swastika*. 1995, pp.80–1.
3. *Verordnungsblatt des Militärbefehlshabers in Serbien* Nr. 8, 31 May 1941, pp.84–9.
4. Royalist partisans.
5. i.e. Tito's partisans.
6. Nuremberg document NOKW 802.
7. Kenrick and Puxon, op. cit. p.119. See, however, Zimmermann, *Rassenutopie*, p.258.
8. Nine rare photographs that record only one such grave of eighteen Orthodox Roma, discovered at the end of the war in Kruševac, are in the Yugoslav State Archives, Fohd.-110, Aj-R2II-1026a.
9. Nuremberg documents MA 6 85 NOKW 1486.
10. See the article in Vol. 2 of this series by Giovanna Boursier.
11. Vuksević, Slavko, *Genocid u Nezavisnoj Držvi Hrvatskoj 1941 – skrivana stvarnost'* in *Vojno-Istorijski Glasnik* 1–2. 1994, pp.79–104.
12. Miletić, Antun, 'Mrtvi u Jasenovcu 1941–1945' in *Vojno-Istorijski Glasnik* 1–2. 1994, pp.145–60.
13. Paris, Edmond, *Genocide in Satellite Croatia, 1941–1945: A Record of Racial and Religious Persecutions and Massacres*. 1961, p.9. By comparison, 25,000 of Germany and Austria's 30,000 Gypsies perished.
14. Heinschink, Mozes F. and Ursula K. Hemetek, *Roma: Das unbekannte Volk: Schicksal and Kultur*. 1994, p.100.
15. Djilas, Milovan, *Wartime*. 1977, pp.11–12.
16. Paris, op. cit. pp.3, 11–12.
17. Ibid. pp.14–58.
18. Hefer, Stjepan, *Croatian Struggle for Freedom and Statehood*. 1979, p.108. Also see Dennis Reinhartz, 'Holokaust kao poslanje' in *Danas*, 15 April 1986, pp.27–8 and idem 'Aryanism in the Independent State of Croatia' in *The South Slav Journal 9*. Autumn–Winter 1986, pp.19–25.
19. Decree Regarding Race Membership. *Narodne Novine*, 30 April 1941, p.1.
20. *Hrvatski Narod*. 19 July 1941, 7. For an excellent document collection,

also see *Zlosini: Na Jugoslavenskim Prostorima u prvom i Drugom Svetskom Ratu. Zbornik Dokumenta. Tom I. Zlosini Nezavisne Države Hrvatske 1941–1945.* 1993.

21. For studies on Jasenovac and the Croatian camps, see Milan Bulajic, 'Jasenovac-System of Croatian Camps of Genocide – Untold Story-Dark Secrecy of the Holocaust in Former Yugoslavia (1941–1945)' [typewritten in Serbo-Croatian], 17pp., presented at The Second International Conference on Jasenovac, in Banja Luka, on 8–10 May 2000; idem *Ustaški Logori Smrti: Srpski Mit?*, 1989; Vladimir Dedijer, *The Yugoslav Auschwitz and the Vatican: The Croatian Massacre of the Serbs during World War II* (1992); and Antun Miletić, *Koncentracioni Logor Jasenovac 1941–1945* (1986).

22. Heinschink and Hemetek, op. cit. p.102.

23. Keller, Larry, 'Witness Ties Artuković, Killing' in *Press Telegram* (Long Beach, CA), 23 April 1986, p.7.

24. For example, see Great Britain, Foreign Office Weekly Political Intelligence Summaries, no. 83, p.15; no. 87, p15; no. 96, pp.15–16; Correspondence of the Foreign Office, Great Britain: Public Records Office. FO371, R791/1068/92, p.7; and FO371, R5331/850/92, pp.15–16.

25. Reprinted from Damodar Singhal, *Gypsies: Indians in Exile*, pp.128–9.

26. See the chapter on Yugoslavia in W. Guy, *Between past and future: The Roma of Central and Eastern Europe*. Hatfield: University of Hertfordshire Press. 2001.

4. Hanisch: Norway – the Final Solution is planned

1. This is Chapter 11 of Ted Hanisch, *Om Sigøynerspörsmålet*. Institut for Samfunnsforskning Oslo 1976, translated by Donald Kenrick and published with the permission of the author.

5. Kenrick: Resistance

1. *Guardian*, 5 February 1985.

2. Parcer (ed.) *Memorial Book: The Gypsies at Auschwitz-Birkenau*. 1993, p.1517.

3. Richter, B, 'Auschwitz, matricola Z.1963' in *Lacio Drom*. 1965/2.

4. *Libération*, 6 March 1995, p.3.

5. Interview with Grattan Puxon.

6. Marcel Courbet p.c.

7. *Roma Rights*. Summer 1997, p.34.

8. Francesca Comisso p.c.

9. See map in M. Gilbert, *The Holocaust: Maps and Photographs*. 1994.

10. p.c.

11. Kuna Cevcet, interviewed by Grattan Puxon.

12. Material in the archives of the Brno Romany Museum.
13. Nečas, Ctibor in *Lacio Drom*. 1994/2, p.19.
14. Acković, Dragoljub, *Ma Bister. Roma suffering in Jasenovac Camp*. 1995, pp.68–9.
15. p.c.
16. *Roma Rights*. Summer 1997, p.32.
17. For Holland, see Leo Lucassen, *En men noemde hen Zigeuners*. 1990, p.221 and *Drom* passim.
18. Sonnemann, Toby, *Shared sorrows: A Gypsy family remembers the Holocaust*. Hatfield: University of Hertfordshire Press. 2002, chapter 5.
19. Reparations claim.
20. Mayerhofer, Claudia, *Dorfzigeuner*. 1988, p.47.
21. p.c.
22. Based on Zekia's claim for residence in Germany after the war.
23. Neilands, Janis, 'Lo sterminio dei Roma in Lettonia' in *Lacio Drom*. 1995–1, pp.13–14.

6. Kalinin: Roma in the Resistance in the Soviet Union

1. *Military Encyclopaedia*. 1988, pp.322–3.
2. Dolgov, Ivan, *Radi zhizni na ziemli* (for the sake of life), Vols. 1–2. 1983, pp.69–71.

7. Ludi: Swiss Policy towards Roma and Sinti Refugees from National Socialism

1. This essay is based on investigations carried out by Thomas Huonker and myself for the Independent Commission of Experts – Switzerland Second World War (ICE), as well as previous research by Thomas Huonker. The full-length report is available as a book Thomas Huonker and Regula Ludi, *Roma, Sinti und Jenische. Die Schweizerische Zigeunerpolitik zur Zeit des Nationalsozialismus*. Zurich, 2001. The study owes its publication to the untiring support given this project by Sybil Milton, until her death in October 2000 vice-president of the ICE, Jacques Picard and Jacob Tanner.
2. Bertogg, Hercli, 'Aus der Welt der Bündner Vaganten' in *Schweizerisches Archiv für Volkskunde* 43. 1946, pp.37–46.
3. Jörger, Josef, 'Die Familie Zero' in *Archiv für Rassen- und Gesellschaftsbiologie einschliesslich Rassen- und Gesellschaftshygiene* 2 (1905) pp.495–559; id. *Psychiatrische Familiengeschichten*. Berlin, 1919. For more detail, see Huonker and Ludi, op. cit. pp.30–8, with the corresponding literature there.
4. Milton, Sybil, 'Persecuting the Survivors: The Continuity of Antigypsism in Post-war Germany and Austria' in Susan Tebbutt (ed.) et al. *Antigypsism in Postwar Germany*. Providence (1998); Gilad Margalit,

'Die deutsche Zigeunerpolitik nach 1945' in *Vierteljahreshefte für Zeitgeschichte* 45 (1997) pp.557–88; Mathias Winter, 'Kontinuitäten in der deutschen Zigeunerforschung und Zigeunerpolitik' in *Beiträge zur nationalsozialistischen Gesundheits- und Sozialpolitik* 6 (1988) pp.135–52.

5. Leimgruber, Walter; Thomas Meier and Roger Sablonier, *Das Hilfswerk für die Kinder der Landstrasse. Historische Studie aufgrund der Akten der Stiftung Pro Juventute im Schweizerischen Bundesarchiv*, ed. Schweizerisches Bundesarchiv, Bern. 1998.

6. *Radgenossenschaft der Landstrasse* (est. 1975) is the umbrella organization of the Jenische. The Foundation Naschet Jenische (est. 1986) and the association Children of the Highway (*Kinder der Landstrasse*, est. 1986) promote the rehabilitation of victims of the coercive measures, while the Travelling Gypsy Centre (est. 1984) and the foundation A Future for Swiss Travellers (*Zukunft für Schweizer Fahrende*, est. 1997) are dedicated to the preservation and promotion of Jenische culture. The Mission Tzigane is also engaged in furthering and protecting the rights of the Travellers.

7. Glaus, Urs, 'Fahrende in der Schweiz: Gefangen zwischen direkter und indirekter Diskriminierung' in Walter Kälin (ed.) *Das Verbot ethnisch-kultureller Diskriminierung: Verfassungs- und menschenrechtliche Aspekte.* Basel (1999) pp.141–8; Andreas Rieder, 'Indirekte Diskriminierung – das Beispiel der Fahrenden' in Kälin op. cit. pp.149–75; Theo van Boven, 'The Concept of Discrimination in the International Convention on the Elimination of All Forms of Racial Discrimination' in Kälin, op. cit. pp.27–46.

8. On the situation of the non-sedentary in the 19th century see Clo Meyer, '*Unkraut der Landstrasse. Industriegesellschaft und Nichtsesshaftigkeit*'. Disentis, 1988; Thomas D. Meier and Rolf Wolfensberger, *"Eine Heimat und doch keine". Heimatlose und Nichtsesshafte in der Schweiz (16-19. Jahrhundert)* Zurich. 1998. On the persecution of the Swiss Jenische in the 20th century, see Edith Gerth, 'Kinderraubende Fürsorge. Die Umerziehung der Schweizer Jenischen durch die Stiftung Pro Juventute' in Mark Müntzel and Bernhard Streck (eds.) *Kumpania und Kontrolle. Moderne Behinderungen zigeunerischen Lebens.* Giessen (1981) pp.129–66; Thomas Huonker, *Fahrendes Volk – verfolgt und verfemt. Jenische Lebensläufe.* Zurich, 1987; Setfan Keller, *Maria Theresia Wilhelm, spurlos verschwunden. Geschichte einer Verfolgung.* Zurich, 1991; Leimgruber, Meier and Sablonier, *Das Hilfswerk für die Kinder der Landstrasse. Historische Studie aufgrund der Akten der Stiftung Pro Juventute im Schweizerischen Bundesarchiv*, ed. Schweizerisches Bundesarchiv, Bern.

9. For a detailed treatment of the problem of source materials, see Huonker and Ludi, op. cit. pp.19–25. For example, the Gypsy Registry, created in

1911, cannot be tracked down, it has disappeared.

10. Independent Commission of Experts (ed.) *Switzerland and Refugees in the Nazi Era*, Bern. 1999, pp.132–6.

11. Bundesblatt. 1906/4, p.350; Amtliche Sammlung, N.S., Vol. 22. 1906, p.417.

12. Egger, Franz, 'Der Bundesstaat und die fremden Zigeuner in der Zeit von 1848 bis 1914' in *Studien und Quellen* 8. 1982, pp.63ff.

13. Swiss Federal Prosecutor's Office.

14. Kaiser, head of the Justice Dept. in the FJPD, to the chief of the FJPD, 18 October 1912, BAR E 21 / 20606.

15. Leupold, Eduard, Programm betreffend Bekämpfung der Zigeunerplage, 3 October 1911, BAR E 21 / 20605.

16. Auszug aus der Zigeunerregistratur des schweiz. Justiz- und Polizeidepartements, 22 April 1914, BAR E 21 / 20608. On the Gypsy Central Office in Munich, see Rainer Hehemann, *Die* 'Bekämpfung *des Zigeunerunwesens' im Wilheminischen Deutschland und in der Weimarer Republik, 1871–1933*. Franfurt/Main. 1987.

17. Kaiser to the head of the FJPD, 18 October 1912; *Ausweisung der Zigeuner*, final report of the Police Department, Leupold, 25 October 1912, BAR E 21 / 20606.

18. District letter of the FJPD, 27 June 1913, BAR E 4260 (C), 1974/34, Vol. 46; Annual Report of the Witzwil Prison 1915, StAB BB 4.2.213. See also Franz Egger, 'Der Bundesstaat und die fremden Zigeuner in der Zeit von 1848 bis 1914' in *Studien und Quellen* 8. 1982.

19. Grivel to the Direction of the Central Police Fribourg, 9 July 1919, ArFR DP d 2630.

20. Bericht von Prof. Heinrich Zangger über die IKPK-Tagung vom 15–20 October 1932, BAR E 4260 (C) 1, Vol. 3.

21. Meier, Thomas D. and Rolf Wolfensberger, 'Eine Heimat und doch keine' in *Heimatlose und Nichtsesshafte in der Schweiz (16–19. Jahrhundert)*. Zurich, 1998.

22. See Hawkins, Mike, *Social Darwinism in European and American Thought 1860-1945. Nature as Model and Nature as Threat*. Cambridge, 1997. For Switzerland, Urs Germann, *Psychiatrie und Strafjustiz*. Bern, 1998.

23. Wippermann, Wolfgang, *Wie die Zigeuner: Antisemitismus und Antiziganismus im Vergleich*. Berlin (1997) p.115; Leo Lucassen, *Zigeuner. Geschichte eines polizeilichen Ordnungsbegriffs in Deutschland 1700–1945*. Köln, 1996; also Piers Beirne, *Inventing Criminology. Essays on the Rise of the Homo Criminalis*. Albany, 1993.

24. Jörger, Josef, *Psychiatrische Familiengeschichten*. Berlin. 1919, pp.4, 1. Josef Jörger was director of the mental asylum Waldhaus near Chur. On his work, see Joachim S. Hohmann, *Robert Ritter und die Erben der Kriminalbiologie. Zigeunerforschung im Nationalsozialismus und in*

Westdeutschland im Zeichen des Rassismus. Frankfurt/Main. 1991, p.41.

25. Maier, Hans W., 'Die nordamerikanischen Gesetze gegen die Vererbung von Verbrechen und Geistesstörung und deren Anwendung' in *Juristisch-psychiatrische Grenzfragen. Zwanglose Abhandlungen.* Halle. 1911, p.4. See similar also in Emil Oberholzer, 'Kastration und Sterilisation von Geisteskranken in der Schweiz' in *Juristisch-psychiatrische Grenzfragen. Zwanglose Abhandlungen.* Halle. 1911, p.137.

26. Waltisbühl, Rudolf, *Die Bekämpfung des Landstreicher- und Landfahrertums in der Schweiz. Eine Untersuchung der rechtlichen und soziologischen Stellung der Nichtsesshaften in der Schweiz.* Aarau. 1944, pp.157, 159.

27. Galli, *Landplage.* 1999, p.120. On race research in Switzerland, see Zürcher, *Tradition,* 1995; Schwank, *Diskurs,* 1996.

28. Maier, Hans W., 'Die nordamerikanischen Gesetze gegen die Vererbung von Verbrechen und Geistesstörung und deren Anwendung' in *Juristisch-psychiatrische Grenzfragen. Zwanglose Abhandlungen.* Halle. 1911, p.24. Hans W. Maier later became director of the Zurich Psychiatric Clinic Burghölzli.

29. Kramer, Brigitte, 'Wie Arme zu Kranken warden. Die Einführung des Eheverbotsartikels im Schweizerischen Zivilgesetzbuch 1907 und seine Anwendung in der Zürcher Gerichtspraxis 1912–1938'. Zurich, 1999 (unpublished master's thesis).

30. Kühl, Stefan, *Die Internationale der Rassisten. Aufstieg und Niedergang der internationalen Bewegung für Eugenik und Rassenhygiene im 20. Jahrhundert.* Franfurt/New York, 1997; for Switzerland see Nadja Ramsauer and Thomas Meier, 'Blinder Fleck im Sozialstaat. Eugenik in der Deutschweiz' traverse 2 (1995) pp.117–21; Regina Wecker, 'Frauenkörper, Volkskörper, Staatskörper. Zur Eugenik und Politik in der Schweiz' in *Itinera* 20 (1998) pp.209–26; Gilles Jeanmonod and Geneviève Heller, 'Eugénisme et contexte socio-politique. L'exemple de l'adoption d'une loi sur la stérilisation des handicapés et malades mentaux dans le canton de Vaud en 1928' in *Schweizerische Zeitschrift für Geschichte* 50, 1 (2000) pp.20–44; Roswitha Dubach, 'Die Verhütung minderwertiger Nachkommen über den Zugriff auf den Frauenkörper. Sterilisationsdiskurs und –praxis in der Deutschschweiz bis 1945'. Zürich, 1999 (unpublished master's thesis). There are still substantial gaps in research in this regard.

31. On giving recognition to eugenic measures in National Socialist Germany, see Rudolf Waltisbühl, *Die Bekämpfung des Landstreicher- und Landfahrertums in der Schweiz. Eine Untersuchung der rechtlichen und soziologischen Stellung der Nichtsesshaften in der Schweiz.* Aarau. 1944, p.157.

32. DDS 11, document 175, pp.542f., files in BAR E 4260 (C) 1974/34, Vol. 22.

33.   Foreword by Heinrich Häberlin, President, Foundation Board of Pro
      Juventute in *Kinder der Landstrasse*. Zurich, 1927; see also Edith Gerth,
      'Kinderraubende Fürsorge. Die Umerziehung der Schweizer Jenischen
      durch die Stiftung Pro Juventute' in Mark Müntzel and Bernhard Streck
      (eds.) *Kumpania und Kontrolle. Moderne Behinderungen zigeunerischen
      Lebens*. Giessen (1981) pp.129–66; Thomas Huonker, *Fahrendes Volk –
      verfolgt und verfemt. Jenische Lebensläufe*. Zurich, 1987; Leimgruber,
      Meier and Sablonier. *Das Hilfswerk für die Kinder der Landstrasse.
      Historische Studie aufgrund der Akten der Stiftung Pro Juventute im
      Schweizerischen Bundesarchiv*, ed. Schweizerisches Bundesarchiv, Bern,
      1998.
34.   There are no precise data. A list based on information of Pro Juventute
      gives 619 cases. Leimgruber, Meier and Sablonier, op. cit. pp.30ff. As late
      as 1968, the psychiatrist Benedikt Fontana justified forcible removal of
      children in a study on the heredity of the non-sedentary trait: Benedikt
      Fontana, 'Nomadentum und Sesshaftigkeit als psychologische und
      psychopathologische Verhaltensradikale: Psychisches Erbgut oder
      Umweltsprägung. Ein Beitrag zur Psychopathie' in *Psychiatria Clinica* 1.
      1968, pp.340–66.
35.   Leimgruber, Meier and Sablonier, op. cit. p.81; see also references to the
      maltreatment and sexual abuse of children in the literary work of Mariella
      Mehr and Peter Paul Moser. *Autobiographie*. Thusis, 2000.
36.   On the ICPC more generally: Fenton Bresler, *Interpol*, 1995; Laurent
      Greilsamer, *Interpol. Le siege de soupçon*. Paris, 1986. The Swiss
      delegates Werner Müller and Heinrich Zangger voted for Heydrich's
      election. See Goldenberg, *La commission de police internationale
      criminelle*. Paris. 1953, p.96.
37.   Errichtung einer Internationalen Zentrale zur Bekämpfung des
      Zigeunerunwesens [þ_], 1935, BAR E 4326 (A) 1991/157, Vol. 1. On the
      importance of such empirical work in regard to racial persecution, see
      Sybil Milton, 'Registering Civilians and Aliens in the Second World War'
      in *Jewish History* 11, 2. 1997.
38.   Bader, Kurt, 'Bekämpfung des Zigeunerunwesens'. Paper at the 11th
      conference of the International Criminal Police Commission 1935. At the
      same conference, the ICPC praised the National Socialist measures against
      habitual criminals as exemplary. BAR E 4326 (A) 1991/157, Vol. 1.
39.   Bresler Fenton, *Interpol. Der Kampf gegen das internationale Verbrechen
      von den Anfängen bis heute*. Munich (1993) pp.93ff.; Adolf Burger,
      Unternehmen Bernhard. Berlin, 1992.
40.   Dressler, Oskar, *Die internationale Kriminalpolizeiliche Kommission und
      ihr Werk*. Berlin-Wannsee (1942) p.28; report by Müller, 1946, BAR E
      4260 (C) 1974/34, Vol. 44. There were no conferences because of the war,
      and relations were maintained primarily through written correspondence.
      For references to relevant sources, see Huonker and Ludi, op. cit. p.49.

41. On this, see the credulous and at times embroidered report by Rothmund in DDS 14, pp.859–69.
42. See Independent Commission of Experts, *Switzerland and Refugees in the Nazi Era*. Bern. 1999, pp.132f.
43. Landjäger Schneller's 'Spezialrapport betreffend übergabe der Zigeunerbande' of 9 January 1931 mentions information about fascist Gypsy policy obtained from an Italian official. BAR E 4264 (-) 1988/2, Vol. 314. See also Giovanna Boursier, 'La Persecuzione degli zingari nell'Italia fascista' in *Studi Storici* 4. 1996, pp.1065–82.
44. Report by Riedtmatten, 7 May 1930, BAR E 4264 (-) 1988/2, Vol. 314. The German expression *Zigauner* that is sometimes found is based on an erroneous etymological derivation of the term *Zigeuner* from the compound *Zieh Gauner* (itinerant thief). See Wippermann, op. cit.
45. Swiss envoy in Rome to Häberlin, 25 May 1930, BAR E 4264 (-) 1988/2, Vol. 314.
46. Unless otherwise noted, the reconstruction of this case is based on official source materials: BAR E 4264 (-) 1988/2, Vol. 314, dossiers P 36529. See also Huonker and Ludi, op. cit. pp.72–80. The dossier on the M. family begins in the autumn of 1929 and extends into 1933 when the last relatives of Carlo M. were naturalized. Important information is also from a personal conversation between Thomas Huonker, Tschawo and Martha M.
47. The death of the child is mentioned only in the accounts sheet of the Ticino authorities for 17 December 1930.
48. Baumann to the Lucerne Chief of Police Walther, 19 December 1936, BAR E 4264 (-) 1988/2, Vol. 314.
49. It is likely that the stateless family of musicians W., some of whose members had been born in Switzerland, was also expelled at this time. Another woman W. with a Swiss place of birth was deported in 1943 to Auschwitz, see *Gedenkbuch: Die Sinti und Roma im Konzentrationslager Auschwitz-Birkenau*. Munich (1993) Vol. I, no. 10056. p.674.
50. Bohny-Reiter, Friedel, *Vorhof der Vernichtung. Tagebuch einer Schweizer Schwester im französischen Internierungslager Rivesaltes 1941-1942*. Konstanz (1995) pp.53 and 125, mentions a Gypsy woman speaking Swiss German who was able to flee from Rivesaltes. There were also Gypsy children in the camp speaking Swiss German and Alsatian German.
51. Note, 7 June 1941, BAR E 4264 (-) 1988/2, Vol. 314.
52. See the dossiers in BAR E 4264 (-) 1988/2, Vol. 317; see also Independent Commission of Experts op. cit. pp.35f.
53. Weiss to Fröhlicher, 27 May 1940, BAR E 27/ 9564. On the May deportation, see Romani Rose, *Der nationalsozialistische Völkermord an den Sinti und Roma in Deutschland*. Heidelberg (1995) pp.88–96; Michael Zimmermann, *Rassenutopie und Genozid. Die nationalsozialistische Lösung der Zigeunerfrage*. Hamburg (1996) pp.173f. On the state of knowledge in Switzerland. Independent Commission of Experts, op. cit.

Bern. 1999, pp.89ff.

54.   Ludwig, Carl, 'Die Flüchtlingspolitik der Schweiz in den Jahren 1933 bis
       1955'. Bericht an den Bundesrat zuhanden der eidgenössischen Räte.
       Bern. 1957, p.234.

55.   Customs Head Office to the Department for Foreign Affairs, 6 July 1939,
       BAR E 2002 (D) 1, Vol. 95.

56.   Katers, Drummers. 1992, p.178.

57.   AEG Ef 2, 71, catalogue card no. 8549; see also Dieter Schulz-Köhn,
       Django Reinhardt. Ein Porträt. Wetzlar. 1960, p.40.

58.   StAB BB 4.2, 2220, dossier 4826/43 (reference from Henry Spira).

59.   Interrogation protocol, 28 August 1944, BAR E 4264 (-) 1985/196, Vol.
       1072. Samuel Plattner made a documentary film on the story of Anton
       Reinhardt: part of the exhibition in the Documentation and Cultural Center
       of German Sinti and Roma in Heidelberg is devoted to that film, see
       Romani Rose, *Den Rauch hatten wir täglich vor Augen. Der
       nationalsozialistische Völkermord an den Sinti und Roma.* Heidelberg.
       1999, pp.331–5.

60.   Report, station Koblenz to the police station Aarau, 29 August 1944, BAR
       E 4264 (-) 1985/196, Vol. 1072.

61.   State Archive Freiburg/Breisgau, F 179/6, packet no. 10–16, running nos.
       119–23, State Prosecutor's Office, notebook no. 5. He either concealed the
       order to report for forced sterilization from the Swiss officials, or they did
       not consider it relevant. In any event, the protocol contains no reference to
       this.

62.   Interrogation protocol, Aarau, 30 August 1944, BAR E 4264 (-) 1985/196,
       Vol. 1072. Anton Reinhardt's mother was married to Johann Bü. Anton
       was the son from her first marriage. In 1941, the family lived in the
       workers' barracks of the Swiss chemical firm Lonza in Waldshut. State
       Archive Freiburg/Breisgau, F 179/6, packet no. 10–16, running nos.
       119–23, State Prosecutor's Office Offenburg, notebook no. 1.

63.   See Ludwig, op. cit. pp.293f.; Independent Commission of Experts, op.
       cit. pp.146ff.

64.   Report, Border Police, 1st Customs District, Benken, 9 September 1944,
       BAR E 4264 (-) 1985/196, Vol. 1072.

65.   For the security camp in Rotenfels, Rottweil district, see Martin
       Weinmann, *Das nationalsozialistische Lagersystem.* Frankfurt/Main. 1990,
       p.172.

66.   State Archive Freiburg/Breisgau, F 179/6, packet no. 10–16, running nos.
       119–23, State Prosecutor's Office Offenburg, notebook no. 1. After the
       war, the War Crimes Investigation Unit conducted an investigation of the
       crime. It is likely that Anton R. was still alive when thrown into the grave,
       since there was no flesh on the fingertips of his exhumed corpse. The main
       perpetrator Karl Hauger was not sentenced to seven years imprisonment
       until 1961, in a verdict handed down by the Karlsruhe district court, 10

July 1961.

67. Lucassen, Leo, *En men noemde hen zigeuners: De geschiedenis van Kaldarasch, Ursari, Lowara en Sinti in Nederland: 1750-1944*. Amsterdam. 1990, pp.217f.

68. Documentation on this in BAR E 4264 (-) 1988/2, Vol. 142. On Dutch policy, see Lucassen, op. cit.

69. Ambassador of the Netherlands to the Police Department, 23 May 1931, BAR E 4264 (-) 1988/2, Vol. 142.

70. Correspondence, 1931, in BAR E 4264 (-) 1988/2, Vol. 142.

71. Swiss Consulate in Amsterdam to Rothmund, 17 March 1938, BAR E 4264 (-) 1988/2, Vol. 142. The Circus Krone appears in the files of the research institute headed by Robert Ritter, BAB, R 165/213.

72. Report by Jezler, n.d. [1938], Zigeuner in Holland, p.1. BAR E 4264 (-) 1988/2, Vol. 142.

73. Ibid.

74. Lucassen, op. cit. p.217. The Italian passports were in part forged; the Guatemalan passports had been issued for humanitarian reasons or for motives of personal profit.

75. Descendants of the family of artists B. who survived the war in the Netherlands are well-known musicians. With their Gypsy Jazz Formation they made the CDs *Basily, Antara* (CLCD no. 8046–040).

76. The other 2,897 Roma were murdered that same day in Auschwitz-Birkenau. See Danuta Czech, *Kalendarium der Ereignisse im Konzentrationslager Auschwitz Birkenau 1939-1945*. Hamburg. 1989, p.838.

77. Czech Danuta, Kalendarium der Ereignisse im Konzentrationslager Auschwitz Birkenau 1939–1945. Hamburg (1989) p.840; Archives of the State Museum Auschwitz-Birkenau; Gestapo tódz, pt. 6, p.100, IZ-8/Gestapo tódz/4a, no. 155917, Archive of the Memorial Buchenwald.

78. Katharina F. is listed in the main registry of the Gypsy Camp Auschwitz under the name of her second spouse W., with whom she probably never had a civil marriage, as are likewise her children Maria, Carolina, Anna, Bertti and Hanny, some of whom were born in Switzerland. On the transport list of Westerbork, she appears under the name Katharina W.-F. List Westerbork no. 160, *Gedenkbuch Auschwitz*, Vol. 1, p.716, no. 10721.

79. Schürch to Brenner, 21 March 1951, BAR E 4260 (C) 1974/34, Vol. 46.

80. Jezler to Chancellor Leimgruber, 20 July 1951, BAR E 4260 (C) 1974/34, Vol. 46. It cannot be ruled out that Roma and Sinti were not recognised as Gypsies at the border and thus were allowed across and found refuge.

81. On this, see in greater detail Huonker and Ludi, op. cit. pp.95–103, where there are also references to continuities in personnel in the ICPC and Interpol, and on Gypsy research in the post-war period.

8. Zimmermann: The National Socialist persecution of the Jews and Gypsies

In this article, I will only reference quotations, detailed studies of individual questions where relevant and recent or especially important literature.

1. For a comprehensive study of the Nazi persecution in addition to those listed, see also Martin Luchterhandt, *Der Weg nach Birkenau. Entstehung und Verlauf der nationalsozialistischen Verfolgung der Zigeuner.* 2000.

2. In a paper dealing with National Socialist persecution of the Gypsies, it is difficult to avoid the term 'Gypsy' (*'Zigeuner'*) despite its pejorative connotations, if the perspective of the state authorities and the majority society is to be presented.

3. See the controversy between Romani Rose and Yehuda Bauer: Romani Rose 'Für beide galt damals der gleiche Befehl: Eine Entgegnung auf Yehuda Bauers Thesen zum Genozid an den europäischen Juden, Sinti und Roma' in *Blätter für deutsche und internationale Politik*, Vol. 43 (1998) pp.467–72; Yehuda Bauer 'Es galt nicht der gleiche Befehl für beide: Eine Entgegnung auf Romani Rose', Ibid. pp.1380–90. There was a similar dispute between Gilad Margalit and Silvio Peritore: Gilad Margalit 'Rassismus zwischen Romantik und Völkermord' and Silvio Peritore 'Die Zigeunerfrage im Nationalsozialismus' in *Geschichte in Wissenschaft und Unterricht*, no. 10 (1999) pp.604–9; Gilad Margalit: Eine Antwort auf Silvio Peritore, Ibid. pp.610–16.

4. Wippermann, Wolfgang, *Wie die Zigeuner. Antisemitismus und Antiziganismus im Vergleich.* 1997, pp.149–72.

5. Lewy, Guenter, *Nazi persecution of the Gypsies.* 2000, pp.224–8.

6. See also Bauer, Yehuda, *Die dunkle Seite der Geschichte. Die Shoah in historischer Sicht* (2001) pp.85–94; Henry Friedlander, *Der Weg zum NS-Genozid. Von der Euthanasie zur Endlösung* (1997) pp.393–476; Peter Longerich, *Politik der Vernichtung. Eine Gesamtdarstellung der nationalsozialistischen Judenverfolgung* (1998) pp.571–3; Luchterhandt, op. cit. p.319f.; Margalit, *The uniqueness*; Michael Zimmermann, 'Zigeunerbilder und Zigeunerpolitik in Deutschland. Eine übersicht über neuere historische Studien' in *Werkstatt Geschichte* 25, Vol. 9. 2000, pp.43–8.

7. Broszat, Martin, 'Soziale Motivation und Führer-Bindung des Nationalsozialismus' in *Vierteljahrshefte für Zeitgeschichte*, 18. 1970, pp.403–6.

8. Mommsen, Hans, 'Auschwitz, 17 Juli 1942' in *Der Weg zur europäischen Endlösung der Judenfrage.* 2002, p.38.

9. Herbert, Ulrich, 'Vernichtungspolitik. Neue Antworten und Fragen zur Geschichte des Holocaust' in idem (ed.) *Nationalsozialistische Vernichtungspolitik 1939–1945. Neuere Forschungen und Kontroversen.*

10. Central Office for the Administration of Justice in the German States (Zentrale Stelle der Landesjustizverwaltungen), Ludwigsburg, AR 72 a/60,

Judgment against Wilhelm Wiebens et al., fols. 34–6.

11. Institute for Contemporary History, Munich, FA 514, *Dr. Koeppen über Hitlers Tischgespräche*, fols. 33ff. – Bericht Nr. 39, Führerhauptquartier, 3 October 1941, dort: 3, Abendessen 2.10.

12. Ibid.

13. For research on the Racial Hygiene Research Centre, see Michael Zimmermann, 'Mit Weigerungen würde also nichts erreicht: Robert Ritter und die Rassenhygienische Forschungsstelle im Reichsgesundheitsamt' in Gerhard Hirschfeld/Tobias Jersak (eds.) *Karrieren im Nationalsozialismus. Funktionseliten zwischen Mitwirkung und Distanz.* 2004.

14. Justin, Eva, *Lebensschicksale artfremd erzogener Zigeunerkinder und ihrer Nachkommen.* 1944, p.120.

15. Schubert, Ernst, 'Die verbotene Existenz der Zigeuner' in Rainer Erb (ed.) *Die Legende vom Ritualmord. Zur Geschichte der Blutbeschuldigung gegen die Juden* (1993) pp.179–200; Karl Härter, 'Kriminalisierung, Verfolgung und Überlebenspraxis der Zigeuner im frühneuzeitlichen Mitteleuropa' in Yaron Matras, Hans Winterberg and Michael Zimmermann (eds.) *Sinti, Roma, Gypsies. Sprache – Geschichte – Gegenwart.* 2003, pp.41–81.

16. From the copious literature on political, social and cultural anti-Semitism, note the study by Shulamit Volkov, *Antisemitismus als kultureller Code.* 2001.

17. Giere, Jacqueline (ed.) *Die gesellschaftliche Konstruktion des Zigeuners. Zur Genese eines Vorurteils.* 1996; Wulf D. Hund (ed.) *Zigeuner. Geschichte und Struktur einer rassistischen Konstruktion.* 1996; idem. (ed.) *Zigeunerbilder. Schnittmuster rassistischer Ideologie.* 2000; Wilhelm Solms and Daniel Strauß (eds.) *Zigeunerbilder in der deutschsprachigen Literatur.* 1995. See also Gilad Margalit, 'The image of the Gypsy in German Christendom' in *Patterns of Prejudice*, Vol. 33 (1999) pp.75-82.

18. Niethammer, Lutz, *Kollektive Identität. Heimliche Quellen einer unheimlichen Konjunktur.* 2000, p.440f.

19. Reichszentrale zur Bekämpfung des Zigeunerunwesens.

20. On the administrative location of the National Centre for the Fight against the Gypsy Menace, see Zimmermann, *Rassenutopie*, p.114. On the Criminal Investigation Department in the Third Reich, see Patrick Wagner, *Hitlers Kriminalisten. Die deutsche Kriminalpolizei und der Nationalsozialismus.* 2002.

21. Lucassen, Leo, *Zigeuner. Die Geschichte eines polizeilichen Ordnungsbegriffs in Deutschland 1700–1945.* 1996, pp.174–213 and 221–3.

22. In German-occupied Poland and the USSR, the definitions of the Nuremberg Laws were not taken into consideration in the practice of deportation and murder. There was likewise no explicit process of definition in the German-occupied countries of Belgium, Denmark,

Greece, Luxembourg, the Netherlands, Norway and Serbia. The allied states of Bulgaria, Croatia, Vichy France, Hungary, Italy, Romania and Slovakia passed regulations that generally copied the Nuremberg Laws. Practical implementation depended there on such factors as pressure from Nazi Germany, at times the counter-influence of the Roman Catholic Church, the point in time when legislation was set up and the geographical extension to old territory or to new territory that had been occupied during the war. See Raul Hilberg, *Die Vernichtung der europäischen Juden*, 1990, esp. pp.225f. (Poland) and 384–6 (USSR). English trans. *The Destruction of the European Jews*. New York. 1961.

23. Essner, Cornelia, *Die "Nürnberger Gesetze" oder die Verwaltung des Rassenwahns 1933–1945*. 2002.

24. Ritter, Robert, 'Die Zigeunerfrage und das Zigeunerbastardproblem' in *Fortschritte der Erbpathologie, Rassenhygiene und ihrer Grenzgebiete*, Vol. 3, no. 1 (1939) pp.2–20; idem, 'Primitivität und Kriminalität' in *Monatsschrift für Kriminalbiologie und Strafrechtsreform*, Vol. 31 (1940) pp.198–210.

25. The intent here was to exclude police informers from deportation.

26. Bundesarchiv Berlin, Erlasssammlung "Vorbeugende Verbrechensbekämpfung", RSHA, 29 January 1943.

27. An especially striking example was the fate of Sidonie Adlersburg. See Erich Hackl, *Abschied von Sidonie*. Erzählung. 1989, esp. p.88–94, and Ursula Baumhauer (ed.) *Abschied von Sidonie von Erich Hackl. Materialien zu einem Buch und seiner Geschichte*. 2000.

28. In Germany within the borders of 1937, between 20 and 25 thousand persons (the precise number is not known) were classified as Gypsies and Gypsies of mixed race. Some 15,000 of them were murdered between 1938 and 1945 (Zimmermann, *Rassenutopie*, p.381).

   In 1933, there were some 500,000 persons of the Jewish faith, and in 1939 there were 238,823 Jews in Germany including the category of *Geltungsjuden* (individuals considered Jews by definition) according to the Nuremberg Laws. Of these, some 165,200 were murdered by the National Socialists (in Arndt und Heinz Boberach, 'Deutsches Reich' in Wolfgang Benz (ed.) *Dimensionen des Völkermords. Die Zahl der jüdischen Opfer des Nationalsozialismus*. 1991, pp.23–65).

29. In the case of Austria, incorporated as the Ostmark into the German state in 1938, the Research Centre for Racial Hygiene gave an estimated figure of 11,000 Gypsies. According to recent estimates, the number of victims was more than 9,000. Österreichische Historikerkommission (ed.), Florian Freund, Gerhard Baumgartner and Harald Greifeneder, *Vermögensentzug, Restitution und Entschädigung der Roma und Sinti*, M.S., Vienna 2002, fols. 49–54; Baumgartner and Freund, 'Daten zur Bevölkerungsgruppe der burgenländischen Roma und Sinti 1945–2001' in *Zeitgeschichte*, Vol. 30 (March/April 2003), no. 2. 'Greifbar! Neue Forschungsansätze zu Roma

und Sinti', pp.91–105.

According to the Austrian census of 1934, there were 191,481 persons of the Jewish faith in the country. By the outbreak of the Second World War, some two-thirds of them had emigrated. Including those deported after 1941 from their countries of emigration, the total figure for Jewish victims of National Socialism from Austria amounts to 65,459 (Jonny Moser, 'Österreich' in Benz, *Dimensionen*, p.67–93.

30.   The number of Czech Gypsies is estimated at 6,500 for the year 1939. Of these, 4,495 were deported to Auschwitz-Birkenau, where more than 3,000 of them perished. In addition, 533 prisoners died in the Gypsy camps in Lety and Hodonín, most as a result of typhoid fever, inadequate nutrition, poor accommodation and exhausting manual labour. Others died in Auschwitz I, Buchenwald, Ravensbrück and other concentration camps where they were supposedly confined as asocial elements. "The real count of the Czech Roma or Sinti who had fallen victim to the mass extermination cannot be ascertained from the incomplete records" notes Ctibor Nečas. "What is certain, though, is that following liberation, a total of 583 Roma ex-inmates who had survived the oppression and suffering of 1939-1945 [...] return to their homes." (Nečas, *The Holocaust of Czech Roma*, p.213).

Of the 118,310 Jews registered on 15 March 1939 in the "Protectorate Bohemia and Moravia", some 78,000 were murdered (Eva Schmidt-Hartmann, 'Tschechoslowakei' in Benz, *Dimensionen*, pp.354–79).

31.   On Estonia, see Weiss-Wendt, *Extermination*. According to that study, nearly all Estonian Gypsies were murdered. That is also true for the estimated 800 to 850 Estonian Jews who fell into German hands in 1941. Gerd Robel, 'Sowjetunion' in Wolfgang Benz (ed.) *Dimensionen des Völkermords. Die Zahl der jüdischen Opfer des Nationalsozialismus.* 1991, pp.499–560 (especially 505–7, 556).

32.   Less than 1,000 persons classified as Gypsies or nomads in Belgium, France and the Netherlands were murdered, a comparatively small number in comparison with Eastern Europe and the Greater German Empire, see Zimmerman, *Rassenutopie*, pp.235–46 and 382. On the individual countries:

Belgium: Gotovitch, José, 'Verfolgung und Vernichtung belgischer Sinti und Roma' in Waclaw Dlugoborski (ed.) *Sinti und Roma im KL Auschwitz-Birkenau 1943–44. Vor dem Hintergrund ihrer Verfolgung unter der Naziherrschaft.* 1998, pp.209–26

France: Peschanski, Denis, *Les Tsiganes en France 1939–1946.* 1994; Marie-Christine Hubert, 'The internment of Gysies in France' in Donald Kenrick (ed.) *The Gypsies during the Second World War: Vol 2 In the shadow of the Swastika.* Hatfield: University of Hertfordshire Press. 1999, pp.59-88

The Netherlands: Sijes, B. A. et al., *Vervolging van Zigeuners in Nederland 1940–1945.* 1979; Leo Lucassen, *En men noemde hen zigeuners. De geschiedenis van Kaldarasch, Ursari, Lowara en Sinti in Nederland (1755–1944)*. 1990.

On the persecution of the Jews in these countries, see Juliane Wetzel, 'Frankreich und Belgien' in Benz, *Dimensionen*, pp.105–35, and Gerhard Hirschfeld, Niederlande, Ibid. pp.137–65.

33. Boursier, Giovanna, 'La persecuzione degli Zingari nell'Italia fascista' in *Studi Storici. Rivista trimestrale dell'Istituto Gramsci* 4 (1996), pp.1065–82 and 'Gypsies in Italy during the Fascist dictatorship' in Donald Kenrick (op. cit., above).

34. László Karsai in *A cigánykérdés Magyarországon 1919–1945: út a cigány Holocausthoz*. 1992, estimated the number of Roma persecuted in Hungary in 1944–5 at some 5,000, and the figure for those murdered at about 1,000. János Bársony ('An overview of the Roma holocaust in Hungary, 1939–1945' in *Civil Rights Booklet*, 2001, 1st issue, 4th booklet, pp.8–17) estimates that the number of victims of persecution was higher, and thinks further research is necessary to establish how many were killed.

See also the article by Katalin Katz in this volume.

On the persecution of the Jews in Hungary, see, László Varga, 'Ungarn' in Benz *Dimensionen*, pp.331–52, and more recently Christian Gerlach and Götz Aly, *Das letzte Kapitel. Realpolitik, Ideologie und der Mord an den ungarischen Juden 1944/45*. 2002.

35. Marushiakova Elena and Vesselin Popov, 'The Bulgarian Romanies during the Second World War' in Donald Kenrick (ed.) (see above) pp.89–94.

36. On the total scope of the murder of the Jews, see Benz, *Dimensionen*, and the texts there on Luxembourg, France, Belgium, the Netherlands, Denmark, Norway, Greece, Bulgaria, Yugoslavia, Czechoslovakia and Poland, and similarly, Eberhard Jäckel, Peter Longerich and Julius H. Schoeps (eds.) *Enzyklopädie des Holocaust. Die Verfolgung und Ermordung der europäischen Juden*. 1993.

37. *Croatia*: Biondich Mark, 'Persecution of Roma-Sinti in Croatia, 1941–1945' in United States Holocaust Memorial Museum – Center for Advanced Holocaust Studies (ed.) *Roma and Sinti. Under-Studied Victims of Nazism. Symposium Proceedings*. 2002, pp.33–48; *Romania*; Michelle Kelso, 'Gypsy Deportations from Romania to Transnistria 1942–44' in Donald Kenrick, Ibid. pp.95–130, estimates that 6,000 survived; Radu Ioanid, *The Holocaust in Romania. The Destruction of Jews and Gypsies under the Antonescu Regime, 1940–1944*. 2000, pp.225–37, states: "It is not really clear how many Gypsies perished in Transnistria. In any case, in May 1944, when the Romanian gendarmerie nominally registered all Gypsies who returned from Transnistria, the lists that were compiled did not contain more than six thousand names." (p.236); Viorel Achim, 'Die Deportation der Roma nach Transnistrien' in Mariana Hausleitner, Brigitte Mihok and Juliane Wetzel (eds.) *Rumänien und der Holocaust. Zu den Massenverbrechen in Transnistrien 1941–1944*. 2001, pp.101–12, arrives

at the following conclusion: "The lists assembled at the time contain only about 6,000 names, but it is likely that the number of survivors was greater. Their listing was carried out only after parts of the territory had been occupied by the Red Army and other areas had become a zone of battle. Many of those returning had not, as yet, reached their villages, so that a by no means insignificant number of Roma were not included in the count. It should also be noted that when the Romanian authorities and the army withdrew, some Roma stayed on in the area and were later dispersed into the interior of the Soviet Union. However, taking all possible sources of error into account, it can be assumed with high probability that about half of the 25,000 Roma deported died in Transnistria." Ioanid and Achim agree that persecution of the Roma under Antonescu did not approach the scope of the parallel persecution of the Jews.

9. Sandner: Criminal justice following the genocide of the Sinti and Roma

1. *FA Z*, 25 January 1991. A similar report also appeared in the Hessische/Niedersächsische Allgemeine (Kassel), 19 September 1991. For further references on this trial, see below. All the judgments cited here refer to the final version that was put into force. Otherwise, a reference is made to the fact that the verdict never became final.

2. Urteil des Landgerichts Siegen vom 4 März 1949, and Urteil im Revisionsverfahren vor dem Oberstem Gerichtshof für die Britische Zone in Köln vom 21 März 1950, in C. F. Rüter et al. (eds.) *Justiz und NS-Verbrechen. Sammlung deutscher Strafurteile wegen nationalsozialistischer Tötungsverbrechen* [hereafter: *Justiz und NS-Verbrechen*]. Amsterdam, 1970, Vol. IV, pp.157–89 and 309–27 (case nos. 124 and 127). For additional material about this trial, see below.
An earlier trial in Mecklenburg for participation in the arrest of Sinti and Roma led merely to the imposition of a non-custodial sentence. Urteil des Landgerichts Schwerin vom 29 Dezember 1947 (Az. Kst Ks 31/47), in C. F. Rüter et al. (eds.) *DDR-Justiz und NS-Verbrechen. Sammlung ostdeutscher Strafurteile wegen nationalsozialistische Tötungsverbrechen* [hereafter: *DDR-Justiz und NS-Verbrechen*]. Amsterdam/Munich, 2000 (case no. 1716).

3. Most of the relevant trials took place in the German Federal Republic. Alongside the already mentioned trial in the Soviet occupied Zone (Schwerin) we can so far only establish three trials in East Germany which featured Roma and Sinti as victims. See Urteil des Obersten Gerichts der DDR vom 6 April 1973 (Az. 1b USt 7/73) in the Rehabilitation Proceedings reversed by Urteil des Landgerichts Chemnitz vom 10 Oktober 1994 (Az. BSRH 491/94), both in *DDR-Justiz und NS-Verbrechen*, Vol. II (case no. 1041).

4. See, for example, H. Boberach, 'Die strafrectliche Verfolgung der Ermordung von Patienten in nassauischen Heil- und Pflegeanstalten nach 1945' in Landeswohlfahrtsverband Hessen (ed.) *Euthanasie in Hadamar. Die nationalsozialistische Vernichtungspolitik in hessischen Anstalten.* 1991, pp.165–74.

5. Bauer, Fritz, 'Im Namen des Volkes. Die strafrechtliche Bewältigung der Vergangenheit' in Helmut Hammerschmidt (ed.) *Zwanzig Jahre danach. Eine deutsche Bilanz 1945–1965.* 1965, pp.301–14, here 309.

6. The Einsatzgruppen were mobile killing squads. See, for example, the extensive files on trial proceedings in the Central State Archive Hesse, Wiesbaden, sec. 631a. See also Matthias Meusch, *Von der Diktatur zur Demokratie. Fritz Bauer und die Aufarbeitung der NS-Verbrechen in Hessen (1956–1968).* 2001.

7. Zülch, Tilman (ed.) *In Auschwitz vergast, bis heute verfolgt. Zur Situation der Roma (Zigeuner) in Deutschland und Europa.* 1979; Donald Kenrick, Grattan Puxon and Tilman Zülch, *Die Zigeuner. Verkannt – verachtet – verfolgt.* 1980; Donald Kenrick and Grattan Puxon, *Destiny of Europe's Gypsies.* 1972.

8. See, for example, Gesellschaft für bedrohte Völker (ed.) 'Sinti und Roma im ehemaligen KZ Bergen-Belsen am 27 Oktober 1979. Erste deutsche und europäische Gedenkkundgebung' in *Auschwitz vergast, bis heute verfolgt.* 1980.

9. Urteil des Landgerichts München vom 20 January 1960 (Az. 1 Ks 3/59) in *Justiz und NS-Verbrechen*, Vol. XVI, Amsterdam, 1976, pp.275–89 (series no. 488), here 280.

10. Urteil des Landgerichts München II vom 22 Dezember 1969 and Urteil des Langerichts Essen vom 8 Mai 1970 in *Justiz und NS-Verbrechen*, Vol. XXXIII (case nos. 721 and 731); Urteil des Landgerichts Kleve vom 15 Oktober 1976 and Urteil des Landgerichts Hannover vom 31 Juli 1981 in *Justiz und NS-Verbrechen* 1945-1999 forthcoming (case nos. 835 and 873). There were some judgements in similar cases in East Germany in the 1950s. Urteil des Landgerichts Magdeburg vom 25 Marz 1952 (Az. 11 StKs 348/48) in *DDR-Justiz und NS-Verbrechen*, Vol. VII, 2005 (case no. 1327); Urteil des Bezirkgerichts Neubrandenburg vom 12 November 1955 (Az. 1 Ks 164/55) in *DDR-Justiz und NS-Verbrechen*, Vol. III, 2003 (case no. 1099).

11. Bauer, p.307.

12. Urteil des Landgerichts Bonn vom 23 Juli 1965 (Az. 8 Ks 3/62) in *Justiz und NS-Verbrechen*, Vol. XXI, Amsterdam, 1979, pp.227–69, here 284; for the complete documentation of the judgments in this complex, see Ibid. pp.221–359 (series no. 594).

13. Urteil des Landgerichts Düsseldorf vom 3 September 1965 (Az. 8 1 Ks 2/64) in *Justiz und NS-Verbrechen*, Vol. XXII, Amsterdam, 1981, pp.19–220, here 20, 143, 146; for the complete documentation of the

judgments in this complex, see Ibid. pp.1–238 (series no. 594).

14. Urteil des Landgerichts Frankfurt a.M. vom 19/20 August 1965 (Az. 4 Ks 2/63) in *Justiz und NS-Verbrechen*, Vol. XXI, 1979, pp.381–837, here 792; for the complete documentation of the judgments in this complex, see Ibid. pp.361–887 (series no. 595).

15. Naumann, Bernhard, *Auschwitz. Bericht über die Strafsache gegen Mulka u. a. vor dem Schwurgericht Frankfurt*. 1968, p.283.

16. Urteil vom 19/20 August 1965, op. cit. p.540.

17. Ibid. p.537; Naumann, p.141–9; Staatliches Museum Auschwitz-Birkenau (ed.) *Auschwitz in den Augen der SS. Rudolf Höß, Pery Broad, Johann Paul Kremer*. 1997, pp.5–24 [here: Jerzy Rawicz, Vorwort, Ibid. p.5–24, esp. pp.7, 19–21; Pery Broad, Bericht, p.95–139, esp. pp.131–3, quotation, p.132].

18. Naumann, pp.23, 247.

19. Urteil vom 19/20 August 1965, op. cit. p.382.

20. Naumann, p.291.

21. Müller-Münch, Ingrid, 'Ein NS-Verfahren von besonderem Tempo' in *Frankfurter Rundschau*, 16 December 1987; press statements of the Central Council of German Sinti and Roma, 22 and 28 August 1991; *Oberhessische Presse* (Marburg), 23 August 1991.

22. Urteil des Landgerichts Siegen vom 24 Januar 1991 in *Justiz und NS-Verbrechen* forthcoming (series no. 909), *Frankfurter Allgemeine Zeitung*, 25 January 1991; *Frankfurter Rundschau*, 25 January 1991; *Hessische/Niedersächsische Allgemeine* (Kassel), 19 September 1991; Ulrich Friedrich Opfermann, *Siegerland und Wittgenstein im Nationalsozialismus. Personen, Daten, Literatur. Ein Handbuch zur regionalen Zeitgeschichte*. 2001, pp.90–6, 235. On the trip in 1964, see Naumann, pp.210–15.

23. Urteil des Landgerichts München I vom 21 Juli 1961 (Az. 22 Ks 1/61) in *Justiz und NS-Verbrechen*, Vol. XVII. 1977, p.658–708 (series no. 519); see also Michael Zimmermann, *Rassenutopie und Genozid*. 1996, pp.259–76.

24. Ibid. esp. pp.677, 683, 690, 697.

25. Urteil des Landgerichts Essen vom 29 März 1965 (Az. 29 Ks 1/64) in *Justiz und NS-Verbrechen*, Vol. XX, Amsterdam, 1979, pp.715–807, here 719; pp.754–8, 800f.; for the complete documentation of the judgments in this complex, see Ibid. pp.715–815 (series no. 588).

26. Urteil des Landgerichts Essen vom 10 Februar 1966 (Az. 29 Ks 1/65) in *Justiz und NS-Verbrechen*, Vol. XXIII. 1998, pp.127–200 (series no. 620), here pp.162–4, 170f. (quotation), 175; see Zimmermann, pp.260, 262.

27. Urteil des Landgerichts Hannover vom 14 Oktober 1971 and Urteil im Revisionsverfahren vor dem Bundesgerichtshof vom 11 Juni 1974 in *Justiz und NS-Verbrechen* forthcoming (series no. 760), see Zimmermann, p.262.

28. Urteil des Landgerichts Mainz vom 17 Juli 1969 in *Justiz und NS-*

Verbrechen forthcoming (series no. 712).

29. Urteil des Landgerichts Karlsruhe vom 6 März 1964 (Az. III Ks 4/63) in *Justiz und NS-Verbrechen*, Vol. XIX. 1978, pp.759–71, here pp.767, 769.

30. Urteil des Landgerichts Kassel vom 26 September 1991 in *Justiz und NS-Verbrechen* forthcoming (series no. 910), Wiesbadener Tageblatt, 18 September 1991; Die Tageszeitung *'taz'* (Berlin), 27 September 1991.

31. Browning, Christopher R., *Ganz normale Männer. Das Reserve-Polizieibataillon 101 und die Endlösung in Polen*. 1993.

32. Sandner, Peter, *Frankfurt. Auschwitz. Die nationalsozialistische Verfolgung der Sinti und Roma in Frankfurt am Main*. 1998, pp.283–91.

33. Copy, Einstellungsverfügung vom 28 August 1950 in Central State Archive North Rhine-Westphalia, Düsseldorf, list 231, no. 1535, fols. 21–37; Sandner, pp.290, 292–7.

34. *Kölner Stadtanzeiger*, 21/22 May 1960.

35. Investigation files: Central State Archive North Rhine-Westphalia, Düsseldorf, list 231, nos. 1535–40 and 1545–7, and Central State Archive Hesse, Wiesbaden, sec. 461, nos. 34141–3. On individual proofs, see Sandner, pp.302–12.

36. Ibid. pp.313–21.

37. Ibid. p.190.

38. Statements by Würth on 14 May 1959 in Stuttgart and Erhardt, 11 June 1959 in Tübingen, in Central State Archive North Rhine-Westphalia, Düsseldorf, list 231, no. 1536, fols. 194f., 217; Benno Müller-Hill, *Tödliche Wissenschaft. Die Aussonderung von Juden, Zigeunern und Geisteskranken 1933–1945*. 1985, pp.152–7, 180, 187; Zimmermann, pp.33, 390.

39. Einstellungsverfügung der Staatsanwaltschaft Stuttgart vom 29 Januar 1982 (Az. 7 [19] Js 928/81) in Central State Archive Hesse, Wiesbaden, sec. 461, no. 34142.

40. Fings, Karola and Frank Sparing, Regelung der Zigeunerfrage in Konkret 11 (1993), pp.26–9, here p.28 (quotation of the attorney); Sandner, p.311; Anklageschrift der Oberstaatsanwaltschaft Köln vom 20 Februar 1964, Verfahrenseröffnung vom 12 Mai 1964 (Az. 24 Ks 1/64) in Central State Archive North Rhine-Westphalia, Düsseldorf, list 231, no. 1547, fols. 664–96, 702a–702b.

41. Urteile des Landgerichts Siegen vom 4 März 1949, Urteile im Revisionsverfahren vor dem Obersten Gerichtshof für die Britische Zone in Köln vom 21 März 1950 in *Justiz und NS-Verbrechen*, Vol. IV. 1970, pp.157–89 (quotation p.169), pp.309–27 (series nos. 124, 127); Opfermann, pp.90–1, 94–6; Zimmermann, p.306.

42. Einstellungsverfügung des Oberstaatsanwalts bei dem Landgericht Frankfurt am Main vom 18 April 1958 (Az. 57 Js 1656/51, 4a Js 8874/54), Central State Archive Hesse, Wiesbaden, sec. 461, no. 32809, fols. 44–7; Sandner, pp.298–302.

43. Einstellungsverfügung der Staatsanwaltschaft beim Landgericht Frankenthal im Ermittlungsverfahren gegen Leo Karsten vom 30 Juli 1960 (Az. 9 Js 153/58), copy in Central State Archive North Rhine-Westphalia, Düsseldorf, list 231, no. 1538.

10. Wipperman: Compensation withheld: The denial of reparations to the Sinti and Roma

1. Quoted in Romani Rose (ed.) *Der nationalsozialistische Völkermord an den Sinti und Roma*. 1995, p.115.
2. Ibid.
3. Greußing, Fritz, 'Das offizielle Verbrechen der zweiten Verfolgung' in Tilman Zülch (ed.) *In Auschwitz vergast – bis heute verfolgt. Zur Situation der Roma (Zigeuner) in Deutschland und Europa*, Reinbek. 1979, pp.192–7; Arnold Spitta, 'Wiedergutmachung oder wider die Gutmachung', Ibid. pp.161–7; Ursula Körber, 'Die Wiedergutmachung und die Zigeuner' in *Beiträge zur nationalsozialistischen Gesundheitspolitik* 6 (1988), pp.165–75; Arnold Spitta, 'Entschädigung für Zigeuner? Geschichte eines Vorurteils' in Ludolf Herbst and Constantin Goschler (eds.) *Wiedergutmachung in der Bundesrepublik Deutschland*. 1989; Anne von Törne, Wiedergutmachung von Sinti und Roma. Bundesrepublik Deutschland, Republik österreich und Deutsche Demokratische Republik im Vergleich, M.A. thesis, Free University Berlin. 1992 (typescript).
4. See remarks by the Roma writer Matéo Maximoff in an essay published in 1946: 'Germany and the Gypsies from the Gypsies point of view' in *Journal of the Gypsy Lore Society* 25 (1946), p.104ff.
5. By contrast, in the *Guidelines for Recognition as Victims of the Nazi Regime*, issued 18 February 1950 by the GDR, it is stated that only those Gypsies should be recognised as victims who after 1945 had also preserved an irreproachable antifascist-democratic attitude. See *Gesetzblatt der Deutschen Demokratischen Republik*, no. 14. 18 February 1950, p.92ff.
6. This continuity in personnel was uncovered and proven by Romani Rose, *Bürgerrechte für Sinti und Roma. Das Buch zum Rassismus in Deutschland*. 1987, p.31ff.
7. See Rose, Ibid. p.35f.; Fritz Greußing, 'Die seltsamen Wege der NS-Zigeunerkartei' in *Pogrom* 12 (1981), no. 80/81, p.174.
8. See Brucker-Boroujerdi, Ute and Wolfgang Wippermann, 'Die Rassenhygienische und Erbbiologische Forschungsstelle im Reichsgesundheitsam' in *Bundesgesundheitsblatt* 32 (March 1989), pp.13–19.
9. This is doubtless a harsh judgment but is supported by the documentation. See R. Rose, *Bürgerrechte für Sinti und Roma*, p.31ff; Volker Berbüsse,

'Das Bild der Zigeuner in deutschsprachigen kriminologischen Lehrbüchern seit 1946. Eine erste Bestandsaufnahme' in *Jahrbuch für Antisemitismusforschung* 1 (1992), pp.117–51; Michael Schenk, *Rassismus gegen Sinti und Roma. Zur Kontinuität der Zigeunerverfolgung innerhalb der deutschen Gesellschaft von der Weimarer Republik bis zur Gegenwart.* 1994, p.368ff.

10. I documented such a case, see Wippermann, 'Mazurka Rose und der Artikel 16 des Grundgesetzes' in *Perspektiven. Die internationale StudenteInnenzeitung*, no. 7/8 (1991), pp.51–3. For a study in greater detail, see Wolfgang Wippermann, Christine Lehmann and Mazurka Rose, 'Two Gypsies in the Grip of German Bureaucracy' in Michael Burleigh (ed.) *Confronting the Nazi Past. New Debates on Modern German History*, London. 1996, pp.112–24.

11. Quoted in Körber, *Die Wiedergutmachung und die 'Zigeuner'*, p.170.

12. As stated in the Law on Compensation for National Socialist Injustice, passed on 12 August 1949 by the Council of States in the American Zone of Occupation. See Reinhard Freiherr v. Godin, *Rückerstattung feststellbarer Vermögensgegenstände in der amerikanischen und britischen Besatzungszone und in Berlin. Gesetze der Militärregierungen mit der Verordnung für Berlin*, 2nd ed. 1950, p.570ff.

13. *Bundesgesetzblatt* I (1953), p.1397ff.

14. 'Bundesgesetz zur Entschädigung für Opfer der nationalsozialistischen Verfolgung vom 29.6.1956' in *Bundesgesetzblatt* I (1956), p.559; 'Zweites Gesetz zur Änderung des Bundesentschädigungsgesetzes (BEG-Schlußgesetz)' in Körber, *Wiedergutmachung*, p.170

15. Several examples in Ulrich König, *Sinti und Roma unter dem Nationalsozialismus. Verfolgung und Widerstand.* 1989.

16. Cavalli-Sforza, Luca and Francesco, *Verschieden und doch gleich. Ein Genetiker entzieht dem Rassismus die Grundlage.* 1994; see also Wolfgang Wippermann, 'Was ist Rassismus? Ideologien, Theorien, Forschungen' in Barbara Danckwortt et al. (eds.) *Historische Rassismusforschung. Ideologien – Täter – Opfer.* Intro. by Wolfgang Wippermann. 1995, pp.9–33.

17. For a detailed treatment, see Wolfgang Wippermann, *Wie die Zigeuner. Antisemitismus und Antiziganismus im Vergleich.* 1997; see also Wippermann, *Antiziganismus – Entstehung und Entwicklung der wichtigsten Vorurteile.*

18. Runderlaß des Reichsführers SS und Chef der Deutschen Polizei im Reichsministerium des Innern vom 8.12.1938 in Ministerialblatt des Reichs- und Preußischen Ministers des Innern, 99, no. 51. 14 December 1938, pp.2105–10, reproduced in Wippermann, *Geschichte der Sinti und Roma in Deutschland. Darstellung und Dokumente.* 1993, p.80ff. [*This decree was issued one month after the 9 November pogrom against the Jews.* Ed.].

19. Ausführungsanweisung des Reichskriminalpolizeiamtes vom 1.3.1939 zum Runderlaß des Reichsführers SS und Chef der Deutschen Polizei im Reichsministerium des Innern vom 8.12.1938 in Deutsches Kriminalpolizeiblatt (Sonderausgabe), 12 (20 March 1939), reproduced in Wippermann, *Geschichte der Sinti und Roma*.

20. They will not be enumerated here. On this, see Brucker-Boroujerdi and Wippermann, *Die 'Rassenhygienische und Erbbiologische Forschungsstelle'*, p.13ff.; Wippermann, *Geschichte der Sinti und Roma*, p.81.

21. Küster, Otto et al., *Bundesentschädigungsgesetzes. Bundesergänzungsgesetz zur Entschädigung für Opfer der nationalsozialistischen Verfolgung (BEG) vom 18 September 1953*. Kommentar. 1955, p.48.

22. Partially reproduced in Tilman Zülch (ed.) *In Auschwitz vergast – bis heute verfolgt*, pp.168–70.

23. Cf. the concurring critique in Greußing, 'Das offizielle Verbrechen der zweiten Verfolgung'; Spitta, 'Wiedergutmachung oder wider die Gutmachung'; Körber, 'Die Wiedergutmachung und die Zigeuner'; Spitta, 'Entschädigung der Zigeuner?'; Schenk, *Rassismus gegen Sinti und Roma*, p.319ff.

24. BGH-Urteil vom 18.12.1963 in *Rechtsprechung zum Wiedergutmachungsrecht*. 1964, p.209ff. See also Schenk, *Rassismus*. p.327f.

25. See the Runderlaß des Reichs- und Preußischen Ministers des Innern vom 26.11.1935 über das 'Verbot der Rassenmischehen' in Ministerialblatt für die inne Verwaltung (1935), no. 49, cols. 1429–34, reproduced in Wippermann, *Geschichte der Sinti und Roma*, p.77.

26. This was the conclusion of a dissertation written at the time: Werner K. Höhne, 'Die Vereinbarkeit der deutschen Zigeunergesetzte mit dem Reichsrecht, insbesondere der Reichsverfassung' diss. jur., Heidelberg. 1929.

27. This resolution in the form of a so-called hardship allowance became law on 26 August 1981, 16 months before the deadline for filing a claim. See Schenk, *Rassismus gegen Sinti und Roma*, p.329; Rose, *Bürgerrechte für Sinti und Roma*, p.59.

28. Drucksache des Deutschen Bundestages 10/6287 vom 31.10.1986, p.34.

29. Ibid. p.471.

30. I rely here on conversations I had in September 2000 with American lawyers in Washington representing clients who had not yet been compensated. I have to date not been able to find any written support for this thesis.

31. For a detailed discussion, see Wolfgang Wippermann, 'Wie mit den Juden'? Der nationalsozialistische Völkermord an den Sinti und Roma in Politik, Rechtsprechung und Wissenschaft in *Bulletin für Faschismus- und*

Weltkriegsforschung, no. 15 (2000), pp.3–29.

32. In the rather voluminous research on these negators, revisionists and Auschwitz deniers, the denial of the Porrajmos goes unmentioned or is noted only very marginally; for a more detailed treatment, see Wippermann, *Wie die Zigeuner*, p.195ff.

11. Tebbutt: History and memory: The genocide of the Romanies

1. Bhabha, Homi (ed.) *Nation and Narration.* 1990, p.4.
2. Acton, Thomas, *Authenticity, Expertise, Scholarship and politics: Conflicting Goals in Romani Studies.*1998, p.6.
3. For cultural imperialism see J. Tomlinson, *Cultural Imperialism: A Critical Introduction.* 1991, pp.70–101.
4. The IRU has also been recognised by the EU and OSCE.
5. Novick, Peter, *The Holocaust and Collective Memory: The American Experience.* 1999, p.223.
6. Zimmermann, M., op. cit. pp.231–9 and notes pp.386–94; L. Jochimsen, 'Wie leben die Zigeuner in der Bundesrepublik?' in *Soziale Welt.* 1962 Heft. 12, pp.370–8.
7. The spelling varies.
8. The Romani term means 'devouring'.
9. Lewy, G., op. cit. p.217.
10. Ibid. p.223.
11. Wippermann, op. cit. pp.135–72.
12. Kenrick, D. (ed.) *The Gypsies during the Second World War: Vol. 2 In the shadow of the Swastika.* Hatfield: University of Hertfordshire Press. 1999, pp.171–89.
13. Op. cit. p.22. On the opposite page are photos of a Gypsy woman prisoner and child.
14. Op. cit. p.241–77.
15. Op. cit. p.275.
16. Heuss, Herbert, *Die Verfolgung der Sinti in Mainz und Rheinhessen.* 1996, p.15.
17. Engbring-Romang, U., *Marburg. Auschwitz: Zur Verfolgung der Sinti in Marburg und Umgebung.* 1998, pp.13–14. See particularly also the section on sterilisation pp.129–40.
18. Benz, W., 'Vorurteil und Realität: Das Lager Marzahn' in *Feinbild und Vorurteil.* 1996, pp.141–2.
19. Fings, K. and F. Sparing, 'Das Zigeunerlager in Köln/Bickendorf 1935/1958' in *1999: Zeitschrift f. Sozialgeschichte des 20 und 21 Jahrhunderts.* 1991.
20. Heuss, op. cit. p.97.
21. See E. Bamberger and A. Ehmann (eds.) *Kinder und Jugendliche als Opfer*

des Holocausts. 1995, p.75.

22.   Ibid. p.80.
23.   Ibid. p.174.
24.   Riechert, op.cit. p.135.
25.   Milton, S., *The story of Karl Stojka: A Childhood in Birkenau.* 1992.
26.   Supple, C., op.cit. p.178.
27.   Yoors, J., op.cit. p.145.
28.   Ibid. p.38.
29.   Said, Edward, *Culture and Imperialism.* 1993.
30.   For an analysis of Ceija Stojka's work see S. Tebbutt (ed.) *Sinti und Roma: Gypsies in German-speaking Society and Literature.* 1998. p.137–9.
31.   Op. cit. p.51.
32.   Ibid. p.105.
33.   Op. cit. p.9.
34.   Op. cit. p.51.
35.   Ibid. p.117.
36.   Relatively little attention has been paid to the experiences of Romani women. Six pages of an account of Auschwitz by Stuttgart-born Elizabeth Guttenberger will be found in Harald Roth (ed.) *Verachtet, verstossen, vernichtet: Kinder- und Jugendjahre unterm Hakenkreuz.* 1995.
37.   Op. cit. p.87.

12. Tegel: Leni Riefenstahl's failure of memory: The Gypsy extras in *Tiefland*

1.   Barkhausen, Hans, 'Footnote to the History of Riefenstahl's Olympia', *Film Quarterly*, 28, 1 (Fall 1974), pp.8–12. Erwin Leiser, *Nazi Cinema*, trans. Gertrud Mander and D. Wilson. London. 1974, quotes (pp.140–1) a letter of Goebbels to the Charlottenburg court dated 30 January 1936: 'The Olympia-Film Co. Ltd. is being founded at the government's request and with government funds...... since the state is unwilling to appear publicly to be the producer of the film.' And one month later: 'It is clearly impracticable to have the Treasury itself acting as film producer.' See also Rainer Rother, *Leni Riefenstahl, The Seduction of Genius*, trans. Martin H. Bott. London, New York: Con 2002, pp.81–3.
2.   Riefenstahl, Leni, *The Memoirs of Leni Riefenstahl: The Sieve of Time.* London. 1992, pp.101–3; Jürgen Trimborn, *Riefenstahl: eine deutsche Karriere.* Berlin: Aufbau. 2002, pp.125–36.
3.   Trimborn, *Riefenstahl: eine deutsche Karriere*, pp.298–300.
4.   Rother, *Leni Riefenstahl*, pp.99–103.
5.   Bundesarchiv, Berlin (cited hereafter as BArch), R 43/810b, Bormann to Lammers, 2 August 1942; Lammers to Funk, 6 August 1942; Funk to Lammers, 17 August 1942; Bormann to Lammers, 9 May 1943.

6. BArch R43II/810b, Bormann to Lammers, 2 August 1942. See also Rother, *Leni Riefenstahl*, pp.124, 234, n.21–3.
7. BArch, R43II/810b, Funk to Goebbels 11 March 1942.
8. BArch R43II/810b, Bormann to Lammers, 9 May 1943. Riefenstahl, p.290 plays down the possibility that Bormann actually consulted with Hitler. Rother, op. cit., p.113 also suggests that it is not clear whether Bormann actually showed the papers to Hitler to obtain his personal approval.
9. BArch, R/109/1211, Riefenstahl to Winkler, 18 June 1944.
10. Rother, op. cit., p.113.
11. Berlin Document Center File, Riefenstahl File, Riefenstahl to Muller-Goerner, 8 April 1945, reproduced in David Culbert (ed.), Leni Riefenstahl's *Triumph of the Will*. University Publications of America. 1986, microform.
12. Fröhlich, Elke (ed.) *Die Tagebücher von Joseph Goebbels*, Part 2, *Diktate 1941–1945*. vi, p.456 (16 December 1942). This entry also appears in Louis Lochner, trans. and ed., *The Goebbels Diaries*. 1948, p.186.
13. Hamann, Brigitte, *Vienna, a Dictatorship's Apprenticeship*, trans. Thomas Thornton. 1999, p.109.
14. Riefenstahl, *The Sieve of Time*, pp.153–6; Trimborn, p.543, n.69.
15. Goebbels recorded on 4 April 1940 that she could not go to Spain as the Mediterranean was too "uncertain". "The Führer thinks that Italy will soon enter the war. God willing!" Fröhlich (ed.) *Die Tagebücher von Joseph Goebbels* Part I, viii, p.34 (4 April 1940).
16. Landesarchiv, Salzburg, RSTH1/346/1940.
17. Rom e V website between August and September 2002.
18. Riefenstahl maintains that she was not there: see *The Sieve of Time*, p.267.
19. Thurner, Erika, *National Socialists and Gypsies in Austria*, trans. Gilya Gerda Schmidt 1998, pp.23, 24. The English edition, a translation of the 1983 book, also incorporates additional material from Thurner's subsequent chapter 'Die Verfolgung der Zigeuner' in Christa Mitterrutzner and Gerhard Ungar (eds.) *Widerstand und Verfolgung in Salzburg 1934–1945*. 1991, pp.24, 33.
20. Landesarchiv, Salzburg, RSTH1/346/1940 and RSTH I/3/1941. Some of the lists, though only for 1940, are reproduced in Henry Friedlander and Sybil Milton (eds.) *Archives of the Holocaust*. 1991, pp.178–80. Some are also reproduced in Thurner, 'Die Verfolgung der Zigeuner' in Mitterrutzner and Ungar (eds.) *Widerstand und Verfolgung in Salzburg 1934–1945*, p.504.
21. There were five from the Reinhardt family, all but one of whom were children, including the thirteen year old Josef; seven from the Winter family, and three from the Kugler family. Their names also appear in Salzburg, RSTH I/3 98/1940, 23 September 1940.
22. Three were Reinhardts. Salzburg, RSTH I/346/1940.
23. Ibid.

24. Salzburg, RSTH I/346/1941. These extras came mainly from five families. Most were children: ten came from the Reinhardt family, including Josef, of whom only two were adults; nine from the Winter family with only two adults; six from the Kugler family with two adults; five from the Herzenberger family with one adult; two Amberger children (ages four and two); four from the Krems family. There were also two new extras: elderly women from the Tyrol.

25. Salzburg, RSTH I/346/1940 and 1941.

26. Dokumentation Östereichischen Widerstands, Vienna (hereafter cited as DÖW) E185 18/3.

27. RSTH 1/3 98/1940, Salzburg.

28. *Revue*, 1 May 1949.

29. Interviews in Nina Gladitz television documentary *Zeit des Schweigens und der Dunkleheit (Time of Silence, Time of Darkness)* (1982). Riefenstahl, *The Sieve of Time,* pp.358–9 cites a letter of gratitude from an Antonia Reinhardt, whose name however does not appear on the Maxglan lists of extras. There is an Anna Reinhardt, but she is Josef's mother and illiterate. Riefenstahl refers to a letter she received from the owner of the barn, Maria Kramer, whose relatives Josef and Katharina Kramer owned the adjacent hotel, confirming their good treatment. See also Thurner, 'Die Verfolgung der Zigeuner', p.479.

30. Thurner, 'Die Verfolgung der Zigeuner'.

31. Dr Reinl's sworn testimony: DÖW, E185 18/3.

32. Landesarchiv, Salzburg, RSTH I/3 98/1940, Memo from Dr Pitter on behalf of the Salzburg Police Director, to the Reichstatthalter Salzburg, 17 October 1940.

33. Rosa Winter, 'Soviel wie eine Asche' in Karin Berger, Elisabeth Holzinger, Lotte Podgornik and Lisbeth N Trallosi (eds.) *Ich geb dir einen Mantel, dass du ihn noch in Freiheit tragen kannst: Widerstehen im KZ, Öesterreichische Frauen erzählen.* 1987, pp.77–81.

34. German Gypsies are often unwilling to be identified, not surprising given the long history of persecution and the detailed 'race' records kept by Robert Ritter's notorious Berlin Institute for Racial Research (*Rassenhygienische und bevölkerungsbiologische Forschungsstelle*). Anna's story was mentioned in a German TV programme, made by Nina Gladitz (ZDF's 'Aspekte', broadcast on 6 August 2003). The commentator states that Krems's release can be verified in the documents. Zäzilia Reinhardt, who also appeared in the same programme, confirmed the incident. Anna's story appeared in print a few days later: 'Offener Brief', *Süddeutsche Zeitung*, 22 August 2002.

35. I am grateful to Nina Gladitz who interviewed Groth-Schmachtenberger, for this information.

36. Groth-Schmachtenberger provided her notes to the publisher of *Revue* who also used some of her photographs: *Revue* no. 12, May 1949, p.18

and DÖW, E185 18/3. Reimar Gilsenbach, *Weltchronik.* 1998 reproduces one of Groth-Schmachtenberger's photographs (p.89) in which the Maxglan extras are described as Rom (p.89) and the Marzahn extras as Sinti (p.90). The latter, he states, were "used a second time" which implies that they were first used in Krün for which there is no extant documentary evidence. Two different photographs are reproduced in Reimar Gilsenbach *O, Django, singt deinen Zorn: Sinti und Roma unter den Deutschen.* 1993, pp.168–9. One of the latter, along with two others, are also reproduced in Reimar Gilsenbach and Otto Rosenberg, *Berliner Zeitung,* 17–18 February 2001. The outdoor photographs will have been taken in Krün and are likely to have been of the Maxglan not the Marzahn extras. Rosenberg, a former inmate of Marzahn, identifies in the photos his grandmother and her sister and states that they were in Krün. He was aware that their names do not appear on the Maxglan lists of extras nor on the Marzahn list, a part of which was reproduced in the article he co-authored in the *Berliner Zeitung.* If his relatives had been used earlier and had been transported from Berlin to Krün, this would have been prior to the introduction of the tax, and thus before any need to produce a list. It was unnecessary for work performed in 1941. Zäzilia Reinhardt claims that three men used in Krün in 1941 came from Berlin-Marzahn. (Interview with Zäzilia Reinhardt, 15 August 2002.)

37. Riefenstahl, *The Sieve of Time,* pp.359–60.
38. See photo, Bildarchiv Preussischer Kulturbesitz, Berlin.
39. Thurner, *National Socialists and Gypsies in Austria,* pp.27–9.
40. Riefenstahl, *The Sieve of Time,* p.287.
41. Ibid. p.288.
42. Gilsenbach, R. and Rosenberg in *Berliner Zeitung,* 17–18 February 2001.
43. Part of the list is reproduced in Gilsenbach and Rosenberg, *Berliner Zeitung,* 17–18 February 2001. The complete listed appeared on the Rom e V website between August and September 2002.
44. Lewy, Guenter, *The Persecution of the Gypsies.* 2000, p.100.
45. According to the production manager, Rudolf Fichtner, testifying on Riefenstahl's behalf in 1949, the Berlin extras were paid between RM20 and 25 and certainly not less than RM15 per day. The production director, Max Hüske, also said that the Berlin extras were paid directly. DÖW, E 185 18/3. These witnesses, for whatever reason though one can surmise a good one, were providing false information.
46. I am grateful to Nina Gladitz for this information. She identifies this role as not being performed by a professional actor.
47. Benz, Wolfgang, 'Das Lager Marzahn: zur nationalsozialistische Verfolgung' in Helga Grabitz, (ed.) *Die Normalität des Verbrechens Kriminalität.* 1994, p.269.
48. *Sterbebücher von Auschwitz, Death Books from Auschwitz.* 1995. 3 vols; *Memorial Book: The Gypsies at Auschwitz-Birkenau.* 1993. 2 vols.

49. Rom e V website.
50. *Tiefland* has been available on video since 1998 Arthaus /Arte edition (1088); copyright remains with Riefenstahl. The video is 97 minutes long in contrast to the 1953 released film at 99 minutes (2695 metres).
51. Riefenstahl, *The Sieve of Time*, p.291.
52. Riefenstahl file, Berlin Document Centre.
53. Tegel, Susan, 'The Demonic Effect: Veit Harlan's Use of Jewish Extras in *Jud Süss* (1940)' in *Holocaust and Genocide Studies* (Fall 2000), 14, 2, pp.215–41.
54. *Revue*, no. 12, 1 May 1949, p.18.
55. Riefenstahl, *The Sieve of Time*, p.349.
56. DÖW, E185 18/3.
57. See note 1.
58. Trimborn, *Leni Riefenstahl*, p.333.
59. DÖW E 185 18/3. The other papers were *Quick*, *Süddeutsche Zeitung* and *Münchener Merkur*.
60. DÖW E 185 18/3. See also *Tageszeitung*, 30 November 1984, which claims that Böhmer referred to Maxglan as a 'philanthropic establishment', a kind of sanitarium (Wohlfahrtsfürsorgelager). Böhme also wrongly claimed that the extras were paid RM15 for adults (over fourteen years) and RM7.50 for children over six years and RM2.50 to 3 for small children and took credit for advising that pocket money of 25 to 50 Pfennig be given.
61. Böhmer lost his post in May 1944 for not following Führer commands and decrees. Initially sent to a concentration camp, but after a rehearing was condemned to hard labour in Salzburg and Hamburg to the end of the war. 'Die Verfolgung der Zigeuner', p.622, n.32.
62. DÖW E 185 18/3.
63. Kurz states wrongly that the extras were used for a period of three months on the first occasion in 1943 (sic) and six weeks on the second. In her memoirs, Riefenstahl recalls with satisfaction that Kurz was immediately tried for perjury and convicted. And that another witness, Josef Reinhart (sic) was subsequently convicted of perjury in 1955. His conviction related to his claim for compensation on behalf of family members, his perjury consisting in miscalculating the number of months that he and his family spent in concentration camps. See E 185 18/3 and Riefenstahl, *The Sieve of Time*, pp.358–9, 365, 385. Thurner also queries Reinhardt's dates: see Thurner, *National Socialists and Gypsies in Austria*, p.148, n.30. Kurz's name does not appear on the Salzburg Criminal Police list of extras. However, since during the trial she is referred to as Frau Kurz, this is likely to have been her married name. There is a Johanna Winter (born 1922) whose name appears on one of the lists: she fits the age of the Frau Kurz whose photograph appears in *Der Spiegel*, 1 December 1949, p.33.
64. The laughter was reported by a reliable observer, Alfred Polgar, the

brilliant Austrian Jewish journalist, who covered the trial and was highly critical of the whole proceedings. *Volksrecht*, 24 December 1949, Biographical Cuttings on Microfilm, Wiener Library, London.

65. *Revue,* 16, 19 April 1952, p.6ff.

66. Rother, *Leni Riefenstahl: The Seduction of Genius*, pp.129–30, 211, n.26.

67. *American Film*, 9, 5 (March 1984), p.13.

68. Riefenstahl, *The Sieve of Time*, pp.362–3.

69. *Der neue Mahnruf*, December 1984, Riefenstahl cuttings, Wiener Library, London.

70. *Tip,* 14 December 1984.

71. *The Times*, 29 November 1984, Riefenstahl cuttings, Wiener Library, London.

72. Ibid.

73. According to the list reproduced in *Berliner Zeitung*, 17–18 February 2001 and on the website, which appeared between August and September 2002.

74. 23 September 1940, RSTH 1/3 98/1940, Salzburg.

75. *Die Zeit*, 9 October 1987. The line cut was: 'I told aunt Leni – as we had to call her – that Maxglan would be dissolved and at the very least at the end of filming and all would be destroyed in Auschwitz. I said to her what we then knew about Auschwitz that no one came back from there.'

76. Riefenstahl, *The Sieve of Time*, p.358.

77. The *Independent*, 20 October 2000.

78. Brownlow, Kevin, 'Leni Riefenstahl', *Film*. Winter 1966, pp.14–19.

79. Sanders-Brahms, Helma, 'Tyrannenmord: *Tiefland* von Leni Riefenstahl' in *Das Dunkle zwischen den Bilder: Essays, Porträts, Kritiken*. 1992, p.246.

80. Ibid. p.262.

81. Rentschler, Eric, *The Ministry of Illusion* (Cambridge, MA: Harvard University Press, 1999), p.48 writes 'for all its putative resistant energy, *Lowlands* still relishes yet another Riefenstahl persona who is patently helpless, indeed subservient to male power', a description which supports her initial attraction to National Socialism.

82. Riefenstahl, *The Sieve of Time*, p.261.

83. von Dassanowsky, Robert, 'Wherever you may run, you cannot escape him: Leni Riefenstahl's Self-Reflection and Romantic Transcendence of Nazism in *Tiefland*', *Camera Obscura* 35 (1995–6), pp.106–29.

84. Fritz, Heribert and Mareen Linnartz, 'Ich bin sehr müde, Leni Riefenstahl über ein Leben im Schatten Hitlers, ihren ersten Film seit 60 Jahren und die Sehnsucht nach dem Tod', *Frankfurter Rundschau*, 27 April 2002.

85. See also Susan Tegel, 'Leni Riefenstahl's "Gypsy Question"', *Historical Journal of Film, Radio and Television*, 23, 1 (January 2003), pp.3–10, which is also reproduced in *Contemporary Literary Criticism*, Vol. 190, pp.258–63.

13. Krokowski: The effects of persecution on the German Sinti

1. Niederland, William G., *Folgen der Verfolgung: Das Überlebenden-Syndrom*. 1980, p.229.

2. This article will not deal with the effects of persecution and its trauma on the subsequent generations of Sinti.

3. [*Most of these are familiar as part of the syndrome of post-traumatic stress disorder*. Ed.].

4. Pollak, Michael, *Die Grenzen des Sagbaren: Lebensgeschichten von KZ-überlebenden als Augenzeugenberichte und als Identitätsarbeit*. 1988, p.12.

Select bibliography for further reading

Autobiographies

Lackova, Ilona, *A false dawn. My life as a Gypsy woman in Slovakia*. Hatfield: University of Hertfordshire Press. 2000

Rosenberg, Otto, *A Gypsy in Auschwitz*. London: London House. 1999

Sonnemann, Toby, *Shared Sorrows*. Hatfield: University of Hertfordshire Press. 2002

Winter, Walter. *Winter Time: Memoirs of a German Sinto who survived Auschwitz*. Hatfield: University of Hertfordshire Press. 2004

General books on the Nazi genocide of the Gypsies

Alt, Betty and Sylvia Folts, *Weeping violins. The Gypsy tragedy in Europe*. Kirksville, MO: Thomas Jefferson University Press. 1996

Kenrick, Donald and Grattan Puxon, *Gypsies under the Swastika*. Hatfield: University of Hertfordshire Press. 1995 (out of print)

Asséo, Henriette and others, *From Race Science to the Camps. Gypsies during the Second World War*. Vol.1. Hatfield: University of Hertfordshire Press. 1997

Kenrick, Donald (ed.), *In the Shadow of the Swastika. Gypsies during the Second World War*. Vol.2. Hatfield: University of Hertfordshire Pres. 1999

Lewy, Guenter, *The Nazi Persecution of the Gypsies*. Oxford: Oxford University Press. 2000

Zimmermann, Michael, *Rassenutopie und Genozid*. Hamburg: Christians. 1996